CLOUD SECURITY HANDBOOK FOR ARCHITECTS

Practical Strategies and Solutions for
Architecting Enterprise Cloud Security
using SECaaS and DevSecOps

by

ASHISH MISHRA

Copyright © 2023, Orange Education Pvt Ltd, AVA™

All rights reserved. No part of this book may be reproduced, stored in a retrieval system, or transmitted in any form or by any means, without the prior written permission of the publisher, except in the case of brief quotations embedded in critical articles or reviews.

Every effort has been made in the preparation of this book to ensure the accuracy of the information presented. However, the information contained in this book is sold without warranty, either express or implied. Neither the author nor Orange Education Pvt Ltd. or its dealers and distributors, will be held liable for any damages caused or alleged to have been caused directly or indirectly by this book.

Orange Education Pvt Ltd. has endeavored to provide trademark information about all of the companies and products mentioned in this book by the appropriate use of capital. However, Orange Education Pvt Ltd. cannot guarantee the accuracy of this information.

FOREWORD

With the increasing demand for digitization, data has been at forefront of every function across different industries, leading to a need for information security. Post the pandemic, information is no longer constrained within the defined perimeter, which has brought forward the need for Cyber Security at the center stage. Recently, Cyber Security has taken a permanent seat in the Enterprise Boardrooms.

With users spread across the globe and thus the need for dynamic data access, Cloud computing has evolved exponentially, thereby bringing multi-fold challenges for Cyber Security professionals. Cloud Security poses unique challenges such as data exposure in the public domain which should have need-based access ensuring data is stored in a secure fashion, complex environments with data movement from on-premises to cloud within an enterprise all the time, increasing compliance requirements with data travelling internationally and cross border.

I have personally known Ashish for the last 3 years and he has been advising many of our customers on cloud security solutions. With over 19 years of experience and 100+ certifications in various fields of cyber security, Ashish has an edge in the field of cloud, network and perimeter security. Known for his expertise in cloud security within the cyber security practice, Ashish has helped many of our customers drive cyber and cloud security roadmaps, develop zero trust frameworks, and adopt cloud security controls ensuring all the compliance requirements are addressed as per the regulatory bodies.

It's heartening to see Ashish bringing his Cloud Security (and in general Cyber Security) knowledge to a wider audience through this book. The book provides a logical flow to adopt a cloud security roadmap, beginning with the need to transform, the building blocks of cloud security and finally maturing the cloud platform with security best practices embedded within the platform.

With Ashish's experience, I am confident that this book will provide a plethora of knowledge to all its readers who are keen to learn and advance their knowledge in the field of Cloud Security.

Sanjeev Garg

Group Delivery Head, Cyber Security, Tech Mahindra

Gurur Brahma, Gurur Vishnu, Gurur Devo Maheshwara !
Guru Sakshat Parabrahma, Tasmai Sri Gurve Namah !!

Dedicated to

All my Teachers and Mentors
and
My wife Madhu and My kids – Aarush and Aarav

About the Author

Ashish Mishra is a seasoned IT professional and author who has more than 19 years of experience in the industry. He holds a strong grip and command of IT (Information Technology), IS (Information Security), and Cyber Security Domains. Ashish is also experienced in managing large IT and IS Operations, Strategy Building, Transformation journey, Project and Program Management, and Service Delivery.

His technical areas of expertise include but are not limited to Public Cloud, Private Cloud, Cloud Security, Network Security, SASE, and Zero Trust.

With the thought process of "Continuous learning is the key to success", he has obtained more than 100 professional certifications across various technologies and platforms related to Public and Private Cloud, Cloud Security, Information Security, Cyber Security, Compliance, Infrastructure management, Leadership, Project management, and many more.

LinkedIn profile: - https://www.linkedin.com/in/amishra1983/

Technical Reviewers

Deepayan Chanda is a highly-experienced Cybersecurity professional with over 25 years of field and domain expertise. He is also an Armed Forces veteran. He has had the privilege to witness and experience the rise of cybersecurity needs for organizations and the community, ranging from simple virus attacks in the early 2000s to complex cyber-attacks against the community and organizations today.

Deepayan has extensive experience in building complex cybersecurity platforms and solutions, as well as developing new technology and products. At present, his primary focus is to help organizations build their strategic solutions, and enhance or fix weak architecture functions. He believes that the majority of security issues can be solved at the ground level by applying the required security controls.

He also takes pride in not only solving cybersecurity issues for enterprises as a primary career, but has also taken a pledge to help build robust, cutting-edge, and sustainable security platforms and products. As part of that personal mission, he has joined multiple cybersecurity startups as a board advisor to assist them with product architecture and business strategies. He is also an established author and a regular contributor to publications aimed at raising awareness about security issues.

Vikram Kolekar is a veteran in the IT industry who has spent the last decade and a half working in Information Technology, Cyber Security, and Cloud Security. He has been involved in Architecture, Design, Implementation, and Technical Program Management from both the IT and Security perspectives.

He has global and domestic work experience in the Security vertical of various sectors such as Banking and Finance, Insurance companies, Product companies, and Service Integration providers.

He holds multiple certifications in Cyber Security Architecture, Risk Management, ERM, AWS, Azure, and Google Cloud.

He abhors the silos that traditional IT creates and the harm they pose to organizations.

Acknowledgements

There are a few people I want to thank for the continued and ongoing support they have given me during the writing of this book. First and foremost, I would like to express my gratitude and thanks to all my teachers (Gurus) and mentors who have played a vital role in shaping my career and defining my path. I could have never completed this book without their support.

The ways in which you all have aided me professionally are too numerous to count. Thank you very much for everything; I only hope I can repay the favor at some point in the future.

I appreciate you all for being good mentors and guiding me in the right direction. You have my eternal gratitude.

Without the encouragement and support of my great wife, Madhu, who urged me not to pass up this opportunity and juggled schedules and duties for almost 7 to 8 months, this book would not have been possible. I'd also like to thank Aarush and Aarav, my children, for giving up their weekends and vacation time so that I could work on this book.

Writing a book requires the contribution of many people, and I did not realize this until I started writing one. I would like to express my gratitude to the publisher and their entire staff for their assistance in getting this book published. I would also like to thank Vikram Kolekar and Deepayan Chanda for taking the time out of their busy schedules to assess the content from a technical standpoint.

Preface

The content of the book is segregated into three parts. The first section is designed to help the audience set the stage and understand the real need to have this transformation journey. This section will primarily focus on the conceptual understanding of cloud security and how this will go with your business.

The next section is primarily meant for technical people, architects, and practitioners, but will certainly help the readers who are getting into the cloud and cloud security space by delving into an in-depth approach to adopting and implementing the right solution. Here we will cover the conceptual framework, architecture, native controls from different cloud providers, adoption of the same, and the compliance umbrella to cover the entire ecosystem.

The final section will touch base on a few real-life problem statements and a pragmatic approach to mitigate them. It also covers the best practices and recommendations that one should consider for their cloud stack along with the future state of cloud security and how enterprises can adopt it.

This book is divided into 3 sections and 9 chapters. The details are listed as follows.

Section I: - Overview and need to transform to Cloud landscape

This section will include the following topics:

- Recognizing the evolution of Cloud computing and its implications for security
- Principles and concepts
- Evaluating the current state of Cloud security
- Choosing and evaluating cloud services for your business

Section II: - Building blocks of Cloud security framework and adoption path

This section will include the following topics:

- Implementing Cloud security in your organization
- Cloud security architecture

- Native cloud security controls - technical components of Cloud security architecture (Asset Management and Protection, Identity and Access Management, Vulnerability Management, Network Security, and Incident Response Management)
- Examining regulatory compliance in the cloud and adoption path
- Creating a Cloud security policy
- Creating a security culture in your organization

Section III: -Maturity Path

This section will include the following topics:

- Predicting security challenges in the Cloud
- Cloud security recommendations
- Checklist, Cloud audit, and compliance
- Security-as-a-service in Cloud

Chapter 1 will explain why you should incorporate cloud services into your everyday operations, the platforms you can use, and how to deal with security issues as you transition from a firm that relies on conventional software to one that uses cloud services.

This chapter also covers measuring your organization's cloud maturity level and the fundamentals of cloud computing. Along with that, you consider how risk has changed in the cloud and what the shared responsibility model means for your company.

Chapter 2 will talk about the basic principles that help us to build the foundation for the cloud security landscape. You will learn about different security principles and concepts that are essential for understanding the cloud landscape. This chapter provides a deep dive into these basic principles and their importance for the cloud ecosystem. In the end, we will explain the strategy you should consider to build your cloud security framework along with a couple of best practices for the same.

Chapter 3 will cover the guidelines and principles for assessing the cloud environment and guide us in choosing the right solution. The initial section of the chapter will help you learn about the different roles and responsibilities across the ecosystem that are important to drive this engagement. In the later section of the chapter, you will learn about the assessment lifecycle and ways to select the right cloud platform for your enterprise.

Chapter 4 will focus on architecting the cloud solution for your business. The chapter will talk about how to build the cloud security architecture, the framework on which the solution will be built, key considerations for your architecture, and an adoption path in the long run. We will also talk about container security and microservices. Container technologies and microservices designs are the new entries to the overall framework which enable new application architectures for legacy programs, refactored apps, and microservices, among others.

The chapter will also give you a quick brief and reference to Autonomic security which provides complete coverage of your cloud ecosystem from a security perspective.

By the end of this chapter, the readers will have a clear understanding of how to define and adopt cloud security architecture for their enterprise, as well as the key considerations they should follow while on their journey of cloud migration.

Chapter 5 will discuss different techniques that will help you to build native security controls in the cloud landscape. We will provide a detailed tour of each of the native cloud security controls that are essential for building overall security and getting aligned with the cloud security framework and architecture.

Chapter 6 will focus on the regulatory compliance requirements for cloud adoption. While our earlier chapters focused on architecture and building blocks, this chapter will cover the importance of compliance requirements in the cloud and its adoption path. This chapter will help us understand the requirements, mapping of controls with technology and business, adoption paths, and best practices. Lastly, this chapter will provide an overview of auditing exercises and checklists along with a risk management approach that should be adopted for the cloud segment.

By the end of the chapter, you will have a complete understanding of how compliance requirements are aligned with overall cloud security and how to adopt them in your landscape.

Chapter 7 will explain the security policy adoption and the approach to adopting the required culture. "Policy and culture" play a vital role in the long run and we must understand the importance of the same and how we should create and adapt them to our organizations. The chapter covers the various roles and responsibilities across enterprise and CSP, and how each of these contribute to a desired cultural state to adopt security as a shared responsibility. We will also talk about how you should inject the training and awareness session with a few examples and recommendations. We will also talk about various security policies such as data protection and encryption.

Chapter 8 will cover the different security services that can be offered from the cloud in a SaaS format. Here, we will discuss a framework for evaluating and delivering cloud-based security services to businesses. First, we'll go through the components of the framework in depth. Then we'll show how to utilize this framework to evaluate and adopt security services through a detailed lifecycle approach. We will also cover a few examples and their adoption path that you can consider for your ecosystem.

By the end of the chapter, you will be able to choose the right security solutions that should be adopted as a service for your cloud transformation journey.

Chapter 9 will explain the various best practices and recommendations across the entire landscape of cloud security. We will also touch base few of the recommendations based on real-life challenges, business scenarios, and alignment with business verticals. To start, we will help your slate with the next steps and the way forward in the journey of defining the security boundary and upliftment engagement.

Downloading the colored images

The images of the book are also hosted on
https://rebrand.ly/bf907c

Errata

We take immense pride in our work at Orange Education Pvt Ltd and follow best practices to ensure the accuracy of our content to provide an indulging reading experience to our subscribers. Our readers are our mirrors, and we use their inputs to reflect and improve upon human errors, if any, that may have occurred during the publishing processes involved. To let us maintain the quality and help us reach out to any readers who might be having difficulties due to any unforeseen errors, please write to us at :

errata@orangeava.com

Your support, suggestions, and feedback are highly appreciated.

DID YOU KNOW

Did you know that Orange Education Pvt Ltd. offers eBook versions of every book published, with PDF and ePub files available? You can upgrade to the eBook version at www.orangeava.com and as a print book customer, you are entitled to a discount on the eBook copy. Get in touch with us at: **info@orangeava.com** for more details.

At **www.orangeava.com**, you can also read a collection of free technical articles, sign up for a range of free newsletters, and receive exclusive discounts and offers on AVA™ Books and eBooks.

Piracy

If you come across any illegal copies of our works in any form on the internet, we would be grateful if you would provide us with the location address or website name. Please contact us at **info@orangeava.com** with a link to the material.

Are you interested in Authoring with us?

If there is a topic that you have expertise in, and you are interested in either writing or contributing to a book, please write to us at **business@orangeava.com**. We are on a journey to help developers and tech professionals to gain insights on the present technological advancements and innovations happening across the globe and build a community that believes Knowledge is best acquired by sharing and learning with others. Please reach out to us to learn what our audience demands and how you can be part of this educational reform. We also welcome ideas from tech experts and help them build learning and development content for their domains.

Reviews

Please leave a review. Once you have read and used this book, why not leave a review on the site that you purchased it from? Potential readers can then see and use your unbiased opinion to make purchase decisions. We at Orange Education would love to know what you think about our products, and our authors can learn from your feedback. Thank you!

For more information about Orange Education, please visit **www. orangeava.com**.

Table of Contents

SECTION II:
Building Blocks of Cloud Security Framework and Adoption Path.......79

SECTION III:
Maturity Path

Overview and Need to Transform to Cloud Landscape

This section will include the following topics:

- Recognizing the evolution of Cloud computing and its implications for security

- Principles and concepts

- Evaluating the current state of Cloud security

- Choosing and evaluating cloud services for your business

CHAPTER 1

Evolution of Cloud Computing and its Impact on Security

Introduction

In cloud and on-premises systems, there are some significant differences even though many security policies and concepts are the same. For this reason, some recommendations for cloud security can surprise those with experience in on-premises security. Although there are undoubtedly legitimate differences of opinion among security professionals in almost any area of information security, the adoption path outlined in this book's recommendations is based on years of experience in securing cloud environments and is influenced by some of the most recent advancements in cloud computing services.

Whether you're a security professional who is relatively new to the cloud or an architect or developer with security responsibilities, the *goal* of this book is to assist you quickly and correctly implement the most crucial security measures for your most crucial assets. You can extend and develop your controls further from this strong foundation.

Starting with this chapter, here we will explain why you should incorporate cloud services into your everyday operations, the platforms you can use, and how to deal with security issues as you go from a firm that relies on conventional software to one that uses cloud services.

You may measure your organization's cloud maturity level and learn about the fundamentals of cloud computing in this chapter. Along with that, you consider how risk has changed in the cloud and what the shared responsibility model means for your company.

Structure

In this chapter, we will discuss the following topics:

- Evolution of cloud
- Cloud computing journey talking about characteristics, service models, types, and industry trends
- Analyzing the risk of cloud services
- Cloud computing privacy concerns
- Cloud maturity assessment
- Shadow IT and Shared Services understanding
- Key considerations for uplifting cloud security

Evolution of cloud

Your entire computing infrastructure, including hardware and software, can be made accessible online via *cloud computing*. It uses the internet and distant central servers to update data and programs. *Gmail, Yahoo Mail, Facebook, Hotmail, Orkut,* and other widely used cloud computing applications are just a few examples. Anyone with an internet connection can check some saved mail, data, or images in the mailbox because the data is stored with the *mail service provider* on a remote cloud.

The method essentially involves the geographic transfer of our data from personal computers to a *centralized server* or *cloud*. For cloud services, customers are often billed based on usage.

It is therefore also referred to as **Software as a Service (SaaS)**. Providing infrastructure and resources online to serve its clients has three main objectives: *dynamics, abstraction,* and *resource sharing*.

It has been impacted by many computer technologies, including virtualization, utility computing, parallel computing, and grid computing. **Web 2.0 technology**, which supports web applications that encourage *user-centered design, interoperability,* and *participatory information sharing,* among other things is the source of cloud computing, which is a relatively new development. There are several Web 2.0 applications, including *wikis, blogs, social networking,* and *video sharing*.

Cloud computing is described by the **National Institute of Standard and Technology (NIST)** as:

A *model for enabling convenient, on-demand network access to a shared pool of configurable and dependable computing resources (for example, networks, servers, storage, applications, services) that can be rapidly provisioned and released with minimal consumer management effort or service provider interaction.*

Cloud computing journey

When utility and grid computing were introduced in the early 1960s, the idea phase began and lasted until the years before the internet bubble. *Joseph Carl Robnett Licklider* was the inventor of cloud computing.

Before the development of clouds, several things happen in the pre-cloud phase. Beginning in 1999 and lasting until 2006 was the pre-cloud phase. With the current landscape and trend, *Application as a Service* is offered over the internet.

The much-discussed actual cloud phase got underway in 2007 after the IaaS, PaaS, and SaaS development classifications were finalized. Over the years, some of the biggest computer and web companies in the world have created some truly amazing cloud computing innovations.

Cloud computing overview

The cloud appears to be present everywhere right now. But let's begin on page one by creating a common cloud terminology, with assistance from our pals at the U.S. *National Institute of Standards and Technology* to make sure we're all talking about the cloud in the same sentence (NIST).

Characteristics of cloud computing

The five key characteristics of cloud computing are listed as follows by NIST in *Special Publication 800-145*:

- **On-demand self-service**: A customer can automatically provision computer resources as needed, such as server time and network storage, without requiring human interaction with each service provider.

- **Broad network access**: Capabilities are accessible via the network and used through common mechanisms to encourage adoption by various *thin-* or *thick-client platforms* (for example, mobile phones, tablets, laptops, and workstations).

- **Resource pooling**: The provider uses a *multi-tenant approach* to pool its computing resources to serve several customers, with various physical and virtual resources being dynamically assigned and reassigned in response to customer demand. Resources include things like *memory*, *computing power*, *storage*, and *network bandwidth*.

- **Quick elasticity**: To quickly scale outward and inward the following demand, capabilities can be elastically provisioned and withdrawn, in certain circumstances, automatically. The capabilities that are available for provisioning frequently look to the user to be limitless and can be used in any quantity at any moment.

- **Metered service**: Cloud systems use metering capabilities at an *abstraction level* appropriate to the type of service to automatically control and optimize resource utilization (for example, *storage*, *processing*, *bandwidth*, and *active user accounts*). Resource utilization can be tracked, managed, and reported, ensuring openness for both the service provider and the client.

Cloud types

Several different types of technologies are referred to as *cloud computing*. Based on the type, application, and place, it is categorized under the following headings:

- **Public cloud**: A cloud that is made available to the public for a price is referred to as a *public cloud*. Customers are not able to see where the cloud computing infrastructure is located. The typical cloud computing model is constructed on top of it. Public clouds include, among others, those offered by *Amazon EC2*, *Microsoft Azure*, *Google*, and others.

- **Private cloud**: An exclusive data center owned by a business that is not open to the public is known as a *private cloud*. As implied by the name, a single consumer is the sole focus of the private cloud. These have greater security compared to public clouds. As a technology, it uses *virtualization*. The private cloud is managed by company servers. Private cloud technology includes products like **VMware** and **Eucalyptus**.

- **Hybrid cloud**: Using both private and public cloud resources, a *hybrid cloud* integrates both types of clouds. When there is a lot of network traffic or a lot of data to handle, businesses use the cloud rather than their infrastructure.

- **Multi-cloud**: Even while major cloud vendors would be happy to meet all of the computing requirements of their business clients, organizations are increasingly attempting to spread the load over several suppliers. *Multi-cloud computing* is now more popular as a result of everything. This method entails a combination of finding the ideal mix of technologies throughout the industry and avoiding becoming overly dependent on a single vendor, which can result in the high costs and inflexibility that the cloud is frequently hailed as avoiding.

Cloud computing service model

As per NIST, the service model of cloud computing is broadly defined into three types and they are:

- **Software as a Service (SaaS)**: The consumer is given the option to use the provider's applications that are hosted on a cloud infrastructure. Through a *program interface* or a *thin client interface*, such as a *web browser* (for web-based email, for instance), the programs can be accessed from a variety of client devices. Apart from a small number of user-specific application configuration choices, the customer does not manage or control the underlying cloud infrastructure, which includes the network, servers, operating systems, storage, or even specific application capabilities.

- **Platform as a Service (PaaS)**: The capacity provided to the customer is the ability to install on the cloud infrastructure user-generated or purchased applications made using programming languages, libraries, services, and tools supported by the provider. However, the network, servers, operating systems, and storage that make up the underlying cloud infrastructure are not under the control of the consumer. Instead, the consumer only controls the deployed programs and possibly the configuration options for the environment where the applications are hosted.

- **Infrastructure as a Service (IaaS)**: This service enables the supply of processing, storage, networks, and other basic computer resources so that the user can deploy and execute any software, such as operating systems and applications. Although the user does not manage or control the underlying cloud infrastructure, they do have control over *deployed apps*, *storage*, and *operating systems*. They may also have limited control over some networking components (for example, *host firewalls*).

Cloud computing trends

Spending on public cloud services is anticipated to surpass $500 *billion* by 2023. The upcoming developments in cloud computing will enable industries through a variety of cloud solutions and increasing expansion.

As a result, cloud computing will account for 22.8% of all corporate IT *investments*. In 2020, the pandemic catalyzed rapid cloud adoption and digital innovation, especially for facilitating remote work, collaboration, and digitalization in hybrid work structures.

Due to their proven scalability, resilience, speed, and flexibility, cloud systems are becoming more prevalent. Utilizing *multi-cloud, hybrid*, and *edge* settings are advancing wireless communications and changing a variety of sectors, including healthcare, mobile banking, and more.

Recognizing the development of cloud

You probably imagine that the majority of people accessing file-sharing services like Box and **Dropbox**, or productivity applications like **Evernote** when you think of cloud growth in business. Enterprise cloud usage, however, goes beyond these services geared towards consumers. The cloud is being used by entire functional departments, such as *marketing, human resources, finance*, and *research and development*.

Justifications for using the cloud

Simply put, employees can complete their tasks with the cloud more swiftly, simply, and adaptably than they can with conventional computing technologies. Here are some factors that each company should consider:

- **Business agility**: People want to be productive now; they don't want to wait for the next software release to take place. Your business can benefit from the newest features because many cloud services provide updates more often than traditional software.

- **Device selection**: The ability to work on any platform, including a *desktop, laptop, tablet*, or *smartphone*, whenever and wherever they like is made possible by the cloud.

- **Collaboration**: The cloud makes it easy for co-workers and business partners to share and use data.

- **Low cost**: On-premises software (as well as the hardware needed to operate it) deployment, upkeep, and updates can be costly. Utilizing cloud services will enable you to lower operating costs and more closely align cost and value.

Your staff is most certainly already using cloud services without your knowledge due to the strong business cases for cloud adoption, which puts your company in danger of data compromise or regulatory non-compliance. By formally using cloud services, you may create standards and guidelines that will protect your company's sensitive data and ensure that you're following legal requirements.

Analyzing the risk of cloud services

Businesses that adopt the cloud must first comprehend, manage, and reduce the inherent risks in any cloud model. Based on objective criteria in the following functional areas, you can assess a cloud service's enterprise readiness:

- Certifications and standards
- Data protection
- Access restriction
- Auditability
- Disaster recovery and business continuity
- Legal and privacy
- Vulnerabilities and exploits

Examine cloud services based on these objective criteria, but keep in mind that while a service's enterprise readiness is crucial, a higher risk may arise from how individuals are utilizing that service.

Inherent risk

You assume a certain level of *inherent risk* when your critical business data is stored outside of your organization. Depending on the capabilities of the public cloud, you may lose the ability to have direct access to the servers hosting your data as you store data. Due to the built-in capabilities of the cloud services where they are stored, sensitive, confidential, or otherwise regulated data may be in danger. Your data is subject to the service's shortcomings, such as if it fails to isolate the data of one tenant from that of another or if it doesn't give sufficient access restrictions.

It is your responsibility as a purchaser, implementer, or approver of such services to confirm that the cloud services your business is using have the inherent security capabilities you require. Anytime your data is stored in a cloud environment and is not under your direct control, it is crucial to make sure the services you select have the security safeguards necessary to keep your data secure and follow your rules.

Techniques to reduce the inherent risk

To reduce your inherent risk, your cloud services should adhere to the following standards:

- **Certifications and standards**: Your services and the data centers where they are hosted should adhere to the laws and professional best practices that are relevant to your organization. The important certifications you ought to think about are mentioned as follows:
  - SOC1 and SOC2
  - SAS-70 / SSAE-16
  - ISO27001
  - HIPAA regulation
  - PCI-DSS security standard
  - TRUSTe certification
- **Data protection**: Services that store your company's data should make it possible for you to protect it following your needs. This could consist of:
  - Categorizing your data and enforcing access and data protection rules following classification levels.
  - Using robust encryption to protect your sensitive and confidential data.
  - Distinguishing your cloud service instance from that of other customers to ensure that there is no danger of data exposure or the corrupted data of one customer impacting the data of another customer.

  Data ownership is related to *data protection*. Be mindful that certain services do not make it clear in their terms and conditions that the consumer owns the data. Choose only services that explicitly state that the data they contain belongs to the user. Additionally, search for conditions that outline how to get your data back if you cancel the service.
- **Access control**: Your services should include access restrictions and policy enforcement comparable to your on-premises controls. It offers functions like *multifactor authentication, single sign-on support*, and *granular access limits*.
- **Business continuity and disaster recovery**: The information about your services' disaster recovery procedures should be very clear. According to the importance of data, those specifics should match your company's needs for data access and uptime. Understand the provider's *disaster recovery plan*, the location of your backup offshore location, and the procedure for backing up and restoring your data.

- **Encryption**: The services you use to store sensitive or regulated data ought to support the encryption of data in transit and provide you with options for managing encryption keys following your policies. They must also make sure that your data is managed independently of that of other tenants in the same cloud.

- **Audits and alerts**: Your services that handle crucial business operations, house sensitive data, or have access to your enterprise systems should have effective administrator, user, and data access logging and alerting tools. This aids in both real-time non-compliant behavior detection and forensic audit trails following a suspected event.

- **File sharing**: Your services that allow for file sharing should handle file sizes that satisfy your needs for large files. As a result, people will be more inclined to use the *corporate cloud services* that are already available to them and less likely to look for a solution that may be of poorer quality and that you are unaware of to meet their file-sharing needs.

Cloud computing privacy concerns

Today, cloud computing is a *hot* topic that has drawn interest from a wide range of sectors, including academia, research, and the IT business. It has suddenly become a popular subject at international conferences and other events all around the world. Huge volumes of data are processed and stored on the servers, which is what's causing the rise in job opportunities. The convenience and simplicity of providing a sizable pool of shared computing resources are key to the cloud model.

More flexibility, cost savings, and product scalability have resulted from the cloud's quick development, but it also presents significant privacy and security problems. Since the idea is still *new* and *developing*, there may be undiscovered security vulnerabilities that must be addressed as soon as they are identified.

The following list of cloud computing's top privacy challenges is provided:

- **Problems with data privacy**: When outsourcing and externalizing particularly delicate and sensitive data to a cloud service provider, data confidentiality for the user is a *crucial problem* to take into account. Users without the right authorization to access it should not be able to access personal data, and one approach to ensure confidentiality is by using strict access control policies and laws. Many people are hesitant to use cloud services due to the lack of confidence that exists between customers and cloud service providers or cloud database service providers regarding the data.

- **Problems with data loss**: One of the main security issues that cloud providers encounter is data loss or theft. More than 60% of consumers would refuse to use a cloud vendor's services if that firm had previously disclosed data loss or theft of crucial or sensitive data. Even from companies like *Dropbox, Microsoft, Amazon,* and so on, outages of cloud services are frequently apparent, which undermines confidence in these services at a crucial moment. Additionally, even if only one storage device is compromised, an attacker can easily access a number of them.

- **Issues with geographical data storage**: Since the cloud infrastructure is dispersed across various geographic locations around the globe, it is frequently possible that the user's data is stored in a location that is outside of the legal jurisdiction, which raises concerns among the user about the legal accessibility of local law enforcement and the regulations on data that is stored outside of their region. Additionally, because it is so challenging to designate a specific server to be utilized for transnational data transmission due to the dynamic nature of the cloud, the user is concerned that local regulations may be broken.

- **Multiple tenant security problems**: A paradigm known as *multitenancy* promotes the idea of sharing computing power, data storage, applications, and services across many tenants. This is then hosted on the same logical or physical platform at the location of the cloud service provider. The provider can maximize earnings by using this strategy, but the customer is put in danger. The possibility of several residences can be exploited by attackers to conduct a variety of attacks against their co-tenants, creating several privacy issues.

- **Problems with transparency**: *Transparency* in cloud computing security refers to a cloud service provider's openness to divulge specifics about its security posture. Some of these specifics violate laws and rules governing security, privacy, and service levels. When assessing transparency, it's vital to include other factors besides willingness and disposition, such as how accessible the data and information genuinely are about security readiness. No matter how accessible a company's security information is, it won't matter if consumers of cloud services and auditors cannot simply grasp it. In this case, the organization's transparency might also be regarded as being *low*.

- **Issues relating to Hypervisors**: *Virtualization* is the mental separation of computing resources from actual physical limitations. However, this presents fresh problems for elements like user identification, accounting, and authorization. The **hypervisor** gets attacked because it oversees several virtual machines. In contrast to physical devices that are separate from one another, virtual machines on the cloud typically exist in a single physical device under the control of the same hypervisor. Consequently, several virtual machines will be at risk if the hypervisor is compromised. In addition, the hypervisor technology is *novel*, offering attackers fresh ways to exploit the system through *isolation*, *security hardening*, *access control*, and so on.

- **Administrative problems**: Cloud privacy difficulties come in both technological and managerial varieties, in addition to non-technical ones. The introduction of vulnerabilities is *inevitable* when a technical solution to an issue or a product is implemented but not managed effectively. Examples include a lack of control, the need to manage security and privacy while virtualizing, the creation of detailed service level agreements, the need to engage in discussions with cloud service providers and users, and so on.

Assessing your organization's cloud maturity

Ironically, although the cloud is present almost everywhere, many businesses manage it incorrectly when it comes to security and compliance, considering it like a distinct, isolated environment. To apply effective protections, IT teams must manually correlate data in a fragmented security environment created by a *siloed security architecture* that uses numerous security technologies from various vendors to address specific use cases. When facing cyber adversaries who employ automation to carry out sophisticated attacks in increasing volumes, this does not scale. Your company will be forced to use its least scalable resource—people—to defend against machine-generated threats if your security ecosystem is unable to inform or collaborate with other products, let alone automatically coordinate or interact with other network capabilities.

The first step in developing a successful plan for cloud security and compliance is understanding the level of cloud maturity inside your firm. Depending on an organization's level of cloud adoption, the following cloud maturity model divides maturity into *three* stages:

- **Cloud evaluators (beginners)**: At this stage, businesses are researching cloud technologies and alternatives to determine which apps to prioritize for deployment in the cloud. Line of business teams frequently test out cloud technology, but the firm as a whole is still defining its cloud policy and best practices. Teams from application development and security collaborate to pilot new strategies.

- **Cloud implementers (intermediate)**: At this point, businesses have shifted their production workloads to the cloud (utilizing either hybrid cloud or single cloud architectures). Teams work together to develop automated **DevOps workflows**, and establish, and execute best practices for cloud deployment and policy. The teams responsible for developing, and deploying applications, and security collaborates on these tasks.

- **Cloud optimizers (advanced)**: At this point, the cloud is used for business-critical tasks and is essential to the organization's digital transformation. For different business needs, the firm may use several cloud ecosystems. An essential corporate strategy entails expanding and automating cloud policy and procedures related to *operations*, *security*, and *compliance*.

Analyzing the development of cloud risk

The security of systems, data, and cloud services must be a top priority for IT as more businesses migrate crucial workloads to the public cloud. The misconception that the cloud is inherently safe is common among cloud users, particularly DevOps teams and certain business units. Oftentimes, making this error puts businesses at greater *cloud risk*.

There are various chances for cloud evaluators to unintentionally add new risks, such as data leaks resulting from poor use of SaaS programs and improperly configured access privileges. In particular, when workloads are deployed via PaaS, security teams have less visibility and control when consumers use SaaS applications, and developers use the public cloud. Since cloud data and applications are essentially available everywhere, there is a significant amount of danger associated with them. For businesses without a clear cloud strategy, this is especially *true*.

It's possible that these firms didn't choose a group of authorized SaaS applications that can be properly secured. Without instruction, staff members use *cutting-edge programs* that have the potential to boost productivity without fully comprehending the risks involved. Unfortunately, its hostile land is filled with fraudsters waiting to prey on gullible customers who may unintentionally misconfigure permissions in a file-sharing service. When sharing files, users can sometimes be careless or make mistakes. These dangers can all reveal private information.

The shift to the cloud has made it possible for many enterprises to embrace a more agile, iterative application development technique. To do this, developers and their workloads require quick, frequently automated, secure access to web-based resources like **GitHub**, **Yum**, **apt-get**, and **OS update methods** for Windows or Linux.

Organizations are more exposed to cloud risk due to a lack of visibility in *IaaS* and *PaaS* environments. Without comprehensive visibility and measures to limit lateral movement, an attacker might travel laterally (east-west) in a data center, including one that uses cloud computing, without being noticed for an extended time. Without visibility, you also face the danger of missing the usage of cloud resources by unauthorized users who do so at your expense to mine cryptocurrencies or perform other tasks.

Last but not least, businesses frequently believe that the cloud provider is in charge of maintaining security. However, cloud providers are in charge of cloud security; customers are always in charge of the security of their *workloads*, *services*, and *data* in the cloud. This is referred to as the *shared responsibility model*, which we will discuss later in the chapter.

Shadow IT and its rise

Shadow IT refers to the use and upkeep of systems and applications by individuals or groups operating independently of IT. When you evaluate the cloud services in your company, you'll probably discover that both *authorized* and *unauthorized* services are used by the staff:

- **Authorized services**: Services that the business offers for use by employees and of which IT is aware are known as **sanctioned cloud services**. These cloud services are typically fully administered by IT, which also looks after them on the company's behalf. Even while IT might be in charge of managing authorized services, the department might not have detailed knowledge of how users are gaining access to them or engaging in specific actions, such as *uploading, downloading, sharing,* or *changing corporate data.*

- **Unauthorized services**: Services that the business isn't aware of and might not approve of. Employees frequently go outside of IT and buy their cloud services if IT either doesn't supply the tools necessary to complete a necessary business function or forbids the usage of such technologies. Without the expertise or aid of IT, employees may simply *locate, pay for, download,* and *manage* these services.

One way in which using *unauthorized services* is advantageous is that it allows staff members to work productively. On the other hand, the firm faces risk from using these illicit cloud services. It is impossible to keep services secure, much alone the data they contain if IT is unaware of them. For services that are not authorized, IT cannot effectively enforce security or compliance. These services and the data included in them are exposed to accidental or deliberate data disclosure without key security features like *robust user authentication* and *audit recording*. Finally, IT is unaware of how users of unauthorized services are using those services.

Enabling the cloud safely entails managing all authorized services as well as identifying any unauthorized ones that are being used. After that, you can start protecting services and data by putting in place robust authentication, keeping an eye on administrator and user activity, preventing data loss or exposure, and defending against dangers like *malware* and *ransomware*. In addition to enforcing security and compliance regulations, IT can reliably manage and secure all cloud services used by the company.

Understanding the shared responsibility paradigm

To increase organizational agility and cut expenses, cloud-based apps and the data they contain are being dispersed more and more throughout various contexts. These settings include *private clouds*, *public clouds* (*hybrid* or *dedicated*), and **Software as a Service (SaaS)** applications, each of which brings its special agility benefits and security challenges. Cloud security is now a top concern due to the fear of data disclosure.

The difficulty now is striking a balance between the organization's demand for agility and strengthening application security and data protection as the data is transferred between different clouds. It becomes crucial across all sites where the apps and data are located to gain visibility into and stop assaults that aim to exfiltrate data, both from an external location and through a lateral attack. The *network team*, *security team*, *applications team*, *compliance team*, or *infrastructure team* are just a few of the entities that may be in charge of an organization's cloud security. However, both the company and the cloud vendor share responsibilities for cloud security. Here are a few of the cloud platform types wherein we have a segregation of responsibilities based on the type of cloud services:

- **Private**: Since the cloud is hosted in businesses' data centers, they are in charge of all aspects of cloud security. The physical network, infrastructure, virtual network, operating systems, firewalls, service configuration, identity, and access management, and so on are all included in this. The enterprise is also responsible for the data's security.

- **Public**: The infrastructure, physical network, and hypervisor are all owned by the cloud provider in public clouds like **Amazon Web Services (AWS)**, **Google Cloud**, or **Microsoft Azure**. Ownership of the workload **operating system (OS)**, applications, virtual network, access to tenant environments/accounts, and data is held by the *enterprise*.

- **SaaS**: SaaS providers are mainly in charge of the platform's security, which covers the building's exterior, its internal network, and its software. These suppliers are not in charge of the applications' usage by consumers or the owners of the customer data. As a result, it is up to the business to ensure that there is security in place to stop and reduce the possibility of *malware infiltration, inadvertent disclosure,* and the *exfiltration of dangerous data.*

As businesses move from private to public clouds or adopt SaaS services, the burden of protecting data, apps, and infrastructure shifts from the organization to the vendor, as shown in the following diagram (*Figure 1.1*). The organization will always oversee making sure that its data is *secure* and *private,* regardless of the platform that is employed:

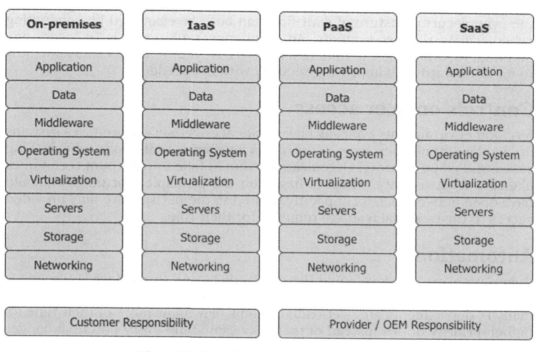

Figure 1.1: *Shared services responsibility matrix*

IT security must be aware of where cloud vendors' security duties end and their own begin to maintain the security of apps and data. Organizations need the proper tools to make sure they are carrying out their security obligations under the shared responsibility paradigm. These tools must offer visibility into activity within the cloud application, in-depth usage analytics to prevent data risk and compliance violations, context-aware policy controls to drive enforcement and remediation if a violation occurs, and real-time threat intelligence on *known* and *unknown* threats to detect and prevent new malware insertion points.

Key considerations for the upliftment of cloud security

Organizations will need to take proactive measures to preserve security in cloud environments if they want to fully benefit from cloud computing. Let's look at some of the most popular techniques businesses can use to enhance cloud computing security.

Risk analysis

The effectiveness of the security controls that are currently in place and the cybersecurity posture of your firm can both be examined by conducting cybersecurity risk assessments. An assessment's objective is to locate any potential security holes or vulnerabilities so that your IT team can decide how to move forward with improving security with knowledge.

Controls on user access

As cloud environments typically have easier access than on-premises systems do, implementing user access controls is another essential part of achieving successful cloud security. Organizations should take into account techniques like *zero-trust security*, which is based on the principle that no one should have open network access implicitly trusted to them. Users are only provided access to the essential features required for their role.

Automation

Cyber attackers are developing their skills daily, and the danger landscape is always expanding. Since there are so many security alerts coming in quickly, many IT departments are overloaded. Teams may focus more of their time on higher-priority duties instead of manually examining every potential danger the network may face by automating important projects like *cybersecurity monitoring*, *threat intelligence gathering*, and *vendor risk evaluations*.

Continual monitoring

The continual monitoring of cybersecurity risk management programs is arguably its most crucial element. *Continuous monitoring* will be even more essential for ensuring adequate cyber hygiene on an ongoing basis as enterprises progressively switch to cloud computing platforms. Rapid changes in the digital landscape make it difficult for enterprises to establish their security posture using point-in-time assessments, and when an issue does occur, it is sometimes too late to take action.

Conclusion

In the current global environment, cloud computing is developing at an extremely rapid rate. Public, private, hybrid, and community clouds are more common nowadays for data storage and data transfer, as well as for *medium-* and *high-use locations*. Since public cloud storage uses more energy during transit, it can have up to five times more control over an environment than private cloud storage, hence demanding more security controls over other types. SaaS serves as the foundation for *on-demand software*, which is built on applications. **PaaS** is a model that relies on the capacity of the *internet's network*, *storage*, and *operating systems*. This model's **IaaS** component refers to **infrastructure as a service**.

Since the data from the cloud computing environment travels and depends on the internet, the issue of data security is more important than it is for traditional networks. On the cloud platform, consumers do not wish to share their data. A major issue with cloud computing nowadays is *privacy* and *security*. Technology and strategy, as well as audit, compliance, risk assessment, and feedback data, all need to be carefully considered when it comes to cloud computing security.

Security examiners in government, business, and public sectors will need to develop more sophisticated and auspicious ways of identifying and preventing intrusions as a result of the complexity of cyber-attacks. Companies will realize that investing in tools like malware detection frameworks, event management, and security data are essential defense mechanisms for digital security. Here, the use of cloud computing services may also be important. Managed security service providers, for example, may be able to offer robust services to businesses that would often be unable to implement comprehensive security measures.

In the next chapter, we will do a deep dive to understand the principles and fundamentals of cloud security along with strategies to adopt the same. We will also cover a few of the best practices you should consider while drafting the fundamentals, objectives, and strategy for your landscape.

Reference

NIST 800-145: https://csrc.nist.gov/publications/detail/sp/800-145/final

CHAPTER 2

Understanding the Core Principles of Cloud Security and its Importance

Introduction

This chapter talks about the basic principles which help us to build the foundation for the cloud security landscape. We will talk and learn about different security principles and concepts in the understanding of the cloud landscape. We will also do a deep dive into these basic principles and their importance for the cloud ecosystem. In the end, we will explain the strategy you should consider to build your cloud security framework along with a couple of best practices for the same.

Structure

In this chapter, we will discuss the following topics:

- Principle and concept understanding
- Architectural consideration
  - o Basic considerations
  - o Additional considerations
- Information classification
- Security awareness, training, and education
- PKI and encryption key management
- Identity and access management
- Strategy to adopt cloud security
- Best practices on cloud security

Principles and concept understanding

In order to start the journey and to set the basic guidelines for cloud security, here are a few of the *critical* and *important* rule games which you should always follow. These *guidelines* will help us to understand the problem statement of the customers and will help build the right cloud security framework and practices to adopt.

Most restrictive

The idea of least privilege states that humans or automated systems should only have access to what is necessary for them to do their duties. It's simple to overlook the automation aspect of this; for instance, a component accessing a database shouldn't utilize credentials that grant write access if write access isn't required.

Your access policies are typically denied by default if the least privilege is used in practice. Users must go through the request and approval processes to obtain any privileges they need because they are typically given no (or very limited) privileges by default.

It is therefore also referred to as **Software as a Service (SaaS)**. Providing infrastructure and resources online to serve its clients has three main objectives: *dynamics*, *abstraction*, and *resource sharing.*

Some of your administrators will require access to the *cloud console*, which is a website that lets you create, manage, and destroy cloud assets like virtual machines. Many cloud service providers grant godlike rights to everyone with access to your cloud panel by default for whatever that service provider manages. Depending on the operating system restrictions on the supplied systems, this can include the ability to *access*, *alter*, or *destroy* data from any location within the cloud environment. Due to this, you must strictly restrict user access to and privileges on the cloud interface, just as you do in on-premises systems with physical data center access, and keep track of their activities.

Defense in Depth

Defense in depth is a strategy that takes into account the possibility of practically any security measure failing, either due to an attacker's level of determination or a flaw in the security measure's implementation. Defense in depth involves building up several overlapping layers of security measures such that even if one is compromised, the one behind it can still stop intruders. This approach will eventually help you to eliminate the *silo-based approach* at the application layer, and help you to have a comprehensive view of how to protect, and establish the defense mechanism for your ecosystem.

With defense-in-depth, you can take things too far, which is why it's critical to comprehend the hazards you can encounter, which are detailed later. The general guideline is that you should be able to say, *What if this fails?* about any one security measure you have. You probably don't have enough defensive depth if the response is an outright failure.

Threat actors as well as trust limits

There are several methods to consider your risks, but I tend to favor an *asset-focused strategy*.

Additionally, it's a good idea to think about the people that are most likely to give you trouble. These are your possible *threat actors*, as they are known in the field of cybersecurity. If you run a business where a criminal can profit from stealing your data or a *hacktivist* would want to deface your website, for instance, you might not need to protect yourself from a well-funded state actor but still need to take precautions. Consider these individuals when creating all of your defenses.

We'll look at four major categories of threat actors that you would need to be concerned about, even if there is a wealth of information and conversation on the subject of threat actors, motivations, and techniques:

- Organized crime or independent criminals who are primarily motivated by financial gain

- Hacktivists who aim to damage your reputation by leaking stolen information, committing acts of vandalism, or interfering with your business

- Insiders who are typically motivated by financial gain or reputational harm

- State actors who may be interested in stealing secrets or interfering with your business

Segregation of duties

To maintain a clear separation of tasks, several requirements must be met before access to sensitive objects or the performance of a specific sensitive activity is granted. The arming of a weapons system, for instance, would require two people with distinct keys and the signatures of two or more people. The separation of responsibilities hence encourages cooperation among entities to undermine the system.

Fail-safe

For a cloud system to collapse safely, it must do so to a condition where neither the system's security nor the privacy of its data is jeopardized. Making a system default to a state where a user or process is prohibited from using the system is one way to put this theory into practice. A *supplemental requirement* would be to guarantee that the system would recover to a secure state and prevent unauthorized access to sensitive data when it does. This strategy relies on employing permissions rather than exclusions. The failed system should only allow access by the system administrator and not by other users if system recovery is not performed automatically until security measures are reinstated.

Economy of mechanism

To prevent unintended access channels from existing or being easily found and eliminated, the economy of the mechanism encourages simple and understandable design and implementation of protection mechanisms.

Complete mediation

Every time a *subject* wants to access something in a computer system, they must first go through a legitimate authorization process that works.

Even when the computer system is being *initialized, shut down, restarted*, or in *maintenance* mode, this mediation must not be suspended or made possible to bypass. The following are the steps involved in full mediation:

- Identifying the entity requesting access
- Confirming that the request hasn't changed since it was made
- Making use of the proper authorization processes
- Reviewing previously approved requests made by the same entity

Open design

The benefits and advantages of security designs that are kept *secret* versus designs that are available for *public observation and judgment* by the community at large have long been a topic of debate. An encryption system is a good case in point. Some believe that keeping the encryption algorithm secret makes it harder to crack. The opposite school of thought contends that making the algorithm public while keeping the encryption key a secret makes it stronger since specialists are more likely to find flaws in it. Except for companies like the **National Security Agency (NSA)**, which employs some of the top mathematicians and cryptographers in the world, the latter strategy has generally proven to be more successful. For most purposes, an *open-access cloud system architecture* that has been scrutinized and put through rigorous testing by a large number of professionals offers a more secure authentication approach than one that has not been thoroughly scrutinized. Protecting keys or passwords is essential to the security of such mechanisms.

Least common mechanism

This idea highlights the need for many users to share a minimum number of security measures since shared access channels can serve as sources of unauthorized information transmission. *Unauthorized data transfers* are made possible via shared access techniques called **covert channels**. The least widespread mechanism supports the least amount of sharing of standard security measures.

Weakest chain

Similar to the adage, *a chain is only as strong as its weakest link*, and a cloud system's security is only as strong as its weakest element. To reduce system risks to a manageable level, it is crucial to pinpoint the weakest security chain and the layer of defense measures and strengthen them.

Making use of the current landscape

Frequently, a cloud implementation's security controls may not be set up correctly or exploited to their full potential. The security posture of an information system will be significantly strengthened by reviewing the status and settings of the existing security mechanisms and making sure they are operating at their ideal design points. Partitioning a cloud system into guarded subunits is another method that may be used to boost security while utilizing current components. In this way, harm to the computing resources will be minimized if a security mechanism for one sub-unit is breached without affecting the other sub-units.

Architectural considerations

Several variables influence the execution and functionality of the cloud security architecture. *Regulatory requirements, standard compliance, security management, information classification,* and *security awareness* are all challenges that are generally present. Then there are more specialized architecturally linked fields, such as trustworthy hardware and software, creating a secure execution environment, establishing secure communications, and enhancing hardware through microarchitectures. In this section, we cover these crucial ideas.

Basic concerns

Cloud security architecture is affected both indirectly and directly by a variety of topics. *Compliance, security management, operational concerns, controls,* and *security awareness* are a few of the things they cover. Cloud security architecture ought to assist in maintaining legal compliance. As a logical extension, the *cloud security policy* should cover information classification, who might have access to information, how access is granted, where the data is located, and whether or not it is acceptable. A suitable *personnel awareness program* should be implemented, and relevant controls should be identified and tested using assurance methods.

Compliance

The service provider in a public cloud environment typically doesn't let the customers know where their data is kept. In *actuality,* one of the core aspects of the cloud is how processing and data storage is distributed. The cloud service provider should, however, work with the client to take into account their needs for data location.

The cloud vendor should also be transparent with the customer by providing details about the storage that was used, the processing characteristics, and other pertinent account information. Accessibility of a client's data by system engineers and specific other workers of the provider is another compliance concern. The acquisition of sensitive information should be monitored, *controlled,* and *safeguarded* by measures such as the separation of roles. This element is a crucial component of providing and maintaining cloud services. The capability of regional law enforcement organizations to access a client's sensitive data is a worry in circumstances where information is held in a foreign country. This scenario, for instance, might take place if a government agency looks into a cloud provider's computer system using computer forensics because they think they may be engaging in criminal activity.

Security control

For cloud computing to be advantageous, security architecture requires efficient security management. *Access control, vulnerability analysis, change control, incident response, fault tolerance, disaster recovery,* and *business continuity planning* are essential areas where management problems should be found via proper cloud security management and administration.

Controls

Reducing vulnerabilities to a manageable level and lessening the effects of an attack are the goals of cloud security controls. A company must ascertain the impact and likelihood of loss to accomplish this. Sensitive information being compromised, money being stolen, reputation being damaged, and resources being physically destroyed are a few examples of loss.

Risk analysis is the process of evaluating numerous dangerous situations and generating a representative number for the *potential loss estimate (risk analysis)*. The purpose of controls is to mitigate vulnerabilities. Although there are many different kinds of controls, they are often divided into one of the four categories as follows:

- **Deterrent measures**: Lessen the possibility of a planned attack.
- **Preventative measures**: Guard weaknesses and render attacks ineffective or less damaging. A security policy violation attempt is prevented by preventative mechanisms.
- **Corrective measures**: Diminish the impact of an assault.
- **Investigative controls**: Identify attacks and activate preventive or corrective measures. Detective controls, which include things like *intrusion detection systems, organizational regulations, video cameras,* and *motion detectors, warn of infractions* or *attempted violations of security policy.*

Additional controls

The following are additional tasks related to managing cloud security:

- Managing and observing service levels and service-level agreements.
- Obtaining sufficient data via dashboards and instruments to recognize and assess problematic situations.
- Reducing important information loss brought on by a lack of controls.
- Adequate data management on a distributed computing system within an enterprise. Organizations with a high volume of laptops and other personal computing devices might lessen the risk of data loss by centralizing their data on the cloud.
- Monitoring of information that is centralized in the cloud, as opposed to needing to look at data that is dispersed throughout an organization on various computing and storage devices.
- Provisioning for quick recovery from problem scenarios.

Additionally, a better ability to perform forensic analysis on cloud-based data utilizing a *network forensic model* should be promoted by *cloud security management*. Utilizing *automatic hashing* that occurs when data is stored in the cloud and other methods, this approach will allow for quick capture and verification of evidence. Additionally, by applying emerging cloud management standards to areas like *interoperable security methods, quality of service, accounting, provisioning*, and *API specifications*, as well as by using *automation* sparingly, and where it makes sense, it is possible to improve cloud security management. Remote APIs should be controlled to ensure that they are consistent and well-documented since they allow for the control of cloud resources through program interfaces.

Scalability, pay-as-you-go billing, on-demand implementation and provisioning, and *moving information management operational tasks to the cloud* are all examples of how cloud security management should address applications to contain enterprise costs.

Information classification

Information classification is a significant compliance-related topic that might impact the architecture of the cloud security system. Disaster recovery and business continuity planning are also supported by the information classification process.

Objectives for information classification

Information classification is advantageous for several reasons. Not every piece of data is equally valuable to a company. For instance, certain data is more valuable to higher management because it helps them decide on *long-* or *short-term* strategic business direction. *Trade secrets, formulas*, and *knowledge of new products* are just a few examples of data that is so important that losing it could have significant ramifications for the business in the marketplace, either in terms of public disgrace or diminished credibility.

These justifications make the higher, enterprise-level value of information classification clear. Not only at the enterprise level or operations level, but across the world, information stored in a cloud environment has an impact on this objective (*maintain the CIA*). Its main goals are enhancing *confidentiality, integrity*, and *availability* while reducing information risk. Additionally, you get a better *cost-to-benefit ratio* by concentrating the controls and protection mechanisms on the information areas that require them the most.

Taking the example of the government sector, information classification has the most experience. It is an essential element when safeguarding trusted systems because its worth has long been recognized. *Information categorization* is largely utilized in this industry to avoid unauthorized disclosure of information and the subsequent breach of confidentiality. Classifying information ensures *regulatory compliance* and meets *privacy obligations*. A business may want to use classification to keep a competitive edge in a challenging industry. An organization may use information classification in the cloud for other good legal reasons like to reduce liability or to safeguard sensitive corporate data.

Benefits of information classification

Employing information classification provides several definite advantages for a company using cloud computing, in addition to the reasons listed above. Following is a list of some of these advantages:

- It shows how committed a company is to security measures.
- It supports the principles of *confidentiality*, *integrity*, and *availability* as they relate to data.
- It helps identify which protections apply to which information. It might be required for *regulatory*, *compliance*, or *legal reasons*. It aids in determining which information is the most sensitive or important to an organization.

Concepts behind information classification

It is necessary to categorize the information that an organization handles under how sensitive the organization is to its loss or disclosure. Setting the sensitivity level of the data is the responsibility of the owner of the information system. Security measures can be properly applied thanks to classification following a defined classification scheme.

The classification words listed as follows are typical of those employed in the private sector and apply to cloud data:

- **Public data**: Information that is comparable to unclassified information; any information about a corporation that does not fall under one of the following categories may be deemed public. Although it may be against policy to disclose material without authorization, the organization, its staff, and/or its clients are not anticipated to be substantially or negatively impacted.
- **Sensitive data**: Sensitive data is information that requires a greater level of classification than regular data. This data is guarded against *loss of confidentiality* and *loss of integrity* brought on by unauthorized changes. This classification applies to data that need extra security measures to maintain their accuracy and prevent unauthorized modification or deletion. It is information that requires a higher level of confidence

than usual in correctness and completeness.

- **Private data**: This category includes any personal data used only internally by the company. Its unauthorized disclosure could have a substantial and negative effect on the company and/or its personnel. Medical records and pay levels are two examples of private information.

- **Confidential data**: Data classified as confidential pertains to the most delicate corporate information that is only to be used internally. Its illegal publication may have a substantial and detrimental effect on the company, its stockholders, its business partners, and/or its clients. Following the rules of *the Freedom of Information Act* and other *relevant federal laws or regulations*, this information is not required to be disclosed. For instance, confidential information includes details regarding the creation of new products, trade secrets, and merger talks.

A company may choose a high, medium, or low classification scheme depending on its CIA *requirements* and whether it needs *high, medium,* or *low protective controls*. A system and its data, for instance, can need a high level of integrity and availability but not secrecy. Subject to senior management assessment, the authorized owners of information are in charge of choosing the data classification levels.

Classification criteria

An information object's classification may be based on several factors, including:

- **Value**: In the private sector, value is the most widely utilized criterion for classifying data. A piece of information needs to be categorized if it is important to a company or its rivals.

- **Age**: If a piece of information loses value over time, its classification may be downgraded. For example, some confidential materials in the US Department of Defense become unclassified automatically after a set amount of time.

- **Useful life**: Information can frequently be declassified if it has become *obsolete* owing to new information, significant company changes, or other factors.

- **Personal association**: Information may need to be categorized if it is directly related to certain people or is covered by a privacy regulation. Investigational data that reveals the identities of informants, for instance, may need to be kept secret.

Procedures for classifying information

The process of creating a classification system involves multiple steps. The priority order for the steps is as follows and also depicted in the following diagram:

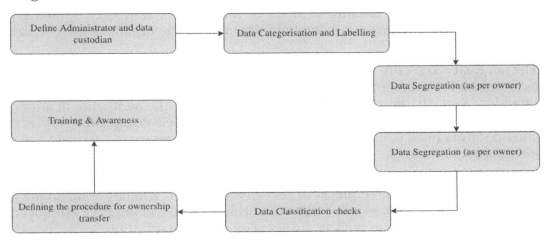

Figure 2.1: *Process for defining information classification*

1. Determine the proper administrator and data custodian in step one. *Data backup*, data *restoration*, and *information security* are all the responsibilities of the data custodian.

2. Outline the standards for categorizing and labeling the data.

3. Sort the information according to the *owner*, who is overseen by a *manager*.

4. Specify any exceptions to the classification policy and record them.

5. Specify the checks that will be used for each classification level.

6. Describe the procedures for declassifying the information or giving the information's custody to a different organization.

7. Develop a program to educate the entire company on classification controls. Data classification should include but not be limited to PI, PII, SPI, PHI, and so on.

Security awareness, training, and education

Because controls, intrusion detection, risk assessment, and proactive or reactive security administration take up the majority of a security practitioner's work, *security awareness* is frequently disregarded as a factor affecting cloud security architecture. Employees need to be aware of how even seemingly trivial activities can have a substantial influence on the organization's overall security posture.

The necessity to secure information and safeguard an enterprise's information assets must be understood by the staff of both the cloud client and the cloud provider. *Security practitioners* need training to implement and maintain essential security controls, especially when using or delivering cloud services, and operators need continual training in the skills necessary to carry out their job functions securely.

The fundamentals of security and its advantages for a company must be taught to all personnel. The three pillars of security awareness training — *awareness, training*, and *education* — will be beneficial since they will improve employee behavior and attitudes as well as the security of an organization.

The following are some ways that computer *security knowledge, training*, and *education* can improve security:

- Increasing understanding of the significance of safeguarding system resources
- Gaining expertise and knowledge to enable computer users to carry out their tasks more securely
- Gaining in-depth expertise as necessary to create, implement, or run security strategies for businesses and systems

Planning, implementing, maintaining, and *periodically evaluating an awareness and training program* for computer security is essential. The following *seven* phases, in general, should be included in a computer security awareness and training program:

- Define the program's objectives, goals, and scope.
- Name training personnel
- Determine the intended audience
- Encourage management and staff
- Execute the application
- Keep up the program
- Assess the scheme

Security awareness

In contrast to training, an organization's *security awareness* refers to how well-informed all of its employees are on the value of security and security controls. Security awareness programs also have the following advantages in addition to the previously listed advantages and goals:

- They can cut down on personnel attempts at unauthorized actions
- They can considerably boost the protection controls' efficacy
- They aid in preventing *fraud*, *waste*, and *abuse* of computing resources

Employees are deemed *security conscious* when they have a solid understanding of how important security is, how it affects viability and the bottom line, and the regular threats to cloud computing resources. To acclimate new hires and refresh veteran personnel, it is crucial to hold regular awareness seminars. Always be *direct*, *easy to understand*, and *concise* when writing.

You should deliver it in a manner that is simple to grasp by the audience, with a good balance of motivation and a minimum of technical jargon. When they show how the audience's interests and the organization's security interests are compatible, these sessions are most powerful.

Instruction and learning

In contrast to *awareness*, *training disseminates security information* in a more organized way, through seminars, workshops, or specialized teaching. Concerning cloud security, the following training options are available:

- Job training for security-related tasks for operators and particular users
- Awareness training for departments or groups of employees holding security-sensitive positions
- Technical security training for IT support staff and system administrators
- Advanced training for security practitioners and information systems auditors
- Security training for senior managers, functional managers, and business unit managers

System administrators, *auditors*, and *security experts* must receive comprehensive training and education, which is often required for job advancement. Additionally, *cloud security software* and *hardware-specific product training* are essential for ensuring the enterprise's security.

The primary goal of any training is to inspire the *employees*, and they must comprehend how important security is to the organization's bottom line. The creation of hypothetical cloud security vulnerability situations and the subsequent solicitation of feedback on potential responses or results are standard training techniques.

PKI and encryption key management

Exchanged data with a cloud should be *encrypted*, calls to distant servers should be checked for embedded malware, and digital certificates should be used and controlled, all of which will help to secure communications. In *public-key cryptography*, people's public keys can be linked to them through a certification procedure. By confirming a person's identification and providing a certificate that attests to the listed person's public key, a **certificate authority (CA)** performs the notarial function. This certifying agent uses its private key to sign the certificate. If the recipient's public key decrypts the data, the recipient is confirmed to be the sender.

Name, **public key**, **certificate authority name**, and the **duration of the certificate's validity** are all included in the certificate. It is necessary to cross-certify the CA's public key with another CA to validate the signature. *Public key certificates* must follow the format specified by the X.509 *standard*. The repository that stores certificates and **certificate revocation lists (CRLs)** that identify revoked certificates receives this certificate after that. The following sections go into further information about digital certificates.

The *public key infrastructure* combines digital certificates and signatures with other *e-commerce-related services* (PKI). For electronic transactions, these services offer *integrity, access control, confidentiality, authentication*, and *non-repudiation*.

Digital certificate

One of the main parts of PKI is the *digital certificate* and *certificate management*. Remember: A *digital certificate's function is to prove to everyone that a person's public key, which is shown on a public key ring, genuinely belongs to that person*. A reputable third-party CA can confirm that the public key belongs to the identified person before issuing a certificate attesting to that fact. The public key of the individual and any associated data is digitally signed by the CA to complete the certification.

Responsibilities between the repository and the CA might be outlined for certificates and CRLs to be stored there. These duties are distributed following the repository access protocol. The repository communicates with users, CAs, and other repositories over one protocol. The repository receives the certificates and CRLs that the CA has deposited. Users can then access the information repository.

Identity and access management

For secure cloud computing, *identity management* and *access control* must be in place. A *user ID* and *password* are used to access a computer system, which is the most basic form of identity management. *Authentication, authorization,* and *access control* must be more stringent for genuine identity management, which is necessary for cloud computing. By utilizing technologies like *biometrics* or *smart cards*, it should be able to ascertain which resources are permitted for a person or process to access and identify instances in which unauthorized parties have accessed a resource.

Identity management

Most access control systems are built around identification and authentication. A user identifying themselves as such to a system is known as **identification**. This usually takes the form of a username or user login ID. Identification creates user accountability for actions performed on the system. User IDs ought to be exclusive and never used by several people. User IDs typically follow standardized formats in many major businesses, such as *first initial, last name,* and so on. An ID shouldn't contain information about a user's position or function to improve security and limit the amount of information that an attacker can access.

When a user logs in, *authentication* is often carried out by verifying their *user password* to ensure that they are whom they say they are. The three sorts of factors used for authentication are as follows:

- **Type 1**: A password or **personal identification number (PIN)** that you are aware of
- **Type 2**: Is something you possess, like an ATM *card* or *smart card*
- **Type 3**: Is something physical about you, like a *fingerprint* or *retina scan*

Two out of the three authentication factors must be utilized in *two-factor authentication.*

Passwords

Passwords must be secured since they are vulnerable to theft. Ideally, a password should only be used once. Due to the need for a new password with each login, this **one-time password**, or **OTP**, offers the *highest level of security*.

The *static password* stays the same each time you log in. *Dynamic passwords* are passwords that alter each time you log in. Between these two extremes, password changes can also fall. Depending on how vital the information has to be protected and how frequently it is used, passwords may need to be changed on a *monthly*, *quarterly*, or *another schedule*. Naturally, the likelihood of a password being compromised increases with the number of times it is used.

A **passphrase** is a string of characters that is typically longer than the permitted password length. The technology turns the passphrase into an arbitrary virtual password. A front-end authentication device or a back-end authentication server, which supports numerous workstations or the host can carry out the authentication in all of these schemes. *Tokens*, *memory cards*, and *smart cards* are just a few examples of gadgets that can offer passwords.

Implementing identity management solution

Effective identity management necessitates a high level of corporate commitment and the allocation of adequate resources to complete the task. The following are examples of typical initiatives for implementing identity management:

- Creating a database of identities and credentials
- Managing access rights for users
- Enforcing security policy
- Developing the ability to create and modify accounts
- Monitoring resource accesses
- Installing a process for removing access rig
- Providing training in proper procedures is the *first five steps*

Software that automates a lot of the necessary procedures can help an identity management effort.

Access controls

Access control is inextricably linked to identity management and is required to protect the *privacy*, *availability*, and *integrity* of cloud data.

These and other related goals flow from the *organizational security policy*. This policy is a high-level declaration of management intent on the management of information access and the individuals that are permitted to receive that information.

Threats to the system, the system's susceptibility to these threats, and the possibility that the threats would materialize are *three* factors that must be taken into account while planning and implementing access control systems. The following definitions are given for these ideas:

- **Threat**: An occurrence or action with the potential to damage information systems or networks.

- **Vulnerability**: A flaw or absence of protection that could be used by an adversary to harm the networks or information systems.

- **Risk**: The possibility of causing harm to an information system or network or of losing data; the likelihood that danger may come to pass.

Controls

To limit risk and the likelihood of loss, *controls* are put in place. Duty separation and the principle of least privilege are two crucial principles in control. For a task or process to be completed, there must be at least two performing entities. A *security policy* can only be broken if the entities conspire, thus that's the only way it can be broken. For instance, in a financial setting, the individual requesting that a check be issued for payment shouldn't also be the person with the power to sign the check.

Control measures can be implemented in an *administrative, logical (also known as technical)*, or *physical manner*:

- **Administrative controls** include rules and procedures, security awareness training, background checks, work habits checks, a review of vacation history, and heightened supervision.

- **Logical or technical controls** include the safeguarding of data and limiting access to systems. These restrictions include *encryption, smart cards, access control lists*, and *transmission protocols*, as examples.

- **Physical controls** include guards and standard building security, such as *locking doors, guarding server rooms or laptops, protecting wires, segregating duties*, and *backing up files*.

For those who access sensitive data in a cloud environment, controls offer *responsibility*. The *audit function* and *access control methods* that demand identification and authentication are used to enforce this responsibility. The security policy of the organization must be adhered to and appropriately represented by these controls. Throughout a cloud information system's complete life cycle, assurance procedures make sure the *control mechanisms* are correctly implementing the security policy.

Controlling access types

Setting up access rules is a necessary step in controlling access by a subject, an active entity like a *person* or a *process*, to an object, or a passive thing like a file. There are *three* categories or models that these regulations might be classified under.

Mandatory access control

The labels on an *object's packaging*, which show the subject's clearance, and the object's classification or level of sensitivity determine whether a subject is allowed access to it. As an illustration, the military designates documents as *unclassified, confidential, secret*, or *top secret*. An individual may be granted clearance of **Confidential**, **Secret**, or **Top Secret**, and may have access to documents classified at or below the level of *his* or *her* particular clearance. As a result, a person with a clearance of *secret* can only have limited access to secret and confidential documents. The requirement is that the person must need to know the classified documents at issue. Therefore, the documents must be required for that person to finish the work that has been allocated to them. The person shouldn't access the material unless there is a need to know, even if they have been cleared for a certain classification level. **Rule-based access control** is a sort of required access control because rules, rather than only the subjects' and objects' identities, define this *access* (such as the correlation between *clearance labels* and *classification labels*).

Discretionary access control

Within certain parameters, the subject has the power to decide which things are accessible when using *discretionary access control*. ACL, for instance, is a type of *access control list*. A list of users with access privileges to a certain resource is called an **access control list**.

User, program, and *file* are the three components of the access control triple, and each user's associated access privileges are listed for reference. In local, dynamic settings where the subjects must have the freedom to decide which resources particular users are allowed access to, this sort of access control is utilized. **User-directed discretionary access control** refers to the situation in which an individual user has the authority to modify the access control for a particular object within specific parameters. Discretionary access controls based on an individual's identity are known as **identity-based access controls**.

The advantages of *user-based* and *identity-based discretionary access control* are sometimes combined in a *hybrid* method.

Non-discretionary access control

Depending on the corporate security policy, a *central authority* decides who is permitted access to particular items. The access controls may be based on a person's position within an organization (*role-based*) or the duties and responsibilities of the subject (*task-based*). Since access controls are based on a person's function or title inside the organization, *nondiscretionary access control* is beneficial in an organization with regular staff changes. As a result, these access controls do not need to be modified whenever a new employee takes over that position.

Single Sign-On (SSO)

SSO eliminates the troublesome requirement of logging in several times to access various sites. Users may employ shortcuts when constructing passwords and IDs when they have a lot to remember, which could make them vulnerable to attack. A user is automatically signed in to all necessary applications when using SSO and only needs to supply one ID and *password* per work session. SSO programs can operate on a user's desktop or authentication servers, however, for SSO security, passwords shouldn't be kept or sent in the open.

Stronger passwords can be used, and SSO makes it simpler to change or remove passwords. It also reduces the amount of time it takes to access resources. Many SSO implementations have the major drawback of allowing users to freely wander the network resources without any *limits* once they have gained access to the system through the initial login. *Smart cards* and *magnetic badges* are only a couple of the authentication tools available. To prevent a user from modifying the configurations that another authority specifies, strict restrictions must be put in place. SSO can be put into practice using scripts that replay users' many login attempts or by employing authentication servers to confirm a user's identity and encrypted authentication tickets to grant access to system services.

Web-based corporate systems with SSO can access control management services from **enterprise access management (EAM)**. There are various ways to offer SSO. The use of non-persistent, encrypted cookies on the client interface, for instance, enables SSO to be applied to web applications running on many servers within the same domain. Each program that a user intends to visit is given a cookie to do this operation. A secure credential could be created for each user on a reverse proxy that sits in front of the web server as an alternative method. Each time a user tries to access protected web apps, they are then required to enter their credentials.

Strategy to adopt cloud security

Here is a set of key considerations you should adopt to build the strategy to engage in a cloud security landscape.

Enabling secure cloud migrations with a cross-platform, integrated segmentation strategy

By segmenting data across several cloud or data storage systems as opposed to storing it all in one location, organizations can improve their cloud security. They must put into practice a multi-cloud or hybrid cloud approach to achieve this.

Businesses can handle various aspects of their cloud journey using a *multi-cloud strategy* by selecting multiple cloud platforms or resources of the same type (public or private). In many circumstances, enterprises will distribute assets across two or more public cloud platforms, such as *Amazon Web Services, Microsoft Azure, Google Cloud*, and others. Government agencies may rely on secret areas in one or more of those public cloud platforms if they need to protect sensitive data that belong to an organization.

Using both on-premises and/or private clouds, along with public clouds, is known as a **hybrid cloud strategy**. Due to the ease with which workloads may be moved between these services, constructing a *hybrid cloud architecture* can increase an organization's agility while managing assets. The *edge*, or the location from which employees will access this information, is where the data is stored in a hybrid cloud, which may also combine public cloud services with edge computing.

Cloud administrators can set precise **identity and access management (IAM)** rules in any scenario. To improve *network security*, administrators can safely divide cloud environments into various compartments using micro-segmentation. Additionally, they have the option of setting up a cloud management service to proactively monitor and immediately address any security vulnerabilities.

Avoiding problems associated with complex, segregated, and bloated legacy data

An *extensive server network* spread over numerous sites may be used for legacy data storage. Businesses can have implemented this storage in some situations as a band-aid without taking security and data integration into account. As a result, the infrastructure becomes unnecessarily complicated and has the potential to *silo data*, making some assets inaccessible to teams, functions, or individuals inside an organization. Of course, this complexity also makes it possible for information security to be *breached* and gives hackers access to *private information*.

These issues can, regrettably, arise again in the cloud. To prevent insecure data sprawl, administrators need a reliable cloud design that takes security into account. Administrators can prevent unnecessarily *siloing* their assets by simplifying the architecture and ensuring it adheres to standard practices. In *multi-cloud* or *hybrid cloud architecture*, administrators can more effectively manage and connect data by reducing silos.

Examining the danger posed by the extended attack surface of the cloud

Public cloud computing platforms allow for more precise segmentation and integration of computer resources. However, if best practices are disregarded and misconfiguration errors go unattended, the security of the cloud environment can go uncontrolled, leaving companies vulnerable to *cyber-attacks*, *data breaches*, and other *vulnerabilities*. With this sprawl, the cloud becomes an *expanded attack surface*, giving criminals and other bad guys access through a backdoor.

Reviewing their cloud infrastructure regularly is required for cloud administrators. Any business can find it difficult to manually check for these hazards. Organizations may identify threats in *real time* and take action before problems result in catastrophic data losses by utilizing a cloud management platform that monitors for security and compliance.

Best practices on cloud security

A few recommended practices have stayed consistent to guarantee the security of cloud systems, although cloud security is continually changing. To prevent sensitive applications and data from getting into the wrong hands, businesses with existing cloud solutions or those intending to deploy them should take into account this advice and resources.

Recognizing the shared responsibility model

In a private data center, all security-related issues are the full responsibility of the business. However, things are far more challenging in the public cloud. The *cloud provider* is in charge of some areas of IT security, even if the cloud customer is ultimately responsible. This is what experts in security and the cloud term a shared responsibility paradigm.

Leading *IaaS* and **platform as a service (PaaS)** providers like **Amazon Web Services (AWS)** and *Microsoft Azure* offer documentation to their clients so that all parties are aware of their respective roles in the various deployment options.

Businesses should evaluate the vendor's shared security responsibility rules to understand who is in charge of each component of cloud security before deciding on a particular cloud vendor. By doing so, confusion and misunderstanding may be avoided. The ability to clearly define roles, however, can help avoid security problems that happen when a specific security requirement slips through the cracks.

Asking detailed security questions to your cloud provider

Organizations should be specific in their inquiries to their public cloud vendors regarding the security protocols and procedures they have in place, along with defining shared responsibilities. Although it's simple to assume that the top companies have security covered, security practices might differ greatly between vendors.

Organizations should ask a variety of questions to better understand how one cloud provider compares to another, such as:

- *Where do the servers of the service physically reside?*

- *What procedure does the provider follow in the event of a security incident?*

- *What is the disaster recovery strategy for the provider?*

- *What safety precautions does the provider have in place for different access components?*

- *How much technical support is the company prepared to offer?*

- *What conclusions can you draw from the provider's most recent penetration tests?*

- *Does the service use encryption for both at-rest and in-transit data?*

- *Which departments or employees of the provider have access to the data that is kept in the cloud?*

- *What forms of authentication may I use with the provider?*

- *What regulations is the provider in favor of?*

Installing Identity and Access Management (IAM) software

A top-notch **identity and access management (IAM)** system can aid in reducing these risks even though hackers' techniques for gaining access to sensitive data are becoming more advanced with each new attack.

To establish and implement access controls based on the least privilege, *experts* advise enterprises to look for an IAM solution. Along with being based on role-based permission capabilities, these regulations should be. Even if hostile actors are successful in stealing usernames and passwords, **multi-factor authentication (MFA)** can further limit the danger of access to critical information.

A *hybrid environment* that combines private data centers and cloud deployments may be another situation in which organizations would like to explore an IAM solution. This can make *authentication* for end-users simpler and make it simpler for security personnel to make sure they are applying uniform policies throughout all IT environments.

Your staff should receive training

Organizations should train their employees on how to identify cybersecurity risks and how to respond to them to stop hackers from obtaining access credentials for cloud computing products. A *thorough training program* should cover both more complex subjects like *risk management* and *fundamental security skills* like how to set a strong password and recognize potential social engineering attacks.

The ability to grasp the inherent risk of *shadow IT* is perhaps the most crucial aspect of cloud security training for staff members. The majority of companies make it far too simple for employees to implement their tools and systems without the knowledge or assistance of the IT department. It is impossible to assess all vulnerabilities without complete insight into every system that interacts with the company's data. Businesses must communicate this risk and its potential effects on the organization.

Creating and enforcing cloud security guidelines

Every organization should have policies in writing that outline *who may utilize cloud services, how they may be used,* and *what information may be stored there.* To protect data and apps in the cloud, they must also specify the precise security technologies that employees must utilize.

To make sure that everyone is adhering to these regulations, security personnel should ideally have automated solutions in place. The cloud vendor may occasionally include functionality for enforcing policies that are sufficient to fulfill the demands of the company. In some cases, the business might have to invest in a *third-party solution*, like a **cloud access security broker (CASB)**, that provides capabilities for enforcing policy.

Protecting your endpoints

Strong endpoint security is still necessary and is even more important when using a cloud service. The new cloud computing initiatives provide a chance to review current tactics and make sure the security measures are sufficient to face changing threats.

Endpoint security has historically relied on a *defense-in-depth* approach consisting of *firewalls*, *anti-malware*, *intrusion detection*, and *access control*. However, the range of endpoint security issues has grown so large and intricate that automation techniques are needed to keep up. EDR instruments and/or **endpoint protection platforms (EPP)** can be helpful in this regard.

Securing data while it is moving and at rest

Any cloud security strategy should include encryption as a major component. Organizations should not only encrypt any data that is stored in a public cloud storage service, but they should also make sure that any data that is being transmitted is encrypted as well, as this is when it may be most exposed to assaults.

Key management and *encryption services* are provided by several cloud computing providers. Encryption options are also provided by some *traditional* and *third-party software providers*. Experts advise looking for an encryption system that integrates naturally with current business procedures, removing the need for end-users to take any additional steps to adhere to corporate encryption regulations.

Utilizing technology for intrusion detection and prevention

Some of the best cloud security options available today include **intrusion prevention and detection systems (IDPs)**. They keep an eye on, examine, and react to network traffic in both *on-premises* and *public cloud environments*. IDPS systems add threats to a log, notify administrators of unexpected activity, and block threats when they come across *anomaly-based*, *protocol-based*, or *signature-based* threats to give administrators time to take appropriate action.

Real-time warnings and *round-the-clock monitoring* are made possible by these solutions. Analyzing network traffic for tell-tale signals of a sophisticated assault is practically impossible without IDPs.

Audits and penetration testing should be performed

All businesses should do penetration testing, according to *experts*, to ascertain whether current cloud security measures are adequate to secure data and applications, regardless of whether an organization chooses to work with an outside security firm or keep security teams in-house.

The skills of all security providers should be examined as part of the regular security audits that enterprises should carry out. This ought to vouch for their compliance with the security requirements that were established. It's important to audit access logs to make sure that only authorized users are using cloud applications and sensitive data.

Conclusion

One of the main concerns of cloud customers is the security of cloud-based applications and data. Protecting cloud services is fundamentally dependent on safe software and secure software life cycle management. The *confidentiality, availability*, and *integrity principles*, as they are used in *distributed, virtualized*, and *dynamic architectures*, provide the foundation for the information security of cloud systems. The *least privilege, division of roles, defense in depth, fail-safe*, and *open design principles* are crucial for developing secure software.

In the next chapter, we will talk about the assessment exercise on the cloud landscape along with choosing the right solution for your enterprise.

References

NIST 800-145: https://csrc.nist.gov/publications/detail/sp/800-145/final.

CHAPTER 3

Cloud Landscape Assessment and Choosing a Solution for Your Enterprise

Introduction

This chapter will help us to understand the guidelines and principles to assess the cloud environment and will guide us to choose the right solution. The initial section of the chapter will help you to learn about different roles and responsibilities across the ecosystem which is important to drive this engagement. In the later section of the chapter, you will learn about the assessment lifecycle and ways to select the right cloud platform for your enterprise.

Structure

In this chapter, we will discuss the following topics:

- Cloud security roles and responsibilities for an organization
- Shared Responsibility Model
- Responsibilities of **Cloud Service Provider** (CSP)
- Responsibilities of the customer
- Roles and responsibilities of the core team and understanding of the team structure
- Risk management framework for CSP and customers
- Cloud security assessment including basic principles, need and benefit to have it, and the execution method
- Selecting the right cloud service provider for your organization

Defining organization cloud security roles and responsibilities

Security and compliance teams shouldn't be a productivity bottleneck and should be in line with business goals and objectives to be effective.

Beyond the *Shared Responsibility Model*, it's crucial to outline individual duties for cloud security within your organization and make sure everyone is aware of the standards.

Initiatives for cloud security must be sponsored by executive leadership teams. Executive sponsorship is essentially required in the current regulatory environment. Even more damaging than (or perhaps as *bad* as) a data breach itself can be the potential financial impact on a company of regulatory noncompliance. For business leaders and other fiduciaries, many regulations often entail criminal consequences in addition to monetary ones.

Executives need to set a good example. Executives shouldn't be granted *one-off exclusions* if company policy mandates that corporate data on mobile devices be encrypted and requires MFA to access SaaS services. Beyond setting a good example, CEOs must make sure that *security* and *compliance* projects have the proper support and funding, and that the effect of strategic business choices on the organization's overall security and compliance posture is always taken into account.

Teams responsible for security and compliance must establish and uphold the proper rules to enable the business securely. Security and compliance teams shouldn't be a hindrance to productivity and efficiency; instead, they should understand and support company goals and objectives.

Working with security and compliance teams also makes it possible to avoid operating in a vacuum with *siloed* cloud technologies and products and to make sure that individual lines of business can benefit from any existing relationships the company may have with vendors or cloud providers to procure services more affordably and quickly when support is required.

Regarding cloud security and compliance, individual end-users are accountable for adhering to corporate governance. They must be aware of the inherent hazards in the cloud and treat the information that has been entrusted to them with the same level of care as their personal information.

Deep-dive into the Shared Responsibility Model

Though not *standardized*, the Shared Responsibility Model is a framework that specifies which security duties belong to the CSP and which belong to the client. To avoid coverage gaps, businesses employing cloud services must be clear about which security duties they delegate to their provider(s) and which they must manage internally.

To learn what the provider covers and what the customer needs to do on their own to secure the company, customers should always check with their CSPs. Every CSPs have a *pre-defined template* that explains the roles and responsibilities between CSPs and customers.

Cloud Service Provider (CSP) responsibilities

Whether it is **SaaS**, **PaaS**, or **IaaS**, the security controls offered by CSPs differ. From SaaS to PaaS to IaaS, the duty of the customer typically grows.

Typically, servers and storage are the sole responsibility of CSPs. They set up the actual data centers, networks, and other gear, such as **virtual machines (VMs)** and power the infrastructure, as well as protect and patch the infrastructure itself. In IaaS contexts, CSPs are often only accountable for these tasks.

CSPs take on more duties in a PaaS environment, such as virtualization, runtime, networking, **operating systems (OSes)**, and runtime security. CSPs also offer application and middleware security in a SaaS environment.

Each provider and consumer may have different security obligations. CSPs providing SaaS-based products, for instance, may or may not give customers access to the security measures they employ. Contrarily, IaaS providers frequently provide *built-in security mechanisms* that let users observe and access CSP security tools, some of which may even have customer-alerting capabilities. Do note that irrespective of the (*IaaS*, *PaaS*, and *SaaS*) models, the customer is always responsible for their data, data classification, and access controls at a minimum.

Customer responsibilities

Customers are often responsible for the application, middleware, virtualization, data, OS, network, and runtime security in IaaS clouds in addition to the CSP security measures mentioned previously. Customers can supplement, replace, or overlay built-in cybersecurity methods in IaaS infrastructures like Amazon **Virtual Private Cloud (VPC)** or Microsoft Azure **Virtual Network (Vnet)**, for instance. Customers often just handle applications and middleware security in PaaS setups, which reduces their security workload. Even less duty falls on the client in SaaS environments.

But regardless of the *cloud delivery architecture*, the client is always in charge of data security and **identity and access management (IAM)**. The customer is also responsible for *compliance* and *encryption*.

Adopting extra controls to further limit risk can be difficult, though, because CSPs control and manage the infrastructure that consumer apps and data operate within. When assessing CSPs and cloud services, IT security personnel ought to become involved as early as possible. To decide whether extra safeguards will need to be implemented internally, security teams must assess CSP's default security tools. By installing one or more network-based virtual security appliances, a corporation can add its security capabilities to cloud environments. Security administrators can fine-tune particular security setups and policy settings with the use of customer-added toolsets. Implementing the same tools in public clouds as they do in corporate **local area networks (LANs)** is frequently more affordable for many businesses. Administrators will no longer need to manually develop security policies using various security technologies in the cloud. Instead, a single security policy may be developed once and then applied to identical security instruments, whether they are located on-premises or in the cloud.

Core cloud team roles and responsibilities

Adopting the cloud is a difficult and uncertain choice. It's the decision to forgo complete ownership and control of the local IT infrastructure in favor of hazy cooperation with unaffiliated cloud and SaaS providers. Despite the astounding variety of resources the cloud offers, mastering it takes expertise.

Finding individuals with the appropriate abilities and knowledge is a crucial component of cloud success. Let's examine the roles and duties required for success in cloud computing, take a deeper look at a modern cloud team organization, and think about some of the most significant jobs.

Understanding team structures

No one cloud team skill set or set of tasks is universal, and there is no single global team structure. A *busy business* may accommodate many cloud teams. But regardless of the organization, the objectives will be the same. The following will be demanded of cloud teams:

- Create new applications that run in the cloud.

- Rebuild existing apps to run in the cloud.

- Migrate workloads from a local data center to the cloud.

- In the cloud, safeguard and save corporate data cloud architectures should be optimized for running app workloads that are designed for high availability.

- To configure and secure cloud data and apps, and create standard policies and processes. Control and maximize the use of the cloud.

- Use the cloud to execute customized projects.

Each of these project examples requires a different set of *abilities, know-how,* and *activities* to be completed. As a result, some teams will just require broad competence, while others would need a more narrowly focused approach.

Think of developing a brand new cloud-based application. Building the proper infrastructure for that application may call for cloud-savvy software developers in addition to cloud architects or engineers. Setting guidelines for setting and safeguarding cloud resources may call for more involvement from security-conscious cloud technologists and business leaders with in-depth compliance knowledge. The key is to match the cloud team members' abilities and perspectives to the unique requirements of the project.

The crucially important cloud team tasks and responsibilities are frequently found in a cloud team structure, even though teams are typically modified to match a project's specific technical and business needs. Here is a list of key roles that are important to build the core team for your cloud security ecosystem:

- **Business Executive**: Business leaders are often the project stakeholders or executive sponsors who oversee the budget for a cloud project and foresee the concrete advantages from the project's end. They act as a point of contact between the cloud team and higher management. They also define the objectives of the cloud project, collect data, and assess success.

  Many, if not all, of a company's cloud projects can be managed by one corporate executive, like a CTO or CIO. In other situations, department or division leaders may be involved in cloud projects, decision-making, the establishment of corporate policies that favor the cloud, and training.

- **Project Manager**: Business executives can manage projects, but they might not have the IT knowledge or skills necessary to organize and manage the technical parts of a cloud project. A *project manager* is frequently used by a company to close this gap. In a cloud team organization, the project manager acts as a liaison between the project's stakeholders and the technical team.

  Outstanding communicators and motivators are essential for project managers. They are frequently involved in staffing, vendor selection, scheduling, and budgeting and are aware of the project's technical and business ramifications. They monitor the cloud project's costs, availability, productivity, and other measurable characteristics using *pre-established key performance indicators.* Exceptional problem-solvers, project managers can spot and fix issues before they cause delays or go over budget.

- **Cloud Architect**: The cloud architect is a senior IT staff member who has in-depth knowledge and experience with cloud applications, resources, services, and operations. They will be able to recognize the finer distinctions between the services offered by each provider since they have in-depth hands-on expertise with particular cloud environments, such as **AWS**, **Azure**, and **Google**.

  Applications are frequently designed with the assistance of cloud architects to ensure that they work well on the cloud. Additionally, they may help build an effective, dependable cloud architecture that provides high availability for apps. The emphasis on design necessitates that architects comprehend cloud technologies in-depth and keep up with cloud advances.

- **Cloud Engineer**: *Implementation*, *monitoring*, and *maintenance* of the cloud are the key duties of a Cloud Engineer. They build and manage the architects' cloud infrastructure. Engineers who can set up and configure resources, including servers, storage, networks, and a variety of cloud services, are required to do this. There may be a large amount of automation involved. Multiple engineers may work on a project to concentrate on various aspects of cloud operations, including networks, computation, databases, security, and so on. Engineers will be the first to offer support and upkeep after the cloud infrastructure has been configured. For instance, engineers would be contacted to look into metric reports of a cloud application's performance flaring. Engineers frequently handle project reporting and documentation.

- **Cloud Security Expert**: While cloud service providers are in charge of cloud security, cloud users are also in charge of cloud security. This is a shared responsibility idea that AWS popularized.

  Occasionally, a cloud security specialist supervises the designed infrastructure and software being developed and makes ensuring cloud accounts, resources, services, and apps adhere to security standards. Security experts also examine activity logs, search for vulnerabilities, conduct event post-mortems, and provide recommendations for security upgrades.

- **Cloud Compliance Expert**: Business data is protected from misuse, loss, and theft by policies and practices that govern access to and use of data. Major compliance regulations, including **HIPAA**, **PCI DSS**, and **GDPR**, are being accommodated by cloud service providers. Compliance experts consult with legal staff and comprehend and keep track of cloud compliance certifications. To satisfy changing requirements, they also design, implement, evaluate, and update procedures. In certain companies, the project's business manager, security experts, or an existing corporate compliance officer may be in charge of compliance. Compliance experts collaborate extensively with the security team since security and compliance have such close ties.

- **Analysts**: Systems and performance analysts gather metrics and make that workload capacity and performance stay within acceptable bounds, although major issues or interruptions are often directed toward engineers and architects. To suggest more updates or enhancements, they might keep an eye on help desk tickets and categorize incidents.

Managing risk in the cloud

The majority of enterprises in the world today have adopted the cloud in one way or another, making cloud risk management a crucial component. In today's world, when more businesses are adopting *work-from-home policies*, cloud risks are becoming more important for CISOs and CIOs. Misconfigured cloud servers continue to pose a serious threat to data security in the wake of data security and privacy. Numerous reports indicate that cloud hazards are to blame for a large number of today's data breaches.

Third-party or *vendor risks* are other names for cloud concerns. According to one of the IAPP and EY reports, *less than 50% of firms had some type of formal audit procedure addressing data privacy, and the majority of those who did depended on ISO 27001 or ISMS, which is primarily about information security and scarcely covers privacy.* External audits were hardly ever utilized by enterprises to manage assurance for privacy threats. Most businesses still manage privacy issues through some form of self-evaluation or their legal departments.

It is more crucial to handle the cloud's data security and privacy threats in light of the fast use of cloud computing and recent rules like the GDPR and CCPA. In addition to fundamental security ideas like *Security by Design* and *Privacy by Design*, adapting a *Risk Management Framework* and a life cycle approach is once again becoming increasingly significant. Despite having a dedicated resource, many small and medium-sized businesses still do not adhere to the Risk Life Cycle Management philosophy. In these enterprises, effective risk management is largely lacking, which increases the risks to *cloud security*, *data security*, and *privacy*.

An integrated, ecosystem-wide risk management framework that takes into account the demands of all cloud actors is necessary for a cloud ecosystem due to the complicated relationships among cloud actors, their particular missions, business processes, and the information systems that support them. As with any other information system, *cloud actors* are in charge of determining their acceptable level of risk for a cloud-based information system, which is determined by their risk tolerance level for the residual risk that exists across the entire cloud ecosystem.

The following high-level components must be implemented to handle information security risks at the ecosystem level effectively:

- Giving cloud actors who are orchestrating cloud ecosystem risk management obligations. *Senior leaders, executives,* and *representatives* of each cloud actor need to be given additional responsibilities internally.

- Establishing a system-wide risk tolerance for the cloud ecosystem and communicating it through their **Service-Level Agreements (SLAs)**, along with details on the decision-making processes that have an impact on risk tolerance.

- Monitoring information security risks in close to *real-time* by each cloud actor and understanding their existence and potential effects on the operation and/or use of the information system utilizing the cloud ecosystem.

- Accountability of cloud actors and exchange of information in close to real-time about *incidents, threats, risk management choices,* and *solutions.*

Risk Management Framework (RMF)

Risk is sometimes defined as a function of the possibility that a negative event will occur and the size of such a negative consequence. Probability is considered in the context of information security as a function of system threats, exploitable vulnerabilities, and the effects of such exploits. As a result, *security risk analyses* concentrate on locating potential hot spots for destructive events within the cloud ecosystem. The *risk-based approach* to managing information systems is an all-encompassing activity that must be thoroughly incorporated into every part of the business, from planning to the activities involved in the system development life cycle to the distribution of security measures and ongoing monitoring. As a result, the **Risk Management Framework (RMF)** offers an organized and disciplined procedure for integrating information security and risk management tasks into the life cycle of a system.

Six clearly defined actions relating to risk should be carried out simultaneously by chosen persons or groups in clearly defined organizational responsibilities, as shown in the following process diagram (*Figure 3.1*) when adopting the *Risk Management Framework:*

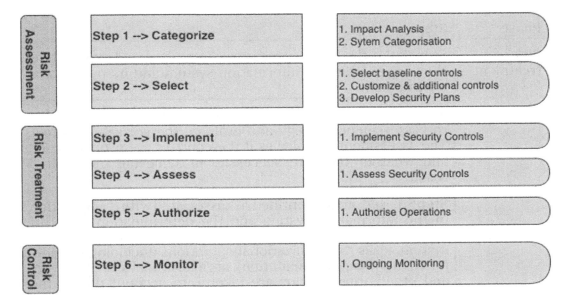

Figure 3.1: *Risk Management Framework for Cloud Service Providers* (CSP)

Along with the risk management activities that were previously explained in this part, these phases or tasks are also listed in the following table (*Table 3.1*):

Phase	Steps
Risk assessment	**Step 1**: Based on a system impact study, classify the information system and the data that is processed, stored, and sent by it. Find out what is needed in terms of operations, performance, security, and privacy.
	Step 2: The information system's initial set of security measures is determined by the security classification (referred to as baseline security controls). Based on the organizational risk assessment and the operational environment's characteristics, then, customize and augment the baseline security controls established. Create a plan for tracking the effectiveness of security measures on an ongoing basis. Keep a record of every control in the security plan. Analyze and accept the security plan.

Phase	Steps
Risk treatment	**Step 3**: Put the security measures into place and explain how they are used in the information system and its operational environment.
	Step 4: Utilizing the relevant assessment methods outlined in the assessment strategy and evaluate the security controls. The assessment establishes if the controls are properly used and whether they are successful in achieving the desired result.
	Step 5: Based on the identified risk associated with the operation of the information system and the determination that this risk is acceptable, authorize the operation of the information system. Risks to organizational operations (including *mission, functions, image,* or *reputation*), organizational assets, people, and other organizations are taken into account during the assessment.
Risk control	**Step 6**: Assessing the efficiency of the security controls in the information system, documenting changes to the system or its operating environment, performing security impact analyses on these changes, and reporting the security state of the system to designated organizational officials are all part of ongoing security control monitoring.

Table 3.1: *Risk management steps explained for CSP*

Cloud consumers are in charge of safeguarding the system and the data in accordance with the sensitivity of the data when orchestrating a cloud ecosystem for a cloud-based information system. The degree of management and direct control that cloud consumers have varies depending on the cloud deployment architecture.

But before obtaining a cloud service, a cloud consumer must assess the risk connected to the adoption of a cloud-based solution for a specific information system and make plans for the risk management and risk control procedures related to the *cloud-based operations* of this system. To do this, a cloud consumer must obtain perspective on the complete cloud ecosystem that will support the operations of their cloud-based information system. The RMF must also be used by cloud consumers in a certain fashion that enables them to:

- Perform a risk assessment
- Identify the best-fitting cloud architecture

- Choose the best cloud service

- Gain visibility into the cloud offering that is required

- Define and negotiate the risk treatment and risk control mitigations that are required

Cloud Service Provider (CSP) risk management process

The creation of cloud architectures and cloud services by cloud providers includes fundamental operational and functional components, as well as security and privacy controls that adhere to minimum standards. With the least amount of customization possible, their solutions seek to meet the demands of a sizable group of cloud consumers. When deciding which security and privacy controls to use and how to implement them, a cloud provider takes into account the *effectiveness*, *efficiency*, and *limitations* of those controls in light of any applicable laws, rules, guidelines, policies, standards, or regulations that the provider must follow. Since it is unknown what exactly the cloud consumers' needs and regulations are, a general core set is proposed.

Although cloud providers have a lot of freedom in defining a cloud service's boundaries, they can only make assumptions about the type of data their cloud consumers will produce when the system is being designed and put into place. As a result, a cloud provider's chosen and implemented security and privacy measures are sets that cater to the demands of many potential customers. A cloud provider can, however, *design highly technological, specialized security solutions* that can give a greater security posture than in traditional IT systems due to the centralized structure of the cloud service that is being offered.

It is crucial to remember that a cloud ecosystem's security posture is only as strong as its weakest functional layer or subsystem. Since the reliability and high performance of a cloud provider's consumers' solutions are essential to its reputation and ability to continue operations, a cloud provider uses the RMF to make up for any potential weaknesses in the solutions of its cloud consumers.

Customer's risk management process for cloud landscape

Organizations are, generally speaking, more willing to tolerate risk when they have more control over the tools and processes that are utilized. When faced with an incident, companies with a high level of control can analyze their options, establish priorities, and take prompt, self-serving action. The ability of the cloud consumer to comprehend the system's cloud-specific characteristics, the architectural components for each service type and deployment model, and the roles of the cloud actors in creating a secure cloud ecosystem are prerequisites for a cloud-based information system solution to be adopted successfully.

Furthermore, the capability of cloud consumers to:

- Recognize all cloud-specific, risk-adjusted security and privacy protections crucial to their company and mission-critical operations.

- Enquire about service agreements and **Service-Level Agreements (SLAs)** with cloud providers and brokers, where the installation of security and privacy measures is the cloud providers' duty, when appropriate and through contractual mechanisms.

- Evaluate how these security and privacy restrictions are being used.

- Keep track of all recognized security and privacy restrictions.

Applying the RMF to these functional layers doesn't necessitate any additional tasks or operations over what would be required in a conventional IT system because the cloud consumers are directly managing and controlling the functional capabilities they implement; as a result, the risk management approach is an excellent example of a widely adopted, thoroughly tested approach. Certain subsystems or subsystem parts with cloud-based services are not under the direct control of the organization of a cloud consumer. Since adopting a cloud-based solution does not automatically ensure the same level of security and compliance with the regulations as in the traditional IT model, the ability to conduct an *extensive risk assessment* is crucial to building trust in the cloud-based system as the first step in authorizing its operation.

Choosing which cloud service offering best meets their cloud computing needs while securing and effectively supporting their mission-critical business processes and services presents a number of challenges for cloud consumers at the moment. In order to demystify the process of *describing, identifying, categorizing, analyzing,* and *choosing* cloud-based services for cloud consumers, this section will apply the Risk Management Framework (RMF) from the cloud consumer's point of view.

In general, a cloud user adopting a cloud-based service must take the following actions:

- Describe the application or service that could use a cloud-based solution.

- List all essential capabilities that must be added to the service.

- List the security and privacy standards as well as the security measures required to protect the service or application. The **Federal Information Processing Standard (FIPS)** 199, *Standards for Security Categorization of Federal Information and Information Systems*, and FIPS 200, *Minimum Security Requirements for Federal Information and Information Systems*, respectively, must be followed by cloud consumers who adopt NIST standards and guidelines. The baseline security control that must be established depends on the effect level of the information system. Low-impact, moderate-impact, and high-impact information systems are represented by three sets of baseline controls.

- Combine a cloud service model and a cloud deployment model (*public, private, hybrid,* or *community*) to analyze and choose the best cloud ecosystem architecture (**IaaS, PaaS, SaaS**).

- Determine and pick the cloud actors responsible for coordinating the cloud ecosystem.

- Recognize the security posture, inherited security and privacy measures, and cloud provider(s) and broker(s). Adapt security and privacy controls to the specific use case's needs or, if more protection is required, establish extra compensating security controls.

- Use explicit assignments and selection statements to give organization-defined security parameters precise values.

- If necessary, supplement baselines with further security and privacy control improvements.

- Give additional specification details for the application of privacy and security rules.

Based on the chosen cloud ecosystem architecture, the organization would keep and be responsible for implementing the security measures established for the cloud consumer, together with an additional set of controls tailored to the consumer's use case.

The RMF is demonstrated in the following graphic (*Figure* 3.2) from the viewpoint of the cloud consumer as it applies to a cloud ecosystem:

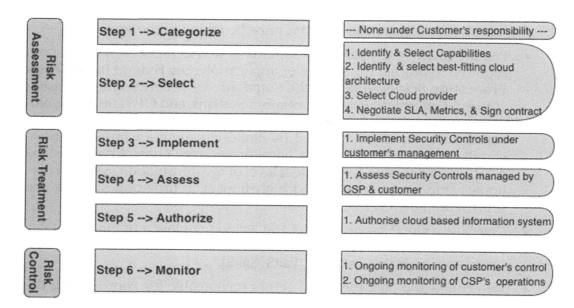

Figure 3.2: *Risk Management Framework for customer*

Monitoring and managing cloud risk

The following *three-step procedure* is advised in order to assist you to implement a straightforward and tested methodology for managing and monitoring cloud risk for your cloud ecosystem.

The same has also been explained in the following diagram (Figure 3.3) :

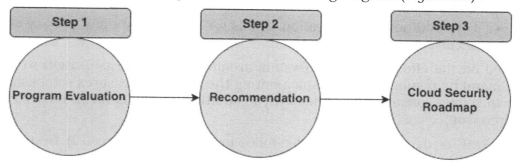

Figure 3.3: *Cloud risk monitoring and management*

- **First step: program evaluation**: We ought to conduct a thorough analysis of every facet of your cloud security at this point. We then compile and evaluate this information to calculate your risk. Finally, we ought to receive in-depth reports summarizing our findings from both technical and non-technical angles.

- **Second step: recommendations**: At this point, we should present a prioritized list of any security concerns we find that are actionable. This list will include both technical and non-technical steps you may take to address each problem we uncover.

- **Third step: a plan for cloud security**: This is the stage when your short- and long-term suggestions for improvement should be represented in a clear, visual manner. We should put these suggestions on a timeline as a result of this exercise to let you know precisely when to make each improvement.

An approach towards cloud security assessment

A review of the company's cloud infrastructure, known as a **cloud security assessment**, is done to make sure the company is safe from various security risks and attacks. The evaluation ought to be planned to:

- Determine the cloud infrastructure's vulnerabilities and potential access points for the company.

- Check the network for indications of exploitation.

- Describe methods for avoiding assaults in the future.

The following *seven* areas are usually the focus of a cloud security assessment:

- Conduct interviews and a documentation review to assess the general security posture of the enterprise cloud infrastructure.

- Review identity and access management, including user accounts, roles, and key management.

- Review segmentation and firewall policies to check for frequent misconfigurations.

- Incident management. Review the cloud infrastructure event response policy, including the roles and processes connected to an incident.

- Evaluate the state of cloud storage, including *object-level storage, block-level storage*, and *related snapshots*.

- Review the security setting of advanced service options that are unique to each cloud service provider.

- Workload security. Examine workload security for *virtualized servers, server-hosted containers, functions,* and *serverless* containerized workloads.

Basic principles for cloud security assessment

There are *four* fundamental elements followed by report submission that typically make up a cloud security assessment:

- **Documentation review and interviews**: This aids in the assessment team's understanding of the environment of the client, its intended architecture, and any changes that are anticipated.

- **Automated and manual testing**: The assessment team uses specialized tools to gather data about the *environment, spot misconfigurations and holes* compared to the ideal architecture, and *assess potential attack chains.*

- **Creation of suggestions**: For each finding, the assessment team develops recommendations and submits them to the client's security team.

- **Presentation**: The assessment team collaborates with the client's internal stakeholders to present findings and respond to inquiries about both specific technical advice and high-level recommendations.

Need to adopt cloud security assessment

In comparison to traditional on-premise servers, cloud computing provides enterprises with considerable operational efficiencies. However, reliance on the cloud and innovation both bring with them new dangers. The quick uptake of cloud-based workloads frequently exceeds the capacity of an organization's security services, creating a severe blind spot for technology leadership. Organizations frequently have several cloud accounts or subscriptions, and because not all of these accounts or subscriptions are subject to the same level of security scrutiny, less *essential* workloads may not have access to certain security measures. Even in previously discounted cloud systems, the effects of a breach can be shockingly severe.

The *cloud environment* needs more sophisticated security mechanisms that offer *anytime, everywhere protection*, unlike a traditional network, which is frequently protected using a perimeter security paradigm. The organization's attack surface may unintentionally expand, raising risk, as more users access cloud-based systems as a result of requirements for working from home.

Misconfiguration is a problem that frequently arises in relation to cloud security. Misconfigurations in the cloud, which are frequently the cause of security breaches, are often the result of mistakes that network engineers unintentionally made when the technology was young. In order to find these problems and any other out-of-date components of the security architecture, a cloud security assessment is essential.

Excessive network permissions are a further frequent problem. Inadvertent access from *untrusted third parties* may come from inbound traffic, and uncontrolled outbound traffic may exacerbate the harm that an organization may suffer from a breach that would otherwise be minor.

Lack of **multi-factor authentication (MFA)**, a security practice that uses two or more independent pieces of evidence to confirm the user's identity, is an example of ineffective user account management. Other examples include having too many privileges, not restricting source IP addresses or source countries, relying on static credentials for users or workloads to authenticate to the cloud service provider, and using excessive privileges. When these problems are combined, it becomes simpler for adversaries to seem to be legitimate activity and manipulate, ex-filtrate, or destroy data. Finally, poor or insufficient logging, which is frequent in cloud-based systems, increases the difficulty of finding, describing, and recovering from hostile activity, which raises costs.

Benefits of adopting cloud security assessment

A *cloud security audit* gives businesses the assurance that their networks and assets are correctly set up, effectively protected, and not currently under threat. The audit, which takes into account the organization's network history, will also pinpoint any points of access or other architectural weak points and provide thorough recommendations on how to bolster security and enhance capabilities going forward.

A cloud security evaluation has the following benefits in particular:

- **Lessened risk from unintentional configuration errors**: The company can lessen the attack surface it faces in the cloud environment by implementing the customized configuration adjustments suggested as part of the cloud security assessment.

- **Lessened chance of missing notifications**: By implementing the suggestions made by the cloud security assessment team, an organization will be better able to identify compromises and take appropriate action before they turn into serious security breaches.

- **Enhanced resilience**: The team providing the cloud security assessment will offer suggestions to assist firms in recovering from a breach more quickly.

- **More effective account management**: Companies with *less-than-ideal identity architectures* can spend less time on account and privilege management while decreasing the likelihood that excessive rights will accidentally be issued.

- **Past compromise detection**: While a cloud security assessment does not include a thorough evaluation of past compromises, it might spot outliers in the organization's cloud settings that might have resulted from a breach.

Ideas to keep in mind before beginning your assessment

You need to know what you are analyzing before you begin a cloud assessment. An evaluation of your current environment, its evaluation, and its mapping into the future are some of the several parts of a cloud security assessment. Following is an explanation of each of these steps:

- **Sketch out your current surroundings**: You can use this step to map your present environment and figure out what you are already doing. You should map both your current internal resources and your surrounding surroundings.

  Infrastructure for the network, control over user access, and user permissions are all *internal resources*. Data storage and network connectivity are examples of external resources.

- **Assess your present environment**: Technology, security measures now in use, and how those measures are put into practice all need to be assessed. Tools like *security analytics and monitoring software*, *security assessment software* and *security scanning software* can all be used for this.

  You should ascertain which elements significantly affect the security posture of your firm. These elements will provide context for your assessment's results.

- **Visualize your potential environment**: You can choose from a variety of cloud service solutions based on your assessment, which come in all different forms and sizes. Based on what you are aware of regarding your present environment, your ideal environment, and your financial situation, you should plan your future environment.

- **Effectiveness of the assessment**: Although it is difficult to foresee, you should plan to map your future environment for 10 *to* 15 *percent* of your assessment time, 65 *to* 70 *percent* of your time will be spent reviewing your current environment, and *the remaining time* will be split equally between those three categories.

- **Price point**: Cloud services might save money, but they also have some security dangers. It's crucial to comprehend how much the tool or service provider you choose will cost. Your financial situation and level of risk tolerance will determine the evaluation you should make.

Executing cloud security assessment

The architecture of a security assessment implementation, as well as instructions and actions necessary for the effective implementation of security assessments as a service, are discussed in great detail in this *portion of the book*. The authors of this content are security architects, cloud engineers, cloud designers, and developers, as well as those in charge of carrying out cloud-based security assessments.

Architecture overview

The architecture of security assessments that can also be offered as a service from a cloud platform can vary. But they will all have some similar architectural elements. The infrastructure that delivers cloud security assessment should be wholly owned and maintained by the service provider in a private cloud, where service providers can deliver their services. This architecture uses a private cloud as the underlying infrastructure, even if the service may be a public, multi-tenant cloud SaaS offering.

The infrastructure of the evaluation platform can also be delivered from a *public cloud* using an *IaaS* or *PaaS* delivery model, which is another option for service providers. A few service providers incorporate SaaS-delivered solutions into the architecture of their platforms for security assessment services.

In response to client worries regarding security assessments, some public cloud service providers have incorporated security assessment capabilities into their *IaaS public cloud infrastructure services*. This architecture offers security assessment capabilities to users of public cloud services without requiring them to install software or virtualized assessment appliances. It may also result in cost savings for users by doing away with the compute and storage requirements for the *security assessment appliance*.

Internal versus internet-based enterprise assessments

Although *cloud-based security assessment services* can evaluate any system that is connected to the internet, internal exams are frequently carried out using managed appliances or software agents that have been installed within the company. Customers of a cloud-based security assessment service should take the following factors into account when choosing a service provider in order to differentiate between the Internet and internal assessments: Appliance users should be able to verify that their appliances are capable of storing and transferring all data securely. Service providers should deploy all appliances in a way that allows access to them to be *monitored*, *recorded*, and *reported*.

The ability of service providers' equipment to ensure that all data on the device is permanently destroyed or deleted upon request and at the conclusion of an assessment should be able to be verified.

Guidelines

The planning and rollout phases are when cloud-based security assessments are implemented, with only a few physical implementation procedures being included. Organizations should concentrate on developing the mechanisms for utilizing the collected data and identifying the goals for the evaluation.

For the purpose of actively managing risk for the vital information and systems of an organization, an accurate inventory, and mapping of the security and compliance state of the *network devices*, *systems*, and *applications* is required.

Account management and user authentication

When choosing a cloud-based security assessment solution, businesses should bear the following principles in mind:

- Account management capabilities ought to make it possible to *create*, *delete*, and *manage* account permissions and roles in a user-friendly web environment.

- The service provider needs to let customers accept or reject the creation of new accounts.

- User authentication requirements must be *precisely defined*, and support for more robust authentication protocols like *two-factor* or *multi-factor authentication* is required.

- The service provider should be able to offer thorough authentication and activity records/logs for user sessions in a manner that the client can access at any time.

- The service provider must be able to keep the data in order to adhere to industry log retention standards.

Vulnerability assessments for network and systems

In order to systematically find and fix vulnerabilities in devices linked to a network, a technique known as **vulnerability management** must be used. The services provided for vulnerability management typically include *asset discovery*, *asset classification*, *scanning profile management*, *vulnerability scanning*, *analysis*, *correlation*, *prioritization of the results*, *reporting*, *remediation management*, *verification of remediation through scanning*, *workflow management*, and *scheduled scanning*.

It's customary to categorize vulnerability assessments as either internal or external. A publicly routable IP network is the target of an external vulnerability evaluation from the internet. Internal evaluations are carried out inside the company, often from inside the perimeter security appliances (firewalls).

External alone, internal only, or both

Choose if you want to evaluate internal systems in addition to internet-facing (external) systems. The deployment of scanning appliances into your internal environment is often required for internal system assessment. The network architecture of your environment is frequently a factor in determining the size of the necessary number of scanning appliances. Additional scanning devices can speed up some security assessment methods, resulting in shorter scanning durations.

You must choose whether to employ authorized scans inside the environment if you opt to conduct internal scanning. In order to gain more access to the system and obtain more information, authenticated scans necessitate the scanning system having a set of credentials.

Server and workstation compliance assessment

Organizations should consider whether a pure cloud-based evaluation will be able to provide them with a complete assessment or if an appliance should be utilized to enable assessment of their environment from both an internal and external perspective. Providers of services should:

- Compile a list of all supported products and devices, and if necessary, include the bare minimum configurations each item needs to be evaluated successfully.

- Possess the capacity to run authenticated/anonymous scans or make use of a resident agent to find server/workstation setups.

- Have the capacity to assess compliance by comparing detected configurations to industry best practices or specific configuration standards.

- Confirm that compliance controls have the capacity to map to industry standards in order to show that each mechanism utilized throughout the assessment complies with each section of the standards being assessed against.

- Give consumers the option to design their own standard templates and import/export their own templates.

- Give clients the option to conduct ad hoc and planned assessments to check for baseline configuration compliance and/or vulnerability detection, both at regular intervals and as assessments on demand.

Network and security system compliance assessment

Organizations should determine whether a pure cloud-based evaluation will be able to provide them with a thorough assessment or if an appliance should be utilized to allow for an assessment of their environment both internally and externally. Service providers ought to:

- Compile a list of all supported products and devices, and if necessary, include the bare minimum configurations each item needs to be evaluated successfully.

- Provide support for a wide range of network and security devices.

- Have the capacity to evaluate not just the device setup but also any particular security or network policies applied by the device (*routing policies, firewall policies, IDS policies,* and so on.).

- Possess the capacity to perform vulnerability assessments against *device-specific flaws* and/or to make use of third-party *scanner-gathered vulnerability* data.

- Be able to offer an interface that resembles a dashboard or report that allows users to view the assessment's findings as well as the overall risk level that was determined based on the findings.

Testing the security of web applications

The practice of scanning online applications for security flaws is automated by web application security assessments. Traditional methods include **white-box testing**, which concentrates on the *web application's source code*, **black-box testing**, which tests the *web application* from the perspective of an external attacker who is unaware of its architecture, and hybrid testing, which combines both outside testing and source code analysis. With rare exceptions, the *black-box methodology* is the main focus of cloud-based web application assessment tools. You should factor in the following recommendations when evaluating these tools:

- **Detection**: The assessment tool should focus on the most prevalent defects, such as *cross-site scripting vulnerabilities, file-inclusion problems, direct object references, directory traversal problems, information leakage, session management problems,* and *SQL injection problems.* You may find a thorough list of the most important problems that assessment tools should be able to identify at OWASP *at their Top 10 rankings* and the SANS *Top 25 software errors* (CWEs).

- **Completeness**: The evaluation tool must be capable of exercising the web application that is being tested to the fullest extent possible. The effectiveness of the evaluation, which finally includes its assistance for following the navigation links utilized by modern web development approaches, depends on the reach of the crawler in the assessment tool (CSS, JavaScript).

Hypervisor layer assessment

It is sometimes possible to evaluate the security of a cloud or virtualized environment in a manner akin to evaluating network and system vulnerabilities. Although the *evaluation tool* must facilitate the detection of potential vulnerabilities inside the virtualization/cloud management layer, it also needs to have a working knowledge of the underlying virtualization technology. The management aspects of the virtual environment are often the focus of virtual infrastructure assessments. These evaluations can be performed in a setting that is under the organization's management or one that is supplied by a third party.

A difficult task is doing a virtual infrastructure security evaluation for a third-party provider. Because testing could negatively affect other customers and possibly reveal flaws of other customers in a *multi-tenant environment*, many providers will restrict the ability of users to test the virtual infrastructure.

Identify and comprehend the virtualization type that the provider is utilizing first. You can then decide which assessment approach is best using this information. It should be determined which security procedures work best for that kind of virtualization. A review of the controls mentioned in those best practices is necessary. Prior to moving to the cloud, a consumer should ideally know this information.

The following areas should be evaluated regardless of the virtualization platform:

- Limitations on who can use the virtualization management system.
- Individuals who have access to the hypervisor's control or management systems.
- Remote access to the hypervisor's control or management systems.
- Virtual operating system separation (virtualized systems should be isolated from each other).

- Services running on hypervisor but not being used (for example, *unused hardware, clipboard, file sharing*, and so on).

- Physical security measures to prevent unwanted access are number *six*. Patch levels for the hypervisor are number *seven*, ensuring the most recent patches are installed (particularly security patches).

- Configurations of virtual switches.

- Security guidelines and vendor advice for the currently used virtualization system.

Reporting and sharing the data that follows

Customers of a cloud-based security assessment service should consider the following factors when choosing a service provider with regard to reporting and sharing resulting data:

- Service providers should provide the resulting assessment data in both formatted *human-readable* and exportable *machine-readable versions* in non-proprietary formats, such as **Cyberscope**, **Security Content Automation Protocol (SCAP)**, **Common Vulnerability Reference Format (CVRF)**, or **Extensible Markup Language (XML)**.

- Clients that want to build repeating assessments, or continuous monitoring and auditing systems, should confirm that the service provider has the capacity to store historical data in a secure environment, perform trend analysis, and compare the data to current assessments.

- Service providers should make it possible to specify the types of data that can be viewed and/or exported as well as who has access to do so.

- Security/risk ratings should attempt to integrate the outcomes of several security assessment types to produce an *overall risk rating* that may be utilized as a gauge of an organization's general security posture.

- There are a number of widely used rating methods, including the **Common Vulnerability Scoring System (CVSS)**.

- When choosing a *cloud-based security assessment*, the rating methodology used by the supplier should be compatible with the organization's present security/risk rating system. Although proprietary rating systems may be employed by service providers, systems that only offer proprietary ratings ought to be avoided. To enable enterprises to customize risk scoring to their organization and organizational business processes, service providers should instead use either proprietary rating systems, industry-standard rating systems, or a combination of these.

- Reports should include thorough explanations of all rating systems applied during the evaluation procedure, as well as any customer ratings that deviate from the norm.

Selecting the right cloud service provider (CSP)

Making proper cloud provider selections is now essential for long-term success as more and more IT systems are being externalized. However, there is a sizable market that is *open*, and a wide range of suppliers offer an even wider range of services. From industry leaders like *Microsoft*, *Amazon*, and *Google* to smaller niche providers of customized services.

Therefore, *how can you pick the best cloud provider out of the many?* The solution is a well-defined selection and procurement procedure that is properly weighted toward your particular set of needs.

We have compiled a comprehensive list of the areas of consideration from the essential factors.

Time to choose the right cloud service provider

You must be aware of your unique business requirements before you can choose a service that can meet them. It might seem rather simple, but by defining your precise needs and minimal standards before evaluating providers, you can be sure that you are comparing each one of them to your checklist rather than to the others. To go from a huge list to a short list quickly, do it this way. You can more effectively interview your chosen set of possible providers if you are clear on the *technical*, *service*, *security*, *data governance*, and *service management needs*.

It's also important to keep in mind that when transferring workloads and applications to the cloud, the particular environments you select, and the services provided by your cloud service provider will determine the configurations required, the work required, and the assistance you can receive from the provider in completing it.

As a result, it is ideal to pick your providers concurrently by analyzing and getting ready to move these workloads to the cloud after you have identified your cloud migration candidates.

Cloud security

You should be fully aware of your security objectives, the security options provided by each supplier, and the methods used to protect your data and application. Additionally, confirm that you fully comprehend the particular areas that each party is in charge of.

Additionally, take into account which security measures are available for *free out of the box* from each vendor you're investigating, which additional paid services are supplied by the providers themselves, and where you might need to supplement with technology from *third-party partners*. As an illustration, the security sections of *AWS* and *Google Cloud*'s respective websites both disclose their security features, paid solutions, and partner integrations, making the procedure quite simple.

In the cloud (and everywhere else these days), security is a primary worry, so it's crucial to pose specific questions that relate to your particular use cases, industry, legal needs, and any other worries you may have. Don't forget to assess this crucial aspect of operating in the cloud.

Standards and accreditations

The best practices and standards in the sector are adhered to by providers who follow recognized standards and quality frameworks. While criteria might not ultimately influence which service provider you select, they can be quite useful in narrowing down the pool of potential vendors.

There are many different standards and certifications offered. The illustration up top shows a few of the more well-known organizations that offer standards, certifications, and good practice recommendations.

Look for structured processes, efficient data management, good knowledge management, and visibility of the status of your services in general. Also, be aware of the provider's intentions for resources and ongoing support for adherence to these standards.

Roadmap for technologies and services

Verify that the provider's platform and preferred technology support your cloud goals and/or are compatible with your present environment. *Do the cloud architectures, standards, and services offered by the provider work for your workloads and management preferences?* Estimate the amount of re-coding or customization necessary to make your workloads compatible with their platforms.

Numerous service providers provide comprehensive relocation services and even aid in the planning and assessment stages. Make sure you have a solid grasp of the support provided, connect it to the project's tasks, and select who will handle what. Service providers frequently have technical personnel on staff who can close gaps in your migration teams' skill sets. To fill in the skills gaps, you might require additional third-party support from some large-scale public cloud providers, so ask them for their suggested third-party partners who have a wealth of relevant expertise and in-depth platform knowledge.

To learn how the service provider intends to stay innovative and expand over time and enquire about their service development plans. *Does their plan meet your long-term requirements?*

Commitments to particular technologies or vendors and the methods used to facilitate interoperability are important issues to take into account. Additionally, *can they show off deployments that are comparable to the ones you're planning?* A *feature, service* and *integration roadmap* is particularly desirable for SaaS companies in particular. You might also want to consider the full range of services that providers can supply depending on your specific cloud plan. If you intend to employ several best-of-breed services from a wide variety of providers, then this is less relevant; but, if you prefer to use just a few major cloud service providers, it is crucial that those providers have a decent selection of complementary services.

Security and data governance

You may already have a data classification strategy in place that specifies the various types of data in terms of their sensitivity and/or data residency rules. You should at the very least be aware of any regulations or data privacy policies that apply to personal data.

Keeping this in mind, a crucial aspect of the choosing process can be the place where your data is stored and the local regulations that are therefore applicable to it. You should search for suppliers who provide you with a choice and control over the country in which your data is *stored*, *processed*, and *managed* if you have certain requirements and duties. Although cloud service providers ought to be open about the locations of their data centers, it is your obligation to do your own research.

If appropriate, evaluate the capacity of data going to or within the cloud to be encrypted in order to secure data in transit. Sensitive volumes should also be encrypted while in transit to reduce susceptibility to unauthorized administrator access. Object storage should *encrypt* sensitive data, typically using client/agent or file/folder encryption.

Look into the provider's data loss and breach notification procedures to make sure they adhere to your organization's risk tolerance and any applicable legal or regulatory requirements.

Dependencies and partnerships for services

It's crucial to comprehend any vendor ties that service providers may have.

It is worthwhile to evaluate the provider's standing with important vendors, their degree of accreditation, their technological prowess, and their staff's credentials. *Do they support multi-vendor environments, and if so, what are some good examples?*

Consider how the provided services would fit into a larger ecosystem of complementary or supporting services.

It's crucial to identify any service dependencies and collaborations that are connected to the delivery of cloud services. It must be obvious how and where the service is being offered because, for instance, SaaS companies frequently construct their services on top of IaaS platforms that are already in place.

When delivering a cloud service, there may occasionally be a complicated network of interconnected parts and subcontractors. It's crucial to make sure the provider is transparent about these connections and is able to uphold the fundamental SLAs stipulated across the entire service, even those elements it has no direct control over. On these subcomponents, you should also try to comprehend the policies regarding liability restrictions and service interruptions.

Consider providers with a short chain of subcontractors cautiously. Especially with data subject to data protection requirements or operations that are *mission-critical* for the company.

According to the *Code of Practice*, service dependencies and their effects on SLAs, accountability, and responsibility must be well explained.

SLAs, commercials, and contracts

There aren't any industry standards for how cloud agreements should be written and defined, which makes them appear more complicated. Many jargon-loving cloud providers continue to use overly complex language or worse, language that is intentionally misleading when referring to SLAs in particular.

Generally speaking, agreements range from *pre-written terms and conditions* that are agreed to online to specifically tailored contracts and **service level agreements (SLAs)**.

Here, a factor is how big CSP is compared to the client. Although smaller CSPs are more willing to engage in discussions, they may also be more ready to accept unique terms that they may not be able to maintain. Always ask providers who are willing to offer flexible terms for further information on how they intend to support variations, who is in charge of variations, and what procedures are employed to control variations.

The service and deliverables should be clearly defined. Find out who is responsible for what aspects of the service (*delivery, provisioning, service management, monitoring, support, escalations,* and so on), and how that responsibility is shared between the *customer* and the *provider. How is accessibility and availability of services handled and ensured? (Maintenance, incident remediation, disaster recovery,* and so on). *How do these policies match up with your needs?*

Analyze a provider's security and data management policies, paying close attention to how they relate to data privacy laws. Make sure there are enough assurances on data ownership, usage rights, and confidentiality, as well as access to, location, and jurisdiction of the data. Examine the provisions for backup and resilience. To learn whether your data might be portable if you decide to leave, review the data conversion policies.

Contracts between *providers* and *clients* should generally include specific clauses relating to *indemnification, intellectual property rights, limitation of responsibility,* and *warranties.* However, it is important to carefully consider the associated parameters. These safeguards are typically the ones that spark the most debate since both customers and providers want to reduce their exposure to potential liability in the event of a claim for data privacy after a breach.

In the service level agreement, there should be the following three main elements:

- Objectives for the service level
- Remediation regulations, fines, and incentives based on these goals
- Disclaimer and restrictions

Accessibility, service availability (often uptime as a percentage), service capacity (what is the maximum number of users, connections, resources, and so on), response time, and *flexibility* are common **service level goals (SLOs)** that are included (or how quickly changes can be accommodated). Depending on how clauses are split between the contract and SLA, there are frequently others as well.

Keep an eye out for SLOs that are *pertinent, clear, measurable,* and *unambiguous.* In the service level agreement, they should be explicitly stated and, if at all possible, audited.

Additionally, SLAs should outline who is responsible for identifying and resolving issues, as well as when this should happen. They will also include available compensation, the procedures for reporting and claiming, restrictions that restrict the SLA's applicability, and a list of exclusions, and caveats.

It's crucial to carefully read these terms because service credit computations are frequently difficult to understand. The request worked samples, or better yet, give each provider on your shortlist the same fictitious outage scenario so you can evaluate the compensation offered.

Performance and dependability

You can evaluate a service provider's dependability using a variety of techniques.

Check the service provider's performance initially against their SLAs for the *previous 6–12 months*. Some service providers make this information public, but all of them ought to offer it upon request. Expecting perfection is unrealistic because any cloud service will occasionally encounter outages. What matters is how the supplier handles the outage. Make sure that the available tools for monitoring and reporting are adequate and compatible with your overall management and reporting systems.

Make sure that the service provider you choose has *developed, documented,* and *tested* procedures for handling scheduled and unscheduled downtime. They should have procedures and plans in place that detail how they intend to get in touch with customers during times of disruption, including how to prioritize issues, communicate on time, and gauge their seriousness. When service faults occur, be aware of the remedies and liability restrictions provided by the cloud provider.

Provider lock-in, exit strategy, and migration support

A scenario known as **vendor lock-in** occurs when a client using a product or service finds it difficult to switch to a competitor. Incompatible proprietary technologies used by competitors can lead to vendor lock-in. However, it can also be brought on by things like contract restrictions or ineffective processes. The portability of your cloud services to other providers or internal operations may be impacted by those that largely rely on specialized or distinctive proprietary components. This is especially *true* if new application architecture is required for platforms provided by service providers.

By minimizing the usage of services that restrict your ability to move or switch providers, or by ensuring that your selected provider uses the least amount of proprietary technology, you can reduce the danger of vendor lock-in.

To reduce the danger of lock-in, choose value-added services that have similar and competitive alternatives on the market and have procedures for routinely reviewing your options. Also watch out for *enhancement creep*, where service providers alter configurations, rules, technologies, and so on and add lock-in elements to your service in the process. The benefits of working with one or a few important providers can be *attractive*, but you should weigh them against the risks of becoming overly dependent on any one supplier.

A *clear exit strategy* should be in place from the beginning of your relationship on the exit provisioning part. It's worthwhile to learn about a CSP's procedures before signing a contract because leaving their service isn't usually a simple or quick transfer.

Also take into account how you'll access your data, its current state, and how long the provider intends to store it.

Conclusion

The finest cloud service provider is one who has the flexibility to adapt to even the most unique business requirements. The importance of having a plan should not be underestimated, but it should also contain very specific execution milestones and very distinct business objectives. Just keep in mind that the secret to a successful cloud transition strategy is to start small, experiment courageously, fail quickly, and learn as the business grows. When evaluating potential providers, take into account both hard and soft criteria. Pay attention to and validate not only the accreditations and standards they uphold, but also what their clients have to say about them in case studies and reviews.

On the risk management part, it is advised that businesses have a strong risk management life cycle that measures and keeps an eye on the most important and high-risk situations in real time. To guarantee that hazards are actually being reduced, it's crucial to specify what needs to be measured precisely as well as the permitted range of variation.

In conclusion, adopting a cloud-based solution for an information system requires cloud consumers to carefully identify their security requirements, evaluate each potential service provider's security and privacy controls, negotiate SLA and SA, and establish trust with the cloud provider before authorizing the service.

In the next chapter, we will talk focus on architecting the cloud solution for your enterprise, key considerations for cloud security architecture, and its adoption path.

References and useful information

- NIST Risk Management Framework
- CCM framework developed by **Cloud Security Alliance (CSA)**
- ISO 27017/18 and ISO 27701 Frameworks
- **Code of practice for cloud service providers**: https://cloudindustryforum.org/8-criteria-to-ensure-you-select-the-right-cloud-service-provider/

Building Blocks of Cloud Security Framework and Adoption Path

This section will include the following topics:

- Implementing Cloud security in your organization
- Cloud security architecture
- Native cloud security controls - technical components of Cloud security architecture (Asset Management and Protection, Identity and Access Management, Vulnerability Management, Network Security, and Incident Response Management)
- Examining regulatory compliance in the cloud and adoption path
- Creating a Cloud security policy
- Creating a security culture in your organization

CHAPTER 4

Cloud Security Architecture and Implementation Framework

Introduction

In the previous chapter, we have assessed and finalized the right solution for your cloud journey. Now, this chapter will focus on architecting the cloud solution for your business. The chapter will talk about how to build the cloud security architecture, the framework on which the solution will be built, key considerations for your architecture, and an adoption path in the long run. We will also talk about container security and microservices. Container technologies and microservices designs are the new entries to the overall framework which enable new application architectures for legacy programs, refactored apps, and microservices, among others.

The chapter will also give you a quick brief and reference to Autonomic security which provides complete coverage of your cloud ecosystem from a security perspective.

At the end of this chapter, the reader will have a clear understanding on how the cloud security architecture should be defined and adopted for your enterprise and the key consideration which you should be following while you are on your journey of cloud migration.

Structure

In this chapter, we will discuss the following topics:

- Key elements and responsibilities of cloud architecture
- Shared responsibilities in cloud ecosystem
- Architecture type and building blocks of cloud security architecture

- Adoption of cloud security architecture along with different service models

- Cloud security principles and framework

- Cloud security adoption path

- Cloud migration strategy inclusive of need and benefit

- Different types of cloud migration scenarios

- Common cloud services

- Microservices and container security

Cloud security architecture overview

A cloud security solution's platform, tools, software, infrastructure, and best practices are what make up its security architecture, often referred to as **cloud computing security architecture** or **cloud security architecture**. A cloud security architecture provides a written and visual model to define how to configure and secure cloud-based activities and operations, including things like *identity and access management, techniques and controls to protect applications and data, methods for gaining and maintaining visibility into compliance, threat posture and overall security, processes for incorporating security principles into the creation,* and *operation of cloud services, policies and governance.*

In general, cloud security relates to the safeguarding of information, applications, data, platforms, and infrastructure that run or exist within the cloud. *Public, private,* and *hybrid* clouds all fall under the umbrella of cloud security. One subset of cybersecurity is cloud security.

Key elements and responsibilities of cloud architecture

Every day, more of our world is shifting to the cloud. We refer to this sea of computers as the cloud, and it contains web apps, mobile apps, personal data, images, and other types of data. It's crucial to analyze security layers as firms undertake this transition or re-evaluate their current security posture. The idea of cloud security architecture will be covered in this chapter, along with how it functions and its practical applications.

Shared responsibilities in cloud security architecture

The kinds of cloud security architectures that are most appropriate depend on the kinds of service models that a firm employs. **Infrastructure as a Service (IaaS)**, **Software as a Service (SaaS)**, and **Platform as a Service (PaaS)** are the *three* service models.

Organizations that provide cloud services frequently follow a shared responsibility paradigm, in which the cloud service provider is in charge of the security of the parts required to run the cloud service (software, computing, storage, database, networking, hardware, infrastructure, and so on). The client is in charge of safeguarding the data and information kept in the cloud as well as the methods by which they can access that data (*identity and access management*). Depending on the sort of service, responsibilities change a little (IaaS, SaaS, or PaaS). Let's take a closer look at all these service types and how the responsibilities are taking the shift.

Infrastructure as a Service (IaaS)

IaaS allows businesses to acquire infrastructure from cloud providers and install their middleware, operating systems, and applications. Azure is an illustration of an IaaS (Microsoft). In an IaaS, the customer is typically liable for the security of everything they install or own on the infrastructure.

Software as a Service (SaaS)

With SaaS, a supplier sells an organization the right to use a *cloud-based application*. *Office 365* and *Salesforce* are two instances of SaaS. In a SaaS, the client is usually only accountable for the security elements related to accessing the software, such as *identity management*, *client network security*, and so on. The backend for security is managed by the software provider.

Platform as a Service (PaaS)

With PaaS, a company buys a platform from a cloud provider to *create*, *manage*, and *operate* applications without creating or managing the platform infrastructure needed for the applications. **Amazon Web Services (AWS)** is one instance of a PaaS. Security related to the *installation*, *configurations*, and *permissions* of the application in a PaaS is the customer's responsibility.

Architectural type for cloud security

Depending on the cloud model you have implemented, defining cloud security architecture is usually necessary. As soon as that is done, you can use the security architecture as a guide to determine what needs to be *configured*, *deployed*, and *managed* to provide the highest level of security for your cloud environment.

It is vital to know which styles you have implemented so that you are aware of your security obligations as each style has shared duties with the cloud provider. Currently, there are three main fashion trends:

- **Infrastructure as a Service (IaaS)**
- **Software as a Service (SaaS)**
- **Platform as a Service (PaaS)**

These cloud services offer users a cloud-native architecture for hosting apps and services from outside their company. When a service or application is specially created to operate in the cloud, such architecture is known as **cloud-native**. The program or service is constructed around cloud infrastructure, and this has been intended from the beginning.

Cloud security architecture building blocks

When a cloud provider adopts a *cloud-native strategy*, security concerns are shared with whoever is offering cloud services. When creating cloud infrastructure or navigating the cloud as a whole, it's important to keep the following things in mind:

- **Layer-by-layer security**: Ensure that the cloud's security stack is *self-defending* at every level. *Defense-in-depth* is essential since each layer may have several components. This relates to things like *automatic operating system updates, secure coding*, and *log monitoring*.

- **Centralized management of components**: This refers to adopting the idea of various components in each tier and controlling them all, notably security, from a single location while taking advantage of efficiency opportunities.

- **Plan for redundancy in case of failures**: Even though most of us detest the idea of failure, we must plan our cloud infrastructure for the chance that it may occur. Order to restore operations entails developing disaster recovery plans and keeping backups on hand. Making sure that all components—or at the very least those that must be online constantly—have resilience built in is another facet of this.

- **Design for elasticity and scalability**: When it comes to elasticity, some design considerations must be made. *Which should be used when sizing—a horizontal scale or a vertical scale? In other words, is it possible to expand the server or add new servers/services? When deploying new systems or services, you must consider the images you'll utilize. What parameters determine whether scaling is increased or decreased? What is the location or area where the additional components will function?* Before you develop your architecture, you must respond to each of these.

- **Pick the best storage for your deployments**: The use cases and requirements of your company must be taken into consideration while selecting storage. As not all options are created equal, take your time to consider your possibilities. Everyone has unique performance requirements as well as security measures. Re-evaluate your data security plans at this time and confirm that you are adhering to all corporate policies.

- **Create an alert and notification plan**: One of the most important components of security architecture design is this. You must make sure that you are being informed and alerted while developing how the components will communicate with one another and how users will engage with those components. As a result, you are always informed about what is happening with your cloud infrastructure. The generated logs are your main source of information, thus it's crucial to enable logging whenever you can, for example, for network, identity, access, and service activities.

- **Centralization, Standardization, and Automation (CSA)**: CSA is a factor that needs to be taken into consideration during design. Using services and resources that can be incorporated into a single dashboard for viewing is known as **centralization**. As a result of *standardization*, the complexity of implementing new services is being reduced while providing architectural security models that are uniform across the large array of cloud services. The ability to scale and respond to accidents and issues more quickly depends on how much of your infrastructure can be automated.

Evolution of cloud security architecture

Serverless and *microservices* architectures are becoming more prevalent in shared cloud environments and cloud architectures. The use of common security technologies, as we are accustomed to, is being eliminated as a result.

The justification is that common tools were not intended to run in containers or a particular service. There is a greater dependency on systems like **CASB**,

Zero Trust, and **Cloud Workload Protection Platforms (CWPP)** as a result of the lack of use of these common monitoring and security technologies.

One of the most important aspects of cloud security overall is its architecture. Businesses may better manage, grow, and monitor their cloud environments by integrating security into infrastructure and services. The environment could be exposed to a security incident that results in data loss if these procedures are not followed.

Responsibilities of cloud security architecture

Here we will be segregating the responsibilities into two types. In the first type, we will address *private* versus *public* cloud. In the second type, we will talk about CSPs versus *customer responsibilities*.

Public cloud versus private cloud

A cloud provider with shared resources and computing among many clients is something you would employ for the public cloud. Customers in the *public cloud* can be compared to tenants renting space because the data and access are hidden from each one of them. In this paradigm, security is typically shared by the *provider* and the *customer*.

The private cloud, on the other hand, is the infrastructure that is controlled by the company that uses it and can either be located on-site in an internet-facing data center or hosted on-premise. Almost everything in this paradigm is the customer's responsibility.

CSP versus customer

The security of the cloud falls under the purview of cloud hosting companies. In other words, they are in charge of ensuring the security of both the infrastructure's hardware (*regions*, *zones*, and *edges*) and software (*compute*, *storage*, *database*, *networking*, and so on).

The onus for cloud security falls on users of cloud service providers. The customer is liable for the security of the usage data in cases where providers handle backend protection. Among them are:

- Data
- Access
- Application development
- **Identity and Access Management (IAM)**
- **Operating System (OS)**

- Firewall administration and configurations
- Network security
- Cryptography/decryption

For the customer in the cloud, this is a lot of data to track. *Gartner* predicts that through 2023, at least 99% of cloud security failures will be the fault of the client. Given the enormous responsibility involved and the substantial move to a cloud model that enterprises must make, this is not a difficult pill to swallow.

Adoption of cloud security architecture on various service models

By far we have learned that there are different service types on the cloud and each one of them is unique from its service offering and underlying component perspective. Similarly, cloud security considerations will also vary for each of these service types. Let's see how far this goes with a different service model.

Software as a Service (SaaS)

An application that is available as a service (SaaS) can be purchased from a cloud service provider or business. With this architecture, the provider normally manages security for the backend, leaving the customer just responsible for managing the application. *Salesforce*, *Microsoft 365*, and *Dropbox* are a few examples of SaaS.

The main risk to businesses using SaaS is fairly similar to that of other applications. *Phishing* is still a major issue with these programs since attackers will try to use your login information to get access. Insider threats and credential exposure will also be things to watch out for in this vein.

Customers should think about **CASBs**, or **Cloud Access Security Brokers**, to help with protecting these apps by providing users with visibility, access controls, and data protection by utilizing APIs, proxies, and/or gateways to counter these dangers in SaaS.

Infrastructure as a Service (IaaS)

IaaS is a cloud service where businesses can buy infrastructure. Systems and networks can be set up quickly, and businesses can install their own operating systems, applications, and middleware. **Azure** and **Rackspace** are two examples that are providers of IaaS.

Normal on-premises security threats apply to IaaS as well. Since corporations are installing the operating systems and apps, they are also in charge of security risks associated with them, including threats like vulnerabilities, malware, insider threats, and credential exposure.

Endpoint Protection (EPP), CASBs, and *vulnerability management* are a few examples of the conventional security measures and cloud-specific solutions you should have in place to combat these threats. *Access control*, *data encryption*, and *network encryption* would be additional components to deploy. By adding layers of security, using these in tandem improves the security strategy. These safeguards are essential, particularly since *Gartner* anticipates that 50% of businesses will have unintentionally and unintentionally exposed certain IaaS storage services, network segments, apps, or APIs to the open internet.

Platform as a Service (PaaS)

A business can buy a platform from a cloud provider in a PaaS arrangement. As a result, the business can *create*, *maintain*, and *manage* applications without worrying about the infrastructure that underlies most application-running systems. AWS, *Oracle*, and *Google* are a few platforms from which PaaS providers can be cited.

You will largely deal with self-inflicted damage when it comes to threats and PaaS. Constraints on the application itself result from using the default setup settings. Permissions on the cloud data and leaving it open to unauthorized access are typically subject of other problems. The use of SSL is one last item to keep in mind because the poor implementation can result in leaks.

Utilizing both common cloud-style security tools and unconventional security software is necessary to secure your PaaS environment. For instance, you'll still need a CASB to impose access and security rules. However, you need additional set up a **Cloud Workload Protection Platform (CWPP)**. You will have protection and visibility into the workload as it moves across environments and suppliers as a result.

Cloud security framework

A secure, *effective*, *efficient*, *resilient*, *high-performing*, and *cost-effective* cloud topology can be designed and operated with the help of the cloud architecture framework for any CSP. It also offers recommendations and describes best practices for *architects*, *developers*, *administrators*, and other *cloud practitioners*.

The architecture framework's best practices and design suggestions are validated by a cross-functional team. The architecture framework is carefully curated by the team to reflect CSP's developing capabilities, industry best practices, community wisdom, and your feedback.

The following diagram depicts the *six* main pillars that make up the cloud architecture framework in practice:

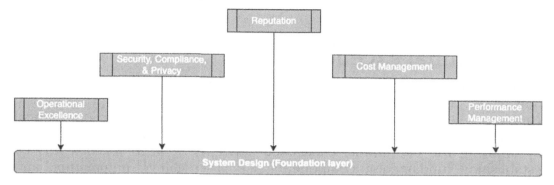

Figure 4.1: *Cloud security framework*

Now, let's take a quick tour of these important pillars of the framework.

System design

You can learn how to define the architecture, parts, modules, interfaces, and data on a cloud platform to meet specific system requirements in this area of the cloud architecture framework. Additionally, you will also get the visibility of different services and tools offered by these CSPs. The framework intends to assist you in designing your *Google Cloud* deployment to best suit your company's requirements. We advise you to do the following actions in order to develop a reliable system:

- Clearly outline your application requirements and base your system architecture on the business criticality of the application.

- To decrease system complexity, facilitate scalability, minimize impact, fail quickly, and enable rapid deployments, decouple your apps.

- To reduce operational overhead and concentrate on application development, use managed services whenever possible.

Key considerations under this pillar must include but are not limited to:

- Support to your commercial applications by choosing certain geographic areas.

- Control cloud resource usage.

- Select and control computing.

- Create an infrastructure for your network.

- Decide on and put a storage plan into practice.

- Optimize your database, please.
- Analyze your data.
- Use artificial intelligence.

Operational excellence

This framework pillar will guarantee effective cloud service operation. It covers how to operate, oversee, and manage processes that generate profit for the company. The various cloud capabilities and services that support operational excellence are also covered. You may lay the groundwork for dependability by applying the operational excellence concepts. It accomplishes this by establishing fundamental components like *observability*, *automation*, and *scalability*.

This architecture framework outlines best practices, offers suggestions for implementation, and explains some of the tools and services that are offered to assist you in achieving operational excellence. The framework intends to assist you in designing your cloud deployment to best meet the requirements of your organization.

The following essential elements for operational excellence should be taken into account as you define this section:

- Make deployments automatically.
- Configure logging, monitoring, and alerting.
- Create mechanisms for cloud support and escalation.
- Manage quota and capacity.
- Prepare for busy periods and launch events.
- Promote an automated culture.

Security, compliance, and privacy

This section explains how to design and manage secure services in a cloud environment.

You need to assess your company's needs, risks, legal requirements, and security measures before moving your workload to the cloud. When creating your framework, keep the guiding concepts in mind. Through the use of policies and controls that are defined across IAM, *encryption*, *networking*, *detection*, *logging and monitoring*, *data and systems* are protected in the cloud through several layered defenses. You can expand on several built-in security features of the cloud, including the following:

- Choices with encryption by default for data at rest and secure options for data in transit.

- Security components that are already included in native cloud services.

- A worldwide infrastructure that incorporates security measures at every stage of the information processing lifecycle and is built for *geo-redundancy*.

- The ability to automate using configuration guardrails and **infrastructure as code (IaC)**.

Key considerations for security, compliance, and privacy which you should consider includes but not limited to:

- Analyze shared accountability and shared destiny on *Google Cloud*.

- Recognize the fundamentals of security.

- Control risks to reduce exposure.

- Organize your resources.

- Manage access and identity.

- Adopt secure computing and container technologies.

- Protect your network.

- Construct data security.

- Install security in applications.

- Control requirements for compliance.

- Establish criteria for data sovereignty and residency.

- Establish rules for privacy.

- Put logging and detective controls in place.

Reputation

Your architecture must have the following components in order to run a *reliable* or *dependable* service which will have direct proportion to your reputation:

- Measurable reliability objectives with timely correction of any discrepancies.

- Design patterns for *scalability*, *high availability*, *disaster recovery*, and *automated change management*.

- Self-healing components and code with instrumentation for observability.

- Operational processes that enable you to quickly identify and address errors while minimizing manual labor and operator cognitive load.

Everyone in engineering, including the development, product management, operations, and site reliability engineering teams, is in charge of reliability. Everyone must take responsibility and be aware of the dependability goals, risk, and error budgets for their application. Teams should be able to set priorities for their work and escalate conflicts between dependability and product feature development. Key elements to consider include:

- Being familiar with the fundamentals of reliability
- Establishing your targets for reliability
- Making your infrastructure and application observable
- A large-scale, highly available design
- Making dependable operating procedures and tools
- Constructing effective warnings
- Creating an interactive incident management procedure

Cost management

By moving your IT workload to the cloud, you can develop at a larger scale, provide features more quickly, and meet changing client expectations. A topology that is optimized for *security*, resilience, *operational excellence*, *cost*, and *performance* is required to migrate existing workloads or deploy cloud-built applications. You need to understand and do a deep dive into the following things in the architecture framework section on cost optimization:

- **Adopt and put into practice FinOps**: Techniques to help you persuade staff to think about the cost implications when providing and managing resources in the cloud.

- **Track and manage costs**: The best *methods*, *programs*, and *tools* for keeping tabs on and managing the costs of your cloud resources.

- **Reduce costs**: Cloud storage, persistent discs, and file store all include cost-optimization settings.

    Reduce costs using smart analytics and databases *BigQuery*, *Cloud Bigtable*, *Cloud Spanner*, *Cloud SQL*, *Dataflow*, and *Dataproc* cost-optimization controls.

    Reduce costs by using *Google Cloud* networking resources with cost-optimization controls.

Cut costs while using the *cloud*. There are suggestions to assist you to reduce the cost of maintaining and monitoring your resources on *Google Cloud*.

Performance management

Performance management is the final but not least option. Here, we need to comprehend the crucial factor for performance management, which is the essential objective for a good environment and delivery. Performance requirements need to be assessed. Decide which of your applications are most important and what performance standards you expect from them. In order to increase scalability and performance with *auto-scaling*, *compute options*, and *storage configurations*, WW should start using scalable design patterns.

A few of the considerations for this last pillar are as follows:

- Use auto-scaling so that the services add or release resources as needed to reflect changes in load.

- There are choices available in the cloud to boost the performance of your workloads. These customized hardware platforms can improve the processing speed of your applications and data.

- You may operate more effective apps by using solutions for application performance management that can help you lower latency and costs.

Adopting cloud security

To begin with, when it comes to cloud transformation, we have all heard that security should be considered before migrating to the cloud rather than after.

There are several security difficulties to overcome, such as deciding whether to maintain cloud-native security controls or incorporate third-party platforms, depending on your cloud strategy and desired speed to market for your application or replacement of your data center.

Furthermore, not *future-proofing* the security architecture is another significant barrier we've seen. This is crucial when taking into account how quickly cloud service providers update or provide new services.

We've observed patterns and techniques emerge based on several successful experiences that can be successfully applied when it comes to implementing cloud security.

Security should be considered before you deploy anything once you've decided to utilize the cloud (or are forced to do so due to an unanticipated catastrophe, such as a global epidemic). If you have already deployed cloud resources, make sure to take full advantage of all the opportunities to increase security. This can entail utilizing both *cloud-native* and *external platforms*.

Setting up your cloud security course involves various phases. But just as with building construction, it's crucial to comprehend building regulations (governance) and make sure you keep inside those restrictions (project management), otherwise you'll end up having to correct costly assumptions. Start by forming two teams: **governance** and **project management**. These teams can be strengthened, and you can teach them about your plan.

To establish the course of action and identify your objectives so they don't need to be addressed later in the process, you may also organize foundational and strategic sessions, such as:

- **Governance team**: Used to specify the requirements for compliance and the course that a business will take.

- **Project management team**: Sets the pace and makes sure the project stays on track. When you consider how quickly events will develop in the environment, this crew becomes essential.

You should consider how the modifications affect both your AWS and Azure installations and SaaS apps. You must pick which environment will be most helpful to achieving your organization's goals, needs, objectives, and security requirements because each environment has a different set of outcomes and criteria.

Five phases of adoption

The first *four* phases of building and executing cloud security are spent defining your security controls and strategy, and the *fifth* phase, or the business layer, is when you deploy the cloud solution(s). The following diagram (*Figure 4.2*) will help you to explain the same followed by a detailed understanding of each of these individual phases:

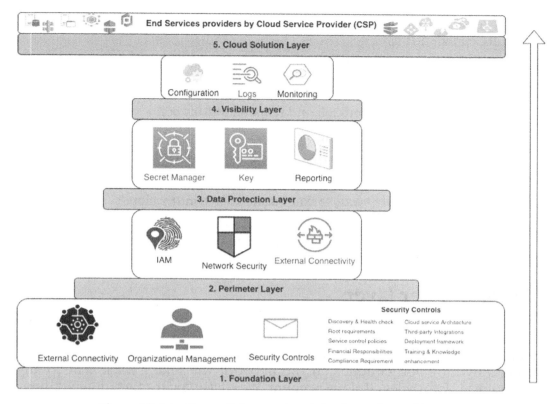

Figure 4.2: Adoption path for a matured cloud security architecture

The foundational layer

Building a solid, solid foundation is the most crucial step in the five phases. To establish your baseline and identify any significant gaps that should be filled sooner rather than later, you must first assess your existing position. You'll need to be able to respond to inquiries like the following as part of this process:

- *Do you know your baseline and present posture?*
- *What will be done to control root accounts?*
- *How will you handle the risks and exposure posed by brand-new cloud services before their adoption or use?*
- *What compliance mandates influence your company and will guide your governance architecture?*
- *It's okay to have a tech stack where we run everything, but how does it affect standardization, security, efficiency, and agility?*

- *Are you comfortable managing several authentication methods independently?*
- *Is your team well-versed in implementing cloud computing?*

The following are some extra topics you should think about:

- *What will each person's job and responsibilities be?*
- *How will you use the services?*
- *Will you employ cloud-native encryption?*
- *Should you begin contacting the vendor to introduce third-party solutions? Possibly because you intend to use many clouds?*
- *Is our staff well prepared to use cloud computing? Are your project managers prepared for integrated teams (DevOps/DevSecOps), as well as for Agile project management?*

The perimeter layer

This stage, which focuses on the new boundary, involves developing your perimeter strategy. While permission and authentication are inadequate, you could have a false sense of security and think your network security is really strong. Anything you conduct on the network will take a back seat to any compromise of a privileged cloud account. We advise you to start thinking about identity access management for the cloud coupled with a robust authorization process as you are developing your program. The actual security posture of your cloud environment will be determined by this. The cloud has seen the emergence of many useful patterns for network topologies and security. When we undertake security audits, we frequently discover hub-and-spoke VPCs and VNets or transit gateways in AWS. After dealing with the perimeter, you should have determined roles, a secure network architecture, and most crucially, a strategy to guarantee that your environment's least privileged policies are upheld(s).

Data protection

Data protection discussions should also take into account *encryption, key management,* and *secret management services.* You should also consider data classification and categorization in this discussion. You must choose whether you want to use a third-party solution for crucial services like *certificate administration, data encryption,* and *secret management.* Another option is to use a cloud-native service.

They can be kept secure with the right implementation and supervision. Although native cloud encryption may be both cost- and operationally-effective, you must ensure that the decision is supported by the appropriate approach. For your ecosystem, it is advised that you make use of the CSP's native key management services.

Visibility

Visibility is crucial, but it can also pose the most difficulties. You need to be able to create a narrative around cloud environment activity when done properly. You require a logging platform that enables you to ingest logs and easily develop search queries, or simply have an efficient approach to detect specific events or abnormalities, to efficiently collect, manage, and obtain the proper performance with your data.

You'll have the ideal foundation on which to develop your dashboards so that you can acquire essential visibility if you can modify the volume of data that is flowing in. You must keep track of network traffic, cloud API use, and infrastructure modifications.

Your OS logs must still be recorded if you are still using **Infrastructure as a Service (IaaS)**. This is why choosing the proper logging platform at the outset is crucial. Inventory management will also be handled by other services, such as tracking and finding fresh stock. Make sure to look for unknown occurrences and risks during the visibility phase. The following capabilities and tasks require a platform that can handle them:

- A logging platform that assists you in understanding cloud events as well as other events so you can correlate activity.

- Record network activity, cloud API activity, and infrastructure changes.

- Automate your change advisory board so that any modifications to cloud resources are tracked and can be undone or prevented.

- Avoid wasting time by delving into irrelevant rabbit holes by being aware of the crucial things to look for, such as an excessive number of API requests that are turned down, unusual cloud API usage (even with effective least privilege policies), and changes to baselines like increased compute capacity or network ingress/egress traffic.

Cloud solution

You may now consider your cloud solutions to have a solid foundation and the other four phases are complete. The following are some considerations for this phase:

- *Is our configuration management and golden AMI process followed by computing instances(virtual servers)?*

- *Do they have hardened or aligned with the recommended hardening guidelines?*

- *Do you just employ roles and service principles when necessary?*

- *Do you have the visibility and ongoing supervision required to guarantee access control improvements?*

- *Have you implemented a web application protection strategy that is suitable for your PaaS architecture?*

- *Are you equipped to deal with public cloud service providers' commonalities and are you ready to welcome the introduction of new cloud services?*

- *Can you conform to industry frameworks to satisfy your compliance obligations?*

Cloud security principles

The following fundamental ideas ought to form the foundation of any well-designed cloud security architecture:

- **Identification**: Knowledge of the users, resources, business environment, policies, vulnerabilities and threats, and risk management techniques (business and supply chain) that are present inside your cloud system.

- **Security controls**: Defines parameters and policies used across users, data, and infrastructure to aid in managing the overall security posture.

- **Security by design**: Specifies control roles, security configurations, and automation for the security baseline, often standardized and repeatable for deployment across typical use cases, with security standards and in audit needs.

- **Compliance**: Ensures that industry standards and regulatory duties are met by integrating components of them into the design.

- **Perimeter security**: Protects and secures traffic entering and exiting an organization's cloud-based resources, as well as the points of connection between the corporate network and the open internet.

- **Segmentation**: To avoid lateral movement in the event of a breach, segmentation divides the architecture into isolated component pieces, and mentions the *least privilege* ideas frequently.

- **User identity and access management**: Ensures knowledge, visibility, and control over all users (*people*, *systems*, and *devices*) who access company resources allowing *access*, *permissions*, and *procedures* to be enforced.

- **Data encryption**: To reduce the impact of a breach, data must be encrypted both while it is in transit and at rest between internal and external cloud connection points.

- **Automation**: Automation enables quick threat detection and supply of security and configuration upgrades.

- **Logging and monitoring**: Logs actions and continuously monitors (sometimes automatically) all activity on connected systems and cloud-based services to ensure *compliance, insight into operations*, and *awareness of dangers*.

- **Visibility**: Incorporates methods and tools to preserve visibility among the many cloud deployments used by a business.

- **Flexible design**: Ensuring that the architecture design is sufficiently flexible to expand and incorporate new components and solutions without compromising intrinsic security.

Autonomic security

Autonomic computing is a *self-managing computing approach* in which computer systems self-heal and reconfigure in response to changing situations. Autonomic computing holds the potential to significantly enhance the security of information systems, and cloud computing in particular, but it will take some time for that potential to manifest. Autonomic systems' capacity to gather and analyze data, offer or implement solutions, and provide for recovery from negative events can significantly improve security.

Autonomic system

The *human autonomic nervous system* serves as the foundation for autonomous systems since it is self-regulating, keeps track of bodily changes, and maintains internal balances. An autonomous computing system's objective is to govern itself to maintain proper operations despite system disruptions. A system of this kind needs sensory inputs, the ability to make decisions, and the capacity to carry out corrective actions in order to maintain an equilibrium state of typical operation. The following are some instances of occurrences that would need to be handled independently:

- Malicious attacks

- Software or hardware issues

- High CPU usage

- Power outages

- Organizational policies
- Unintentional operator mistakes
- System interaction
- Software updates

Autonomic protection

Autonomic self-protection entails recognizing a dangerous circumstance and acting to lessen it. Additionally, these systems will be created to identify issues through the analysis of sensory inputs and to start implementing solutions. Based on network knowledge, connected resource capabilities, information aggregation, the complexity of the issue, and the effect on affected applications, an autonomous system's security response is determined.

The autonomic computing decision-making component can change the strength of necessary authentications or alter encryption keys while taking into consideration the current security posture and security context of the system to be protected. When creating a higher-level representation of the system security status, the security context is created using data gathered from network and system supervising elements. The fact that configuration changes and additional autonomous operations designed to solve other computing domains might result in *security vulnerabilities* is a frequently ignored element of autonomic systems. Therefore, the following principles should be followed by autonomous protection systems:

- Reduce the need for overhead.
- Follow security guidelines strictly.
- Increase the efficiency of security-related factors.
- Minimize any performance-related effects.
- Minimize the possibility of creating new vulnerabilities.
- If issues are brought about by modifications, perform regression analysis, and go back to earlier program versions.
- Make sure reconfiguration procedures are safe.

Autonomic healing

It can be *difficult, time-consuming,* and typically involves a lot of labor to diagnose and fix IT system faults. Without the need for human interaction, autonomous self-healing systems may discover *hardware flaws, find and fix software bugs,* and *detect software errors.* To identify the issue, the autonomic process would gather data that had been logged and tracked and conduct an analysis. Typically, this approach is carried out by an autonomic manager, who has control over computing resource elements with clearly defined interfaces that support the diagnostic and mitigation activities. In addition to having defined performance characteristics and connections to other computational components, managed elements are in control of their internal states.

Maintaining the elements' ability to function in accordance with their design specifications is the goal of the autonomous self-healing process.

Evaluating the cloud security maturity model

The **cloud security maturity model (CSMM)** talks about recommendations that might or might not work for any enterprise. It serves as an excellent starting point for directing investment choices toward particular cloud environment areas. There are several maturity models from diverse organizations. It is best to research the option that makes the most sense for your company. Given the numerous attempts to compromise this access point and user identities, authentication ought to be given top priority. The following are things to check for or bring up with your cloud service provider:

- *Do you have methods for multi-factor authentication?*
- *Does Single Sign-On (SSO) support exist?*
- *Do you interact with enterprise directories and authentication?*

When assessing how they handled earlier security occurrences and their numbers, it is important to consider previous security-related difficulties. Several of the following can be used as examples:

- *How many data breaches has the business had overall?*
- *Has their cloud ever housed malware?*
- *Do they regularly run environments through penetration tests?*

Documents and ideologies such as policies, compliance data, and documents are equally significant. You may learn a lot about your cloud service provider's security practices by looking at how they manage their security. *Will they notify you if there is a breach and provide you with the information?* These are all excellent concerns to have when assessing service providers.

It's best to look everywhere while assessing your cloud security provider. You should not take your organization's security lightly, thus while making judgments, you should have as much information as you can. Keeping this in mind, not all cloud security models are made equal. In one, you could control the majority of the environment's security, but in the other, you would only have authority over a few specific places. Before defining your cloud security architecture, understand your cloud model.

Cloud migration

Let's take some time and talk about the migration strategy to the cloud as it's important to understand the journey towards the cloud ecosystem. The compute plan is described in this section along with certain factors that business should take into account while *creating, implementing,* and *maintaining* cloud-based digital services. The following steps should be taken by agencies to ensure a smooth and secure transition to cloud services:

- **Develop software for the cloud**: To build a reliable and secure cloud environment, decide which services and capabilities to include right away.

- **Create a cloud migration strategy**: Develop a plan tailored to your agency to move data and services from an on-premises environment to the cloud.

- **Adopt a Development, Security, and Operations (DevSecOps) strategy**: Utilize coding and include support staff to produce dependable automated digital services.

- **Centralize common cloud services**: Choose the CSPs that will be applied throughout the organization, and streamline the administrative and purchasing processes.

- **Invest in people**: To successfully migrate to the cloud, organizations need to develop specific capabilities.

Software development for the cloud

Organizations can integrate services in support of their goals by using the cloud's flexibility. As early as feasible in the **Software Development Life Cycle (SDLC)**, organizations should endeavor to integrate security measures into their cloud-based digital services (SDLC). Customers who enable **DevSecOps** with automated security testing will be able to create *scalable, repeatable, trustworthy* architectures that adhere to the *zero-trust principle*. To create digital services, agency teams must collaborate during this process. IT teams can support DevSecOps in conjunction with centralized SaaS to enable security testing of products prior to deployment. Digital services that use the cloud can include IaaS, PaaS, and SaaS. Accountability for various system design levels varies between these service models and the on-premises model. Agencies must verify the products and services that their suppliers are – and are not – offering.

Need to shift software to cloud

It is possible to create software that is more *dependable, scalable,* and *predictable* by shifting digital services and software from an on-premises data center to the cloud. With the use of cloud services, organizations may swiftly increase capacity when necessary without having to invest in additional data centers and have disaster recovery available in other locations. Before attempting to migrate larger services, organizations might first move smaller, internal projects, and tools to the cloud to build knowledge and comfort using new environments. In order to enable daring advancement or modernization, moving to the cloud presents an opportunity to rebuild existing digital services.

Building *zero-trust architecture* and more secure apps can be made easier in the cloud, which is just one of many well-known advantages that agencies should take into account. The *five* pillars of zero trust—**identity**, **devices**, **networks**, **applications**, and **data**—can all be addressed by CSPs, and they can also provide the visibility required to start developing cross-pillar interactions. Enterprises can often speed up an **Authority to Operate (ATO)**, facilitating the migration process, by checking for the proper **FedRAMP** approval level for cloud services. DevSecOps teams or other administrators may be in charge of properly setting up these services, creating useful IAM roles, and safeguarding confidential data with encryption offered by a **Key Management System (KMS)**.

When managing their cloud deployments safely, businesses should take into account the security benefits of leveraging APIs or data services. The same data can be accessed through services from CSPs and other suppliers without requiring organizations to *develop, validate,* and *maintain* complicated software. APIs offered by CSPs and others are frequently supported by a large team of developers and other specialists who specialize in these systems. The purpose of an agency may suffer as a result of the time and money required to establish a comparable team within the organization.

Strategy for cloud migration

Moving corporate activities and missions into the cloud is referred to as cloud migration. For many agencies, this entails moving from legacy infrastructure that might no longer serve their needs to a modern infrastructure that supports a more flexible and cost-effective solution for an agency's application. A mentality change from on-premises solutions is a necessary part of cloud environments. **Infrastructure as code (IaC)** principles, for example, allow some cloud functions to perform in ways that on-premises functions cannot. These ideas include dynamic resource provisioning and decommissioning based on how elastic the demand for services is, as well as temporal-based maintenance to replace specific infrastructure components for security reasons.

The amount of planning required for cloud migration depends on the scale of the application ecosystem, how old the existing systems and apps are, how many users there are, and how much data there is. Agencies should take into account the age and volume of data present in their application ecosystem because transferring data to the cloud might become more difficult as data accumulates over time. Agencies should consider the advantages, dangers, and difficulties associated with adopting *cloud-based technologies* before deciding to shift their application ecosystem to the cloud.

Real-time challenges while migrating to cloud

Every large-scale software project faces difficulties, but transitioning from on-premises to the cloud presents certain special obstacles related to staff, money, and data. The following *Table 4.1* shows typical problems that organizations run into when moving to the cloud.

Challenges	How does it affect the migration
Implementing change	Aside from technical changes, adopting a cloud architecture calls for process changes as well. The discomfort of change might be lessened by acknowledging this and making space to reimagine the procedures.
Policy support	Existing application/project ATOs may need to be upgraded or changed in order to accommodate cloud migration, which typically pushes the limits of existing ATOs.
Staffing	The number of employees is important because as a project develops, a specialized team may be required to support the migration effort.
Infrastructure support	A team new to cloud migration may want assistance setting up servers, network support, application, and database in the cloud.
Onboarding	A successful migration for their application should be facilitated by giving staff additional time during onboarding to be trained on the new technologies.
Financials/ Funding	An overlap in financing requirements may be necessary before cost benefits can be realized because the application infrastructure and data may be present for a while in several contexts. Costs related to data transfer are also involved. Transferring data out of a CSP can be more expensive; in certain cases, moving data into a CSP is *cheap* or even *free*. This depends on the CSP, the design, and the technique.

Table 4.1: *Potential list of real- time challenges during cloud migration*

In addition to the difficulties stated previously, the organization should think about the technical difficulties of data migration. Migration, validation, and support of large amounts of data take longer. If there are additional demands that result in little to no application downtime or if the underlying data changes often, the difficulty of the migration is exacerbated. Technical issues with data migration to the cloud are listed in the following *Table 4.2*:

Technical challenges	How does it affect the migration
Network assistance	An agency should understand the latency and throughput characteristics of the network when a lot of data is moving across the infrastructure of the network as part of data migration. Decisions about how to move the data to the cloud vendor's environment more effectively can be influenced by these measurements. Developers who must transfer data and apps around and end users on home networks may both experience problems with bandwidth.
Data integrity	By using encryption, the migration must guarantee both the integrity of the data once it has arrived at its final storage site and the security of the data during transfer.
Cut downtime	Since many organization applications are accessible during working hours, weekends might be used for downtime. More strict downtime requirements might apply to selective applications. It takes planning and, in many advised circumstances, an iterative rollout of the application in the cloud when replacing a system to minimize downtime during the move.

Table 4.2: Potential list of technical challenges during cloud migration

Benefits of cloud migration

Since so many business and mission operations are cloud-centric, cloud services provide agencies with a variety of operational and financial benefits. *On-demand self-service, broad network access, resource pooling, quick elasticity,* and *measurable service* are listed by NIST as the *five* fundamental characteristics of cloud computing in SP 800-14529. A fundamental departure from conventional hardware procurement and management is possible with gear that can be provisioned in accordance with tenants' needs.

In lieu of making a hardware reservation, tenants might choose **virtual machines (VMs)**. Additionally, renters have the option to use the CSP's platform instead of creating any servers at all (*virtual* or *bare metal*). As a result, agencies can delegate to the CSP some of the routine tasks associated with patch management and health monitoring, albeit agencies would still be responsible for the security of their own systems. Instead of being contained in a single place like a server room or data center on premises, provisioned resources may instead be spread across many *geographical locations* and *availability zones* within regions. Agencies should think about their own needs and resources while evaluating various cloud services to decide which ones are best for their purposes. The following table (*Table 4.3*) will talk about a few of the important benefits of this migration journey:

Benefits	How does it affect the migration
Cybersecurity	To avoid requiring each customer to develop their own security support, CSPs frequently offer alternatives for various security-related issues. Enterprises must, however, *educate* themselves on the available options in order to deploy and configure the ones that are best for them.
BCP and DR	Organizations using off-premises cloud infrastructure and data are better prepared to respond to and recover from unfavorable events at agency offices.
Cost	CSP services enable organizations to focus financial resources on mission-critical tasks while increasing efficiency.
Uptime	In order to relocate running code with the least amount of disruption, cloud services can manage failures of the application's underlying infrastructure.
Scalability	A wide range of horizontal scalability, or the capacity to add more machines to an application's resource pool, is supported by cloud services. For distributed systems, scalability is essential.
Design flexibility	Managed services offered by cloud providers include document storage, database replication storage, and application interfaces for automation.
Support coverage	A variety of cloud suppliers and support options are available to agencies.

Table 4.3: Notable benefits in the journey of cloud migration

Approaches to cloud migration

When transferring an application, organizations can need to apply several different methodologies. Agencies must take into account their unique demands when they move because not every application is made to function in a cloud environment. A CSP might not be able to deliver the speed that an application needs, for instance, if it depends on the low latency offered by a local network. Some of the key cloud migration tactics that have been made popular by industry partners are listed in the following table (*Table 4.4*):

Techniques	Description
Rehost	The previous configuration is transferred onto cloud servers using this technique, which recreates the application architecture in a *lift and shift* paradigm.
Re-architecture	With the intention of leveraging cloud-native services from a code and design standpoint, this approach restructures the application into use cases.
Re-platform	A portion of the program can be migrated and enhanced to use cloud-native services after revision. Utilizing managed cloud-native databases is a common choice because of how little maintenance work is required.
Rebuild	When rebuilding an application, the old application must be discarded and the new application must be created using cloud infrastructure. This depends on building the application into a cloud-native solution or placing it there.
Replace	By moving the use cases to a SaaS environment with a third-party provider, this method does away with the necessity for the legacy application.

***Table 4.4**: Cloud migration techniques*

The *Rehost approach*, *Refactor*, and *Revise* strategies are hotly contested, therefore enterprises should carefully examine which is best for them. Due to the deprecation of legacy systems, it is occasionally required to shift an application to the cloud; nevertheless, it is not practical to do a *Refactor* at the same time. In that scenario, the best course of action might be to proceed with the Refactor once the Rehosting is finished. There are numerous ways that cloud-native services from an IaaS or PaaS can *minimize complexity*, *increase performance*, and *lower hosting costs*, therefore the Refactor should still be taken into consideration.

An enterprise may need to take into consideration when moving to the cloud the subtleties of moving various types of services to and between cloud environments. An enterprise might decide to move development procedures, for instance. In this situation, DevSecOps can be used to address the distinct scalability and flexibility requirements of on-demand infrastructure as well as to sustain newly *integrated cloud-native solutions* over time. An enterprise might choose to use containerization, for instance, to make it easier for service users to orchestrate their computing needs.

Scenarios for cloud migration

Giving general advice on how to accomplish the conversion is difficult because every cloud migration is as unique as the original application. Following the steps listed as follows, however, can improve your odds of success:

- **Plan**: Choose the strategy to employ, the CSP and service category, and the application's path map.

- **Design**: Create the application's architecture, paying particular attention to the system's distributed nature. Try out CSP's cloud-native features.

- **Pilot**: Construct a **Minimum Viable Product (MVP)** to show that the cloud-based application will function.

- **Migrate**: Prepare the cloud version for production, including transferring any necessary data.

- **Maintain**: Continue to enhance the cloud application, whether from the perspective of the features of the product or from a standpoint of performance.

Common cloud services centralization

Their organization may assist developers by managing and maintaining shared services as they *migrate*, *build*, and *deploy* apps on the cloud. Agencies enable developers to spend more time concentrating on the purpose and less time on administrative or upkeep responsibilities by offering shared services. This list of services is divided into *four* categories:

- Consumer PaaS

- Resources and services for development

- Public-facing services

- Security solutions

By reducing administrative burden and freeing up time to consider other overheads that might be reduced, sharing some services at the agency level can assist teams in implementing cloud native practices more quickly. A team can switch from operating entire **virtual machines (VMs)** for web servers to operating servers in containers, and then switch from containers to using **Functions-as-a-Service (FaaS)**.

Just to educate readers, FaaS is a class of cloud computing services that gives users a platform to *create*, *use*, and *manage* application capabilities without having to worry about creating and maintaining the infrastructure that is generally needed to create and launch an app.

The utilization of specialized roles has undergone another metamorphosis as organizations switch from conventional on-premises servers to IaaS. Teams will still want specialist knowledge to comprehend how to make databases performant, even if they will no longer require someone committed to administrating the server that the database is on. Database administrators are able to concentrate on the strategic operations under this paradigm, as well as serve as consultants for the organization.

Need to centralize common services

The centralization of IaaS, PaaS, and SaaS within an organization serves *two* key purposes: **resource conservation** and the **creation of a common user experience**. New equipment and software purchases require a lot of resources. Organizing a centralized team to conduct research, make purchases, and provide training on the tools that other teams use will help agencies cut costs overall. Additionally, by streamlining maintenance and compliance initiatives, centralizing services (such as those in the following categories) can help save resources.

By providing shared tools to various teams within an agency and encouraging collaboration, centralization also enables agencies to create a shared experience. Knowledge may be shared between teams thanks to centralized documentation. Teams can collaborate more easily when they are using the same ticketing, pager, and monitoring system.

As staff members change teams within an agency, it also makes onboarding easier. Teams that have worked on cloud-based projects can also share their best practices and difficult areas so that other teams can benefit from their expertise. The total investment in people can be increased by experienced team members mentoring younger teams to share their knowledge and expertise. Cloud tool centralization is a good idea for *two* reasons: **reducing resource usage** and **removing organizational silos**.

Consumer PaaS

Businesses can centralize access to current IaaS tools by purchasing cloud infrastructure in bulk and granting access to various teams as required. This will guarantee that the right level of access is allowed and enable newer teams to use the infrastructure right away. The customer's cloud team can behave more like a PaaS by providing configurations to *standardize logging, software libraries*, and *operating systems*. These ideas will work together to accelerate the creation of cloud-based digital services while conserving resources. While starting to lighten the load of security paperwork like ATOs on development teams, a centralized IaaS can promote normative practices and enforce compliance. The majority of IaaS solutions allow for compliance checks, such as *alerting teams* when a storage container is *public* or *not* encrypted so teams can swiftly resolve the problem. When all teams utilize the same platform, they can inherit organizational account NIST SP 800-5334 controls and use standard language in their **software support program (SSP)** agreements for quicker paperwork.

To enable teams to share the IaC containers they use, customers might centralize *gold image* VMs and set up *artefact* repositories. The logging standards can also be configured for the containers and virtual machines. The conflict between usability and security is evident in this situation; while customers can add security monitoring to the base images, it's crucial to maintain the images' performance by avoiding overtaxing the systems with additional processing. Enforcing consistent patching across the board will increase security further.

By supplying the program with certificates on the web server, encryption services can guarantee that the application uses *secure communication routes* (like TLS). Additionally, these systems have the ability to directly encrypt data at rest or use managed services to do so as appropriate.

Key and **password management** allows apps to cycle keys and passwords on a set schedule without the application being interrupted. In the event of a compromise, this service must also have the ability to *revoke* keys.

Resources and services for development

To build and manage apps fast and effectively, you need development tools and services. Although not all-inclusive, this section does include common tools and services used in application development.

The software development lifecycle and DevSecOps heavily rely on collaboration tools, requirement tracking, and documentation to provide current status evaluations both inside and between teams. Collaboration and documentation procedures across the entire organization foster collaborative and sharing cultures.

The basis of a CI/CD pipeline is the source control software because it determines which tools can be utilized for *developing, testing*, and *delivering* code. Another crucial component of CI/CD that can be standardized throughout the organization is code quality control using *linters*, which can examine code for problems that would prevent execution or make it difficult to read, and checking for coding *anti-patterns*, which can prevent using bad coding conventions that result in insecure or underperforming code.

It's crucial to centralize and standardize security testing across an agency since consistent security implementation results in improved overall processes. This can be done by integrating security testing into the CI/CD pipeline. The first line of defense against unintentionally releasing defects into production can be provided by static and dynamic security testing.

Public facing services

Centralization would help several parts of the digital services that organizations offer to the public. Obtaining a domain, establishing the site's **domain name system (DNS)** entries, and installing certificates for **secure hypertext transfer protocol (HTTPS)** are routine steps in launching a new website. The agency is aided in keeping an accurate inventory of its web presence by centralizing these activities.

Applications and APIs need to be protected from malicious traffic if they are to be accessed over the internet. **Content delivery networks (CDNs)** that also serve as **DDoS** defense mechanisms, API gateways, and WAFs are some examples of protection. WAFs can regulate network access in general and examine web server request packets for common website assaults. Multiple APIs can be protected by the same API gateway, which regulates access to APIs for specified users.

In addition to offering a means of storing cached material closer to consumers for speedier delivery, CDNs frequently have the capacity to absorb more traffic during **denial-of-service (DoS)** assaults or restrict network traffic via firewalls. This protection will be required for all online properties owned by an organization, and purchasing in bulk can reduce costs.

Security services

In as much of the company as feasible, customers should implement centrally integrated security services. The agency's attack surface is diminished by having fewer distinct instances of the same service. Applications are protected by security services, which also *offer logging, authentication, authorization, encryption*, and *key management*.

The improved incident response depends on centralized logging. It decreases the significance of locally stored logs' deletion by making them superfluous. A response to an occurrence requires less time to investigate when logging is centralized. Additionally, across CSPs and on-premises solutions, centralized logging makes threat hunting easier.

IAM via **single sign-on (SSO)** is the perfect place to start for customer service, as the CIO probably already has the ability to allow staff to log in to services like email. **Lightweight Directory Access Protocol (LDAP)**, which can be used even on-premises, can broker access to cloud services, removing the need for staff members to remember yet another password.

When onboarding a new SaaS product to a centralized IAM system, the customer should aim for *minimal* friction. Prior to widespread acceptance and integration, they should look at ways to prototype or pilot connecting such services. Agencies may be able to address their initial performance and security-related issues thanks to this, which may also give them more information for more seamless integration.

In many cases, IAM services also *offer authorization*. Application-level enforcement of authorization is occasionally necessary, though. Teams working on development projects must be able to regularly ask for information on authorization. The authorization process will change from *role-based* to *attribute-based* as clients continue their journey toward *zero trust*, and will need to include data from many pillars. The centralized approach also helps with the overall authentication process and workflow.

Human impact

Changes to processes and procedures are needed for the stakeholders and users of these technologies as well as the staff working on deploying tools and apps in order to build scalable, repeatable architectures via CSPs. To deliver projects using the cloud, customers will need to invest in people. Additionally, they will need to *revamp procedures, train the entire workforce*, and *enable dependable access*.

Spending money on people

The secret to a successful project is investing in the best people to deliver cloud-based initiatives. Training, hiring, and purchasing are the three components of this. Enterprise professionals who previously worked in traditional software development environments can be retrained in cloud technology, but doing so requires enterprises to invest in their employees through outside trainings, certifications, and workshops, as well as the use of work time to learn new technologies. Training in contemporary project management techniques might also be a part of this. Customers must give staff members opportunities to put their newly learned abilities into practice in order to reinforce the trainings (for example, through access to sandbox environments that allow for experimentation with these new technologies). Employees that are new to cloud technologies will develop their abilities and provide superior digital services with the assistance of experimentation, iteration, and the freedom to *fail fast*.

Another way to invest in people is by hiring fresh, qualified workers who have prior expertise with cloud-based initiatives. The skill pool is often small, making it difficult to fill a new position.

The **Subject Matter Expert Qualification Assessments** are one of the tools you can use to hire technical candidates more effectively. Rather than taking a broad approach, these assessments help you find talent that is more appropriate and aligned with your unique needs. This enables clients that require similar personnel, such as designers or product managers, to share job requisitions, screen applicants using technical tests and provide a pool of eligible individuals from which they can individually select.

Support staff

Agencies should work to help federal workers by providing prompt access to resources and extra training through onboarding and other documented procedures. Both on how to use the new CSP technologies and how the usage of cloud tools alters the *security paradigm*, additional training will be required for all staff. Anti-phishing and appropriate data handling are two topics covered in security training. Both individuals directly involved in the design of digital services (such as those working in DevSecOps) and those supporting digital services from a non-technical standpoint will need to adapt to this new security paradigm.

Silos that may have developed over time can be broken down through better communication between *development teams* and *stakeholders*. Information silos will be broken down and collaboration will be facilitated by combining development, security, and operations. Timely access also lessens the possibility that staff may create **shadow IT services** that evade IT or security teams' monitoring and degrade the client's overall cybersecurity posture.

Microservices and container security

Growing in popularity is the usage of *microservices-based architecture* to implement complicated, dynamic applications. Component replacement or update during flight is much simpler thanks to microservices. Additionally, it enables independent work on various facets of the entire solution by several engineers.

However, security issues unique to the microservices design exist. In order to guarantee that data is *secure* and *private*, as well as that the system is available when needed, anybody who might wish to use it must carefully consider these difficulties from the beginning.

Microservices-based architecture

Instead of typical monolithic programs, which handle a wide range of duties, microservices are *compact, containerized* application services that carry out a single task or a small group of related tasks. Utilizing security technologies for containers that were specifically created for the microservices architectural environment is crucial.

As a direct result of its modular design, microservices architecture has certain special risks. Microservices architecture is a complex and open development model for applications. They have a significantly wider attack surface than more conventional application models.

Application Programming Interfaces (**APIs**) used by microservices for communication are independent of the machine architecture and even the programming language. In comparison to conventional subroutines or features of a major application, which only communicate with other components of the same application, they have a greater exposed surface. There are therefore more possible attacks against them.

The quick development cycle and the **continuous integration/continuous delivery** (**CI/CD**) strategy for the microservices architecture mean that code testing is not done as a *one-time activity* at the conclusion of development but rather as a continuous operation. They need to handle this testing carefully.

Last but not least, the container-based solution where microservices are implemented may be vulnerable to a specific set of risks. This can be caused by the integrity of the container images themselves, how they are handled, the degree of isolation between containers, vulnerabilities within the containers, such as packaged libraries, and the security of the **operating system** (**OS**) that hosts the containers.

Securing the microservices architecture

Although this may seem like a difficult effort, protecting your microservices just requires putting several best practices into place that make security an essential part of how your development teams operate—without sacrificing productivity.

To preserve the integrity of your microservices architecture, your teams can take the following steps:

Adopting security while designing the solution

Developers must include layers of security into programs to safeguard the data they contain, much like construction workers must carefully layer rebar and concrete to create sturdy foundations for buildings. Being *safe by design* inside a microservices architecture entails maintaining security at the forefront of all production phases, from *design* to *build* to *deployment*.

This entails putting in place a continual stress test on your architecture when it comes to writing your code. Testing your **continuous integration (CI)** and **continuous delivery (CD)** pipelines is a necessary component of this. **Static Application Security Testing (SAST)** and **Dynamic Application Security Testing (DAST)**, respectively, are examples of security unit tests that can be used to do this:

- Both your code and the libraries you import will be vulnerability-checked by SAST. A scanner that is compatible with your programming language is necessary because it operates from the inside.

- DAST searches for vulnerabilities from the outside, simulating hostile attacks. It is independent of a particular language, in contrast to SAST.

These unit tests can be incorporated into your delivery process to lessen the amount of time that developers might have to spend performing manual security checks. To assist your team in putting best practices into practice as they create software, the **Open Web Application Security Project (OWASP)** also provides a number of resources and analytics tools.

Verifying dependencies

A large portion of the code that is released to production contains *third-party dependencies* because many libraries used to develop software depend on other libraries in turn. Because of the potential for creating extensive chains of dependencies as a result of these relationships, security becomes much more of a worry.

These failure points can be removed by routinely and carefully examining an application's source code repository, fresh code contributions, and deployment pipeline for weak dependencies (including updated release versions).

While most programs include *release notes*, only 75% of them disclose security problems, and only 10% do so for common vulnerabilities and exposures. By being aware of your dependencies, you can assist verify that your code is current at the time of deployment and that there are no vulnerabilities brought on by recent pull requests.

Adopting HTTPS for everything

This can seem like a simple idea, but it's crucial to apply it consistently as the basis for both your internal and exterior activities.

When putting in place security infrastructure, most IT professionals focus on conventional threats like *phishing* and *credential stuffing* but it's also critical to mitigate assaults that could occur from within your network. You can achieve this in part by integrating HTTPS into your microservices design.

HTTPS secures data integrity and privacy by encrypting communication over HTTP, also known as **Transport Layer Security** (**TLS**). Consider it this way: just as driving necessitates the possession of a license, which certifies your identity and grants you access to the use of motor vehicles, HTTPS demands the possession of a certificate, which verifies your identity and grants you access to encrypted communications via *Public Key Infrastructure*. Once you've obtained your certificates, you can keep improving your security posture by automating certificate generation and renewals, thwarting malicious parties that might try to compromise your architecture.

Making use of identity and access tokens

A microservices architecture might include everything from the backend services that give the data to the middleware code that communicates with the data storage to the **user interface** (**UI**) that presents the data in a logical and comprehensible fashion. The delivery of secure and efficient authentication and authorization across these microservices depends on the establishment of the appropriate tools and protocols.

Industry-standard protocol **OAuth 2.0**, for instance, provides a means of authorizing users in distributed systems. A *secure server-to-server connection* between an API client and an API server is made possible inside the framework of microservices via OAuth 2.0's client credential flow.

By submitting an access token to a user information endpoint, OIDC and OAuth 2.0 also allow you to check the identification of a user. Through the use of OIDC *discovery*, the path to this endpoint can be found. By eliminating the need for each microservice to contain its own authentication system, OAuth 2.0 lessens the workload on your developers. A combination of OAuth 2.0 and OIDC can pull off the following things:

- Find provider metadata for **OpenID**
- Follow OAuth flow instructions to get an access token and/or ID token
- Get **JSON Web Key Sets (JWKS)** for signature keys
- Verify identity tokens (for example, JSON web tokens)
- Get extra user attributes together with access tokens from user information endpoints

Securing secrets via encryption

When you design microservices that communicate with authorization servers and other services, those microservices probably have some sort of secret information that they use to communicate with one another. Examples of this information include API *keys*, *client secrets*, or *credentials* for simple authentication.

Your source control management system shouldn't contain these secrets. It's likely to cause issues while your team is working on production code, even if you develop code in a private repository. Instead, placing secrets in environment variables is the first step in protecting your microservices' secrets. Better still, programmers should use encryption software like **HashiCorp Vault**, **Microsoft Azure Key Vault**, or **Amazon KMS** to protect secrets. With Amazon KMS, for instance, you may create a master key, and encrypt your data with special data keys that are then encrypted by the master key, creating an encrypted message that is stored as a file, or in a database. With this method, you can be sure that the keys required to decrypt any data are always *secure* and *unique*, *saving your team time* from having to manage additional security measures.

Knowing how to secure your cloud and cluster

The *four* Cs of cloud-native security—**code**, **container**, **cluster**, and **cloud/co-lo/corporate** datacenter—should be understood by your team members if they are responsible for managing your organization's production clusters and clouds.

The security of the squares they fit in determines how each of the *four* Cs works. If you simply address security at one level, protecting microservices is essentially impossible. The code, container, cluster, and cloud can all be enhanced with the necessary security, though, strengthening an already solid foundation. We've discussed how to write *secure code* effectively and how to work in a *secure cloud environment*. The following diagram (*Figure* 4.3) will depict the same understanding:

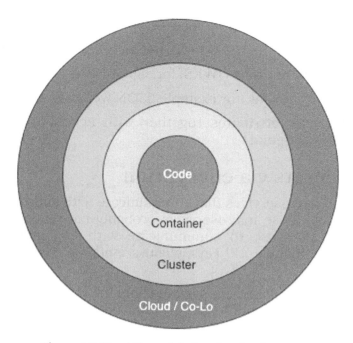

Figure 4.3: *The 4C's model of native cloud security*

The integrity of your containers and their base images must be guaranteed for container security, though. This is accomplished by the following:

- Making use of Docker content trust and signed images
- Creating an internal registry
- Implementing safe container versioning
- Checking container images for flaws and problems
- Protecting configurations
- Using *least-privilege techniques* to prevent container breakouts
- Adding features for authentication (this is *true* across all *four* Cs)
- Staying current with container security best practices; keep in mind that what's secure now could not be secure tomorrow

The following are the steps you should take to safeguard your clusters and strengthen their resistance to an attack:

- Use TLS everywhere (as we discussed previously).
- Make *role-based access control* with the least privilege available.
- Opt for audit logging instead of attribute-based access control.

- Utilize an external supplier of authentication, such as *Google*, *GitHub*, or *Okta*.

- Change your encryption keys frequently to reduce weaknesses.

- Employ network controls to restrict traffic among pods.

- Start the service mesh.

Covering all of your security bases

There are three practical methods (mentioned previously), your team may strengthen the security of your microservices in addition to the previously mentioned strategies:

- **Use rootless mode**: *Docker* 19.03 and later offers a rootless mode that was created to lessen the security footprint of the Docker daemon and enable Docker functionality to systems where users cannot obtain root rights. This feature provides an additional level of protection if you operate Docker daemons in a production environment.

- **Use time-based security**: Time-based security assumes that your system is *never* completely protected. As a result, you need to be able to see anomalies and act swiftly in addition to being able to stop intruders from accessing your application infrastructure. Products like *Okta*'s **Advanced Server Access (ASA)** slow down invaders by authorizing them on the basis of customizable access regulations, authenticating server login requests via Single Sign-On and multi-factor authentication, and blocking access without authorization. To aid your team in detecting security issues immediately, ASA also creates rich request events that can be consumed through API or delivered straight to a SIEM like **Splunk**.

- **Check the settings of Docker and Kubernetes for vulnerabilities**: Since microservice architectures frequently use Docker containers, they must be adequately secured. This entails taking the actions we've listed previously for protecting both images and containers.

Conclusion

It is crucial to take the time to comprehend the shared responsibility model, the various cloud security best practices, and the best ways to approach cloud security in the context of your business needs, obligations, and risks as you begin the process of developing a strong cloud security architecture. Cloud security architecture can vary in complexity based on the sorts of cloud services your business uses. It's crucial to remember that creating a strong and reliable security architecture takes time and expertise. Instead of trying to create a *unique* cloud security architecture on your own, think about collaborating with a cloud security provider.

While some security experts are familiar with the basics of cloud systems, others only need a blueprint. It is important to be aware of both historical and contemporary concerns. *Is multi-cloud something to think about when looking ahead?* A *manageable procedure* that integrates security with your company's activities can be achieved by establishing project management patterns for cloud computing.

Building confidence in the cloud computing paradigm requires a strong security architecture for the cloud. Providing a secure execution environment, securing cloud communications, enabling microarchitectures, and leveraging trusted computing mechanisms are all necessary for confidence in the use of the cloud.

Development and DevOps teams are changing how they work as a result of the shift to microservice architecture. Microservices enables teams to be more flexible, economical, and better able to scale their systems by replacing what has typically been a monolithic approach to developing systems and applications. It's vital that you provide your team with the appropriate tools and resources to secure these dispersed features as this approach to design becomes more commonplace inside your organization.

In the next chapter, we will learn and talk about the native security controls of public cloud and how these building blocks will help you to build a baseline and sustainable foundation layer for cloud security. We will also touch base on *third-party security controls* as an additional layer which will strengthen the overall security posture.

References and useful information

- Cloud Security Technical Reference document published by CISA: https://www.cisa.gov/sites/default/files/publications/CISA%20Cloud%20Security%20Technical%20Reference%20Architecture_Version%201.pdf
- NIST SP 800-204

Questions

1. Define the importance of shared responsibilities in the cloud security ecosystem.
2. What are the three major types of architecture you can have in the cloud ecosystem? Explain them in brief.

3. Explain the various building blocks of cloud security architecture.

4. How will your responsibilities vary under the shared service model? In your opinion, which side is heavier than the other in terms of accountability?

5. What are the various service models offered by the cloud ecosystem to the end users? Explain them in brief.

6. Define the importance of cloud security framework.

7. How many pillars does the cloud security framework hold and what is the importance of each one of them?

8. Explain the five phases of cloud security adoption.

9. What do you mean by autonomic security? Help to understand the importance of the same.

10. What do you mean by autonomic healing?

11. How do you evaluate the maturity of your cloud security architecture?

12. Explain the real-time challenges you may face while migrating your workload to the cloud ecosystem.

13. What are some of the key benefits of migration to the cloud landscape?

14. Define Microservices.

15. What are some of the key considerations you should adopt while defining the Microservices architecture in your landscape?

CHAPTER 5

Native Cloud Security Controls and Building Blocks

Introduction

This chapter will talk about different techniques which will help you to build native security controls in the cloud landscape. We will take a detailed tour of each of the native cloud security controls which is essential to building the overall security and getting aligned with the cloud security framework and architecture.

Structure

In this chapter, we will discuss the following topics associated with cloud security:

- Asset management and protection explaining data classification and regulatory requirements
- Cloud-based data management and protection including tokenization, encryption, and key management
- Asset tag in the cloud
- Identity and access management explaining B2B, B2C MFA, and SSO
- Vulnerability management on the cloud
- Network security on the cloud along with its adoption path
- Security incident response management

Asset management and protection

Data asset management and cloud asset management make up asset management. The crucial data you own, such as client names and addresses, credit card numbers, bank account numbers, or login credentials to access such data, is referred to as a **data asset**. Your data is stored and processed by your cloud assets, which include platform instances like databases and queues, object stores for storage, and computing resources like servers or containers.

Although the notion of managing data assets in the cloud is the same as managing those on-premises, several cloud technologies can be useful in actual practice.

Classification and identification of data

The **CIA** triumvirate of **Confidentiality, Integrity, and Availability** is one of the more well-known information security paradigms. A **threat actor** attempting to compromise the confidentiality of your data intends to steal it, usually to sell it for cash or to make you look bad. A threat actor attempting to alter your data integrity would like to manipulate your data, for example, by changing your bank balance. Threat actors attempting to compromise your data availability want to shut you down for entertainment or financial gain, or they want to encrypt your files with ransomware.

Classification level for data

The following guidelines offer a decent, straightforward place to start when determining the worth of your data and, thus, the danger of a breach, even if every organization is unique. All business sizes and types will be affected by this:

- **Low**: Although the public release of the material in this category *may* or *may not* be intentional, the impact on the organization would be extremely little or non-existent. A few examples which explain this:
  - Public IP addresses for your servers
  - Application log data free of sensitive information, secrets, and value to attackers
  - Documents used to install software that doesn't contain any secrets or other elements attackers would find valuable
- **Moderate**: Without appropriate nondisclosure agreements, this material shouldn't be shared outside of the organization. The *need-to-know principle* should be followed when disclosing this kind of

information within an organization, especially in larger ones. Most information will fit into this category in organizations. Consider these examples for quick understanding:

- Detailed knowledge of the architecture of your information systems that an attacker could use

- Information about your employees, which might be used by attackers to launch phishing or pretexting assaults

- Usual financial data, such as purchase orders or travel reimbursements, could be utilized

- **High**: The organization depends on this information, and its reputation may suffer greatly if it were to be disclosed. Multiple safeguards should be in place and access to this data should be securely restricted. Such information is sometimes referred to as the *crown jewels*. Consider these instances:

  - Financial data or information regarding future strategies that might provide rivals with a major competitive advantage

  - Trade secrets, including the recipe for your favorite soft drink or fried chicken

  - Keys to the kingdom, such as full access information for your cloud infrastructure

  - Private data, such as your client's financial information, that has been given to you for protection

  - Anything else that may make news if there was a breach

Relevant regulatory or industry requirements

This chapter is about *security*, not *compliance*. As a sweeping generalization, compliance is about demonstrating your security to a third party, which is much simpler to do if you have truly secured your systems and data. Although the material in this book will aid you in being safe, you will still need to perform additional compliance tasks and documentation once your systems have been made secure. Your security design, however, might be influenced by some compliance requirements. Therefore, even at this early level, it's crucial to be aware of a few industry or legal requirements:

- **EC GDPR**: No matter where personal information is located in the world, it may be subject to this law if it belongs to a citizen of the *European Union* or the *European Economic Area*. GDPR mandates that you organize, safeguard, and audit access to *any information related to an identifiable person who can be directly or indirectly identified in* *particular by reference to an identifier.* Some of the GDPR criteria may be easier to complete with the strategies in this chapter, but you must ensure that the personal data you're protecting includes any pertinent ones.

- **FedRAMP**: Even though the *Federal Risk and Authorization Management Program* certification can be used with various agencies, the *FedRAMP Federal Information Security Management Act* requires you to categorize your data and systems in line with *FIPS 199* and other US government requirements. Use the *FIPS 199* classification level if you work in a field where you might require one of these certifications.

- **US ITAR**: You must select cloud services that support *ITAR* if you must adhere to *ITAR* requirements in addition to your controls. Some cloud service providers offer these services, which are only run by *Americans*.

- **PCI DSS**: The **Payment Card Industry Data Security Standard** requires you to implement specified controls and lists specific data categories that you are not permitted to maintain if you handle credit card information.

- **HIPAA**: The **Health Insurance Portability and Accountability Act** requires that you put any **protected health information (PHI)** you deal with in your list and protect it, which frequently entails encryption if you are a US resident.

- **Digital Personal Data Protection Bill (India)**: Only personal information that is gathered online or offline but has been digitalized is covered by the law. If the processing of personal data takes place outside of India and is related to activities such as supplying goods or services inside *India* or creating profiles of *Indian* principals, then the legislation will be applicable to that processing. The law also exempts the processing of data pertaining to persons outside of India who are subject to a cross-border contract; this essentially covers the offshore/outsourcing sector.

Around the world, there are other laws and industry standards, including MTCS (*Singapore*), *G-Cloud* (UK), and *IRAP* (*Australia*). Review the data categories they are intended to protect if you believe you might be affected by any of these so you can be sure to classify and safeguard your data appropriately.

Cloud-based data asset management

The majority of the previously provided knowledge is a solid and acceptable general practice and is not unique to cloud systems. However, cloud service providers are in a unique position to assist you in identifying and categorizing your data. They will be able to identify all of your data storage locations because they want to charge you for them. Additionally, using cloud services naturally results in some sort of standardization. Instead of being dispersed across tens of thousands of different discs connected to numerous physical servers, your persistent data in the cloud is frequently stored in one of the cloud services that store data, such as object storage, file storage, block storage, a cloud database, or a cloud message queue.

You are provided with the capabilities by your cloud service provider to both inventory these storage areas and access them (in a carefully regulated manner) to learn what kinds of data are kept there. There are cloud services that can automatically classify where your vital data is located by scanning all of your storage locations. Then, you can utilize this data to tag your data-storing cloud assets.

Cloud resource tags

Tags are a feature of the majority of cloud providers and container management systems like Kubernetes. Typically, a tag is made up of a name (or *key*) and a *value*. These tags can be used for a variety of things, including classifying resources in an inventory, deciding who has access to what, and selecting what to alert on. For anything that contains personally identifiable information, for instance, you might have a key of *PII-data* and a value of *yes*, or you might use a key of data type and a value of PII.

It is obvious *what the issue is: tags won't be very helpful if everyone in your organization uses different tags!* The same tags should be used across different cloud providers and applied automatically (that is, by automated tools) when resources are produced. Create a list of tags with descriptions of when they should be used. Even if one of your cloud providers doesn't expressly support tags, there are frequently other description fields that can be utilized to store tags in *simple-to-parse formats* like JSON.

Although cloud providers do place a cap on the number of *tags*, a resource can have (often between 15 and 64 *tags per resource*), tags are free to use, so there's no reason to create a lot of them. They are simply ignored if you don't need to use them for later categorization or decision-making.

Some cloud providers even provide automation to ensure that tags are correctly assigned to resources, allowing you to identify untagged or incorrectly tagged resources early on and fix them. You can run automated scans to detect any resources where the tag is absent or where the value isn't one of the classification levels you have agreed upon, for instance, if you have a rule that states that each asset must be tagged with the highest data classification allowed on that asset. At the time of writing, not all of the main providers offer comprehensive coverage of these services, even though all of them support tags in some way. It's possible, for instance, that you can designate virtual machines you make but not databases. You will need to proceed manually with a list of instances of such services in cases where tags are not provided. The following *Table 5.1* depicts different names used by different CSPs for tagging:

CSP name / infrastructure	Feature providing tagging service
AWS	Tags
Microsoft Azure	Tags
GCP	Labels and network tags
IBM Cloud	Tags
Kubernetes	Labels

Table 5.1: Tagging with different CSP

Data protection in the cloud

Many of the on-premises data security strategies covered in this section may also be used in the cloud, but many of them offer *quick, standardized,* and *less expensive* solutions to protect your data.

Tokenization

Why keep the data when you could keep something that works similarly but is useless to an attacker? **Tokenization** substitutes a sensitive piece of data with a token, which is typically used with credit card information (usually randomly generated).

The benefit is that since the token typically has the same properties as the original data (such as being 16 *digits long*), existing systems that were created to accept that data don't need to be altered. Only one location (a *token service*) is aware of the actual sensitive information.

Encryption

We want to *encrypt everything* because encryption is the panacea for data protection. The situation is, regrettably, a little more complicated than that. Three states for data exist: *in use* refers to data that is now being processed in a computer's CPU or stored in RAM. It can also be in motion (being transported via a network) (on persistent storage, such as a disk). A crucial control that is covered in detail in the section that follows is the encryption of data in motion.

The remaining two states will be covered in this section:

- **Data is being encrypted**: Since it is still relatively new as of this writing, very high-security contexts are the main focus of data encryption *in use*. The hardware platform must support it, and the cloud service provider needs to make it accessible. The most popular method of implementation is to encrypt process memory, making it impossible for anyone, not even privileged users (or malicious software acting as privileged users), to access it. The *processor* can only read it when that particular process is active. You should look for a platform that supports memory encryption if you operate in a very secure environment and your threat model calls for protecting data in memory from privileged users.

- **Data encryption while it is at rest**: The most challenging encryption to appropriately deploy can be for data that is at rest. The encryption of the data is not the issue; numerous libraries can handle this. The issue is that after encrypting the data, you now have an encryption key that can be used to decrypt it. *Where do many people put this? Next to the data!* Imagine locking a door and then hanging the key on a hook next to it with the helpful label *key*. You need effective key management if you want true security rather than merely checking the box that says you've encrypted data. Thankfully, cloud services are available to support this.

  Please note that once the data is *encrypted*, it can't be compressed effectively, hence it's recommended that you should first compress the data and then encrypt it.

You would buy a **hardware security module (HSM)** to retain your encryption keys in conventional on-premises systems with strict security needs. HSMs often take the shape of expansion cards or network-accessible modules. Significant logical and physical security measures guard against unwanted access in an HSM. With ordinary systems, anyone with physical access can quickly gain access, but an HSM features sensors that can delete the data the moment someone tries to disassemble it, run X-rays over it, tamper with its power supply, or even just glare menacingly in its general vicinity. The majority of on-premises deployments cannot afford HSMs because of their high cost. But in cloud environments, cutting-edge technology like HSMs and encryption key management systems are now affordable for projects with limited funding.

Some cloud service providers give you the choice to rent a specific HSM for your environment. A *dedicated* HSM is still pricey in a cloud environment, even though it can be necessary for environments with the highest levels of security. Another option is a **key management service (KMS)**, a *multi-tenant service* that safeguards keys using an HSM on the backend. There is a slight increase in risk because you must have faith in both the HSM and the KMS, rather than simply the HSM. But KMS offers outstanding protection at no or very little expense compared to doing your key management, which is frequently done wrong. In projects with more modest security resources, you can still reap the benefits of proper key management. Key management options associated with various CSPs are discussed in the following *Table 5.2*:

CSP name / infrastructure	Dedicated HSM options	KMS
AWS	CloudHSM	Amazon KMS
Microsoft Azure	None	Key Vaults
GCP	None	Cloud KMS
IBM Cloud	Cloud HSM	Key Protect

Table 5.2: *Key management with CSP*

Key management

So, *what is the proper KMS use*? Things start to get a little difficult at this point. The most straightforward method of managing keys is to create a key, use it to encrypt data, place the key within the KMS, and then write the encrypted data to the disc with a notation identifying the key that was used to do so. This strategy suffers from two key issues:

- It heavily burdens the weak KMS. Every file should have a unique key for a variety of reasons, so a KMS with a large client base would need to store billions or trillions of keys with near-instantaneous retrieval.

- You can't leave any backup copies of the key lying about if you want to securely remove the data; you have to rely on the KMS to delete the key permanently after you're done with it. Another option is to completely wipe the encrypted data, which can take some time.

You might not want to wait several hours or days before overwriting a significant amount of data. It's preferable to have the ability to rapidly and securely destroy data objects in *two* separate ways: by removing a key at the KMS, which might effectively erase several different objects at once; or by deleting a key where the data is kept, to delete a single data item. For these reasons, you normally have *two levels of keys*: **a key encryption key** and **a data encryption key**. The *key-encryption key* is used to encrypt (or *wrap*) the data encryption keys, as the names imply, and the *wrapped keys* are kept exactly next to the data. To maintain security, the key-encryption key often never leaves the KMS. When necessary, the wrapped data encryption keys are sent to the HSM to be unwrapped. The *unwrapped keys* are then used to encrypt or decrypt the data. The unwrapped keys are never recorded. You put them out of your mind once you've finished the current encryption or decryption operation.

Take the following real-life scenario for a better understanding. You decide to sell your home, which houses all of your data, and you give your realtor the key to open the door. This home key functions as a direct access key, similar to a data encryption key (data). This key will be secured by the *Realtor* with a code issued by the Realtor service and placed in a key box on your door. The service used by Realtors to distribute codes is analogous to the key management service, and this code is comparable to the encryption key for keys. In this very strained example, you take the key box to the KMS, and it gives you a copy of the key inside with the understanding that you won't make a duplicate of it (write it to disc), and you'll melt (forget) that copy when you're finished with it. The code to open the box is never actually visible.

As a result, you can see the data key when you approach the home (data), but you need another *key* or *password* to open it. The key could, of course, be extracted from the box in the real world with the help of a hammer and some patience, or you could smash a window without a key. Trying to figure out the key or password used to secure the data key is the cryptographic equivalent of using a hammer. This is typically accomplished by the use of *brute force* or, in the case of passwords, a *dictionary attack* that involves testing numerous popular passwords. The predicted time for the *hammer* to enter the box is longer than the age of the universe if the encryption technique and its implementation are accurate.

Encryption on both the client and server sides

The fantastic news is that *you usually don't have to handle most of this crucial management yourself!* If you use the storage service of the majority of cloud providers along with their KMS and enable KMS encryption for your storage instances, the storage service will generate data encryption keys automatically, wrap them in a *key-encryption key* that you can control in the KMS, and store the wrapped keys alongside the data. Although you don't have to ask the KMS to encrypt or decrypt your data for you and you don't have to handle the encryption or decryption procedures yourself, you may still control the keys that are stored in the KMS. Your data can be decrypted by the multitenant storage service, therefore if there is a bug in that storage service, an unauthorized user could be able to ask it to do so. Due to this, performing the *encryption* and *decryption* across the storage service is not quite as secure as performing it within your instance—even if you implement it appropriately and make use of well-known libraries and processes. *Client-side encryption* is another term for this. However, unless you have an extremely *low-risk tolerance* (and a budget to match that low-risk tolerance), I suggest that you use *tried-and-true cloud services* and let them take care of the encryption and decryption on your behalf.

You should be aware that when *client-side encryption* is used, the server cannot read the encrypted data because it does not own the keys. Therefore, no server-side indexing, calculating, virus scanning, or other high-value functions can be carried out. As of this writing, *homomorphic encryption* is too slow to be useful, but it may make it possible to conduct operations like addition correctly on encrypted data without decrypting the data.

Cryptographic erasure

In reality, erasing vast volumes of data with confidence is challenging. Even after a thorough erase, there can still be duplicates of the data lingering. **Cryptographic erasure** will allow us to resolve this. This method involves merely saving an encrypted version of the data on the *disc*, not the clear-text equivalent. If we wish to render data irretrievable, we can erase or revoke access to the key-encryption key in the KMS, rendering any data encryption keys *wrapped* with that key encryption key useless, no matter where they may be located. We can successfully make a multi-terabyte file unrecoverable by overwriting a *256-bit key* by wiping out just the wrapped data encryption key for a specific piece of data.

Enabling encryption to protect against different attacks

As we've discussed, *data encryption at rest* can thwart attackers by limiting their options; data is only accessible in the open in a limited number of locations, depending on where the encryption is being used. Let's examine some typical successful attempts to see how much annoyance the attackers might experience due to our encryption choices:

- **Unauthorized access is gained by the program to physical media**: Attackers may be effective in stealing tapes while they are being transported or discs from the data center or trash. Data on physical media is protected by encryption at rest, which prevents an attacker from using the data even if they manage to access the media (such as by breaking a password). This is *fantastic news*, even if this kind of attack normally doesn't pose a significant risk because of the physical and media protections that the majority of cloud providers deploy. (It is even more crucial for portable devices like smartphones and laptops.) If encryption is just used to *check the box*, it frequently only serves to lessen the risk of physical theft. In some cases, even this security is ineffective if the keys are kept on the same storage medium as the data.

- **Unauthorized access is gained by the attacker to physical media**:

Attackers may be effective in stealing tapes while they are being transported or discs from the data center or trash. Data on physical media is protected by encryption at rest, which prevents an attacker from using the data even if they manage to access the media (such as by *breaking a password*). This is fantastic news, even if this kind of attack normally doesn't pose a significant risk because of the physical and media protections that the majority of cloud providers deploy.

- **Unauthorized access is gained to the platform or storage system by the attacker**: It's possible that you have an attacker or rogue employee who has access to your data in a *database, block storage, file storage*, or *object storage* instance. Depending on the technical controls in place inside the storage system, the attacker will frequently be able to mislead the system into giving it the data if the storage system itself is in charge of completing the encryption. However, this will at least leave auditable trails in a completely unrelated system (the *key management system*), so it could be possible to limit an attack if the key access behavior appears weird and someone sees it fast enough.

  However, the attacker will only be able to access a useless *bag of bits* if the program only transfers data that has already been encrypted to the storage system. The data's integrity and confidentiality cannot be compromised, but they can make the data unavailable.

- **Unauthorized access is gained to the operating system by the attacker**: There are *two* possibilities to consider if an attacker acquires unauthorized access to the operating system your application is running on:

  - The attacker's access to the operating system is constrained. The only functional controls at this time are those provided by the operating system. If the attacker has access to the *process, files*, or *storage* that contains the decrypted data, they will still be able to access the data even though it has been encrypted at rest.

  - The attacker has full control over the operating system. An attacker with restricted operating system access can frequently get full rights because of the abundance of privilege escalation exploits.

- **Unauthorized access is gained to the program by the attacker**: All bets are off if an attacker acquires unauthorized access to the application because it needs to be able to read the data to work. The attacker might not be able to view any data besides the data that the hacked program has access to, though, if encryption and other access controls are used properly.

Tagging cloud assets

It makes sense to classify and organize your assets as you are producing them so that you are aware of what they contain and how to use them. *Automation and access control* can be greatly facilitated using tags. You must tag other sorts of assets in the same way that you tag data assets with the types of data they include to identify the data types that are processed by those assets as well as their purpose. For a consistent view of where your data is kept and processed, it's crucial to utilize the same data tags to identify the different types of data processed on computing assets. The possibilities for other operational tags, however, are virtually limitless, whereas creating a set of data classification levels or a list of compliance requirements is rather straightforward.

The following are a few *illustrations* of the many tags that can be helpful:

- Function of the asset
- Environment type for the asset
- Applications or projects for which the asset is utilized
- Department in charge of the asset
- Version number
- Automation tags indicating whether the asset should be chosen for action by scripts, scanners, or other automation

The same has been illustrated in the following diagram (*Figure 5.1*). *Automated security checks* may be possible with proper tagging. Consider the very reasonable policy you may have in place prohibiting the storage or access of sensitive data on systems used for testing and development. You must maintain a consistent set of *tag names* and permitted values for *tags* to be effective, which calls for having a tagging policy and adhering to it. The *tagging policy* ought to be used uniformly throughout smaller enterprises. A bigger organization will need to accept some tags that apply to the entire organization in addition to permitting tags unique to business units. In either scenario, the tagging policy should have a clear owner who updates the official list of tags as necessary.

If your company or business unit has a tagging policy, you might wish to implement automation to gather all of the tags that are currently being used and report on any that are not mentioned in it:

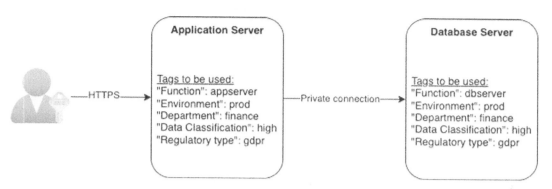

Figure 5.1: *Sample diagram representing the usage of tags*

Identity and Access Management (IAM)

One of the most crucial sets of security measures is **identity and access management (IAM)**. Lost or stolen credentials have been the attackers' *go-to weapon* for numerous years in breaches affecting web services. No amount of firewalls and updates will be able to keep an attacker out if they have legitimate credentials to access your system. It's vital to recognize that identity and access management are two separate ideas even if they are frequently discussed together:

- Each entity (such as a *user*, *administrator*, or *system*) requires an identity. Authentication is the procedure used to confirm their identification.

- Ensuring that entities can only carry out the tasks they require is the goal of access management. **Authorization** is the process of verifying the appropriate level of access for an object.

IAM on cloud

To access their cloud services, several cloud providers offer IAM services at no additional cost. With the help of these solutions, you can manage the identities of your company's cloud administrators as well as the access you've given them to all of the services the cloud provider provides from a single, central location.

This may be of great assistance. It can be challenging to determine how much access a particular person has if you use dozens or even hundreds of services from a cloud provider. When a person leaves your company, it can be challenging to make sure all of their identities have been destroyed.

Examples of identity services to authenticate your cloud administrators with cloud provider services are provided in the following *Table 5.3*:

CSP name / infrastructure	Identity system on the cloud
AWS	Amazon IAM
Microsoft Azure	Azure Active Directory
GCP	Google Identity
IBM Cloud	Cloud IAM

***Table 5.3**: Identity services on different cloud*

Enterprise-to-Employee (B2B) and Enterprise-to-Consumer (B2C)

You might need to handle identities for your end users, whether they are outside clients or your staff, in addition to the identities your business uses to access cloud provider services. Although you can handle *client identity management* on your own by simply adding rows in a database with passwords, this is frequently not the best option for your end customers since they will need to remember yet another *login* and *password*. There are other important security mistakes to avoid while checking passwords. There are *two* preferred alternatives:

- Make use of the current identity service. For your staff or the employees of your customer, this might be an internal identity service. An external service like *Facebook*, *Google*, or *LinkedIn* might also be available to end users. You must have faith in the identity service to authenticate users on your behalf in a trustworthy manner. Furthermore, it makes your affiliation with the identity provider clear to your end users when they check-in, which isn't always ideal.

- Use client identities specific to your application and manage these customer identities using a cloud service.

These **Identity-as-a-Service (IDaaS)** services occasionally have titles that are not entirely descriptive of their functions. Examples from both big cloud *infrastructure providers* and *independent providers* are listed in the following table. This is not a recommendation of any specific *third-party suppliers* since there are several in this market and they frequently change. The majority of these IDaaS services can also access your employee data repository, such as your internal directory, for *business-to-employee* scenarios:

CSP name / infrastructure	Identity system on the cloud
AWS	Amazon Cognito
Microsoft Azure	Azure Active Directory B2C
GCP	Firebase
IBM Cloud	Cloud Identity
Auth0	Customer Identity Management
Ping	Customer Identity and Access Management
Okta	Customer Identity Management
Oracle	Oracle Identity Cloud Service

Table 5.4: *Consumer Identity services (CIAM) on different clouds*

Multi-Factor Authentication (MFA)

One of the greatest ways to protect against faulty or stolen credentials is *multi-factor authentication*, which if implemented correctly will just be an extra step for users. Most of the identity services listed in the above table enable **multi-factor authentication (MFA)**.

Multi-factor authentication uses multiple of these factors to authenticate users, as the name suggests. It is of little assistance to use two of the same factors, such as two *distinct* passwords. Using something you know (like a password) and something you have (like your cell phone), **two-factor access (2FA)** is the most widely used approach.

If implemented properly, MFA should be the default for the majority of access because it adds very little extra work for most users. If you have privileged access, access to view or change sensitive material, or access to systems like email that may be used to reset other passwords, you should utilize 2FA there. These are all places where the consequences of lost or stolen credentials would be considerable.

Unauthorized administrative access to the cloud portal or APIs poses a very significant risk to you if you are in charge of maintaining a cloud environment since an attacker who gains that access can frequently use it to compromise all of your data. Since most cloud providers already allow *two-factor authentication*, you should enable it for this kind of access. As an alternative, your SSO provider might already handle MFA for you if you're utilizing a **single sign-on (SSO)**.

Many services provide a variety of 2FA options. The most widely used techniques are:

- **Sending texts to a mobile device (SMS)**: This approach is quickly losing effectiveness. favor due to the simplicity with which one can take someone's phone number and spam with text messages through various ways, therefore new implementations should not use SMS, and existing implementations ought to switch to a different technique. To receive SMS messages, you do need network access.

- **One-time passwords based on time (OTPs)**: To use this technique, a mobile device must get an initial *secret* (usually transferred by a 2D barcode). The *key* is a formula for creating a one-time password roughly once every minute. The initial secret should be forgotten or stored in a physically secure location after usage because it can enable any device to generate valid passwords. The *one-time password* only has to be kept secure for a few seconds. The mobile device just needs a synchronized clock after the initial secret has been delivered; network connectivity is not necessary.

- **Push notifications**: With this approach, a mobile device's client application that has already been authorized connects to a server, which *pushes* back a one-time use code as necessary. This requires a network connection for the mobile device but is secure as long as the authentication for the client application that has previously been validated is secure.

A hardware device that can deliver a one-time password when required, such as one that complies with the *FIDO U2F standard*. These gadgets will undoubtedly become commonplace in the not-too-distant future, connected with smartphones or wearable technology like *watches* and *rings*, and will probably be the sole type of verification necessary for lower-risk transactions.

API keys and passwords

Passwords are no longer your only form of security if you're using multi-factor authentication. Having said that, it's still crucial to pick strong passwords as of this writing, despite claims that *passwords are dead*. This is frequently even more true in cloud setups because an attacker can frequently guess passwords straight over the internet from anywhere in the globe. Although there is a lot of discussion and advice on good passwords, my suggestions for selecting passwords are straightforward and as follows:

- Reusing passwords is never a good idea unless you don't care at all whether someone else has access to the resources that the password protects. You should always presume that the website's administrators are evil when you enter your password since they might use it to access other websites. For instance, you might use the same password on a dozen different forum platforms if you don't care whether someone else writes on any or all of those boards in your place.

- You'll accumulate many passwords if you don't reuse them, so use a *trusted password manager* to manage them. Keep duplicates of any master passwords or recovery keys in a physically secure location, such as a reliable safe or a bank safe deposit box.

- Take advantage of a safe random number generator for passwords that you don't need to remember. *Twenty characters* is a good goal; however, you could come into systems that won't take that many; for them, utilize a character set that is as diverse as possible.

Although API *keys* and *passwords* are fairly similar, people rather than automation are the intended users. Because of this, API keys must be lengthy random strings and cannot employ multi-factor authentication. Instead of having a public user ID and a secret password like other user identities, you only have a private API key that serves as both an identification and authentication.

Shared credentials

Shared credentials are identities for which more than one person has the password or other authentication information, such as the system's default root or administrator accounts. Similar to how they are handled on-premises, they can be challenging in cloud systems. Users should often use personal IDs rather than shared IDs. For some activities, they might adopt a persona or employ a different, more privileged ID. If you do need to use shared IDs, you should be able to identify the specific user that accessed any data using that ID. In actuality, this typically indicates that you have a check-in/check-out procedure.

Single Sign-On (SSO)

The concept of federated identity is the foundation for **single sign-on (SSO)** technology implementations. Each website required a unique *login* and *password* in the bad old days (granted, this concept is still prevalent today). Users will need to remember a lot of passwords in this case. Users frequently use the same password on various websites, which is an expected outcome. As a result, the password is only as secure as the site with the lowest security.

The concept is that a website should not request a user's ID and password, but rather should transfer them to a trusted centralized **identity provider (IdP)**. To authenticate the user, the IdP will employ tools such as a *username* and *password* and, ideally, an extra authorization factor like ownership of a phone or hardware key. Once the user's identity has been validated, it will redirect them back to the original website. Sometimes, the IdP will communicate additional data (such as *group membership*) that the website can use to decide whether to grant the user access as a regular user, as an administrator, or not at all.

Generally speaking, SSO is only effective for websites and mobile applications. **LDAP**, **Kerberos**, **TACACS+**, or **RADIUS** are some examples of different authentication protocols you need to use for non-web assets like operating systems or network devices. It's uncommon to discover something that offers higher security while also making use easier. Users only need to remember one set of login credentials, and as these credentials are only ever seen by the identity provider (and not by any of the different sites), they are safe from compromise if one of those sites is compromised. The main negative is that this is a little trickier for the website to implement than inadequate authentication methods like comparing against a plaintext password or an insecurely hashed password in a database.

SAML and OIDC

The most popular SSO technologies as of this writing are **OpenID Connect (OIDC)** and **Security Assertion Markup Language (SAML)**. Despite having somewhat distinct methods, the outcomes are comparable. Since 2005, there has been a version of *SAML called 2.0*. It is among the most widely used SSO solutions, especially for complex enterprise applications. There are various in-depth analyses on how SAML functions, but the following is a greatly condensed version:

1. You point your web browser to the service provider, or SP, that has the website you want to view.

2. According to the SP website, *Hey, I don't know who you are because you don't have a SAML cookie. You are directed to this identity provider website to obtain one by clicking here.*

3. After arriving at the IdP, you log in with your *username, password,* and perhaps an additional factor.

4. The IdP sends your browser a cookie with an XML *assertion* that declares, *I'm the identity provider, and this user is authenticated," after which it sends you back.*

5. Your web browser returns the cookie to the top website (SP). The SP confirms the cryptographic signature and declares, *You succeeded in persuading the IdP of your identity, so that's good enough for me. Welcome inside.*

A far more recent authentication layer built on top of **OAuth 2.0** is called **OpenID Connect**, and it was finalized back in 2014. It employs a somewhat different language and replaces XML with JSON Web Tokens. *Authorization Code Flows and Implicit Flows* are both available through OIDC. The applications you're authenticating with never see your actual password, and you don't have to re-authenticate for every application even though there are many distinctions from SAML, the final effects are identical.

SSO with legacy applications

What if you want to enable a single sign-on for an outdated program that doesn't support it? In this situation, you can add a component that processes SSO requests and then communicates the user's identity to the legacy application. The legacy application must only accept connections from this frontend service (typically a *reverse proxy*), which it will trust to handle authentication. When transferring an existing application to the cloud, methods like these are frequently required. Many of the *Identity-as-a-Service* companies previously mentioned have means of enabling SSO for legacy applications.

Vulnerability management

Vulnerability management and patch management have a lot in common. Instead of addressing functional bugs or adding features, patch installations are frequently performed to address vulnerabilities. Since improper configurations can frequently result in vulnerabilities, even if you have diligently applied all security patches, there is also a significant overlap between vulnerability management and configuration management. In the interest of practicality, we'll discuss all of the tools and procedures for managing vulnerabilities, configuration, and patches in this section.

Unfortunately, *managing vulnerabilities* rarely involves simply turning on automated patching and walking away. Vulnerabilities in cloud systems can be identified at many different layers, including the physical infrastructure, the computational hardware, the operating system, the code you've written, and the libraries you've used. The *cloud shared responsibility model* described in an earlier chapter can help you understand which vulnerabilities are your cloud provider's responsibility. The information in this chapter will help you manage your duties. To deal with various types of vulnerabilities, you'll typically require several unique tools and procedures.

Differences in traditional IT

Compared to on-premises environments, the rate of change in cloud environments is frequently significantly higher, and these ongoing changes may render obsolete more established vulnerability management procedures. To prevent missing new systems as they go live, you must use inventory from cloud APIs to input each system into your vulnerability management tool as it is produced.

In addition to the rate of change, prominent modern hosting models like *containers* and *serverless hosts* alter how you handle vulnerabilities because existing technologies are either ineffective or inapplicable. In every container, as you could in virtual machines, you cannot install a powerful vulnerability management solution that consumes a small percentage of your CPU. There would probably be hundreds of instances of the agent operating on the machine, leaving no CPU time for the actual work. Furthermore, even though **continuous integration** (CI), **continuous delivery** (CD), and microservice architectures are unrelated to cloud computing, they frequently accompany cloud deployment. The use of these methods may also fundamentally alter vulnerability management.

The traditional approach is logically constructed to balance the risk of a security incident against the risk of an availability incident in operational situations. It's trickier to secure environments while keeping them functional. But as the cloud landscape becomes more prevalent in our ecosystem, we have choices for lowering the risk of an availability problem and shifting the scale. Let's look at the following options:

- The environment definition can be included in the code thanks to cloud services and infrastructure as code. Instead of installing on an existing computer and integrating the environment and the code later, this enables the testing of new code and environments simultaneously. Furthermore, you can lower the possibility of running into a situation where you are unable to roll back immediately by creating a new production environment for each deployment and switching back to (or recreating) the old one simply if necessary. This is comparable to *blue/ green deployments* in conventional environments, but with the cloud, you do not always need to pay for the *green* environment, allowing infrastructure as code to be used even for smaller, less expensive applications.

- The deployment of minor changes to production in each iteration is made possible by continuous integration and delivery. Smaller adjustments lower the possibility of catastrophic failures and facilitate debugging for issues that do occur.

- To reduce the likelihood that changes in one microservice would have unintended consequences for other microservices, microservice architecture might disconnect services. Because each container is separate from the others, this is especially true in systems where microservices are container-based.

- The program is spread among many computers and containers as necessary to accommodate the load in microservice designs, which also tend to scale horizontally. This implies that adjustments can be made gradually throughout the environment and that potentially disruptive scans will only partially impair the application's functionality.

Each of these factors tips the scales in favor of increased availability, allowing security updates to be more *proactive* without affecting the system's overall availability. Your overall risk is lowered as a result. The new vulnerability management procedure appears as follows:

- As part of routine development work, automatically download security upgrades. Updated code libraries or operating system components, for instance, can fall under this category.

- When testing an application for deployment, include the updates. The only time you need to take a step back and decide whether the changes need to be added is if you discover a problem at this point.

- Deploy the updated version, which instantly generates a *fresh production environment* with updated configuration, security patches, and code. If you are unsure that it won't disrupt service, you might only deploy to a portion of the systems that are currently in production.

- Add any additional test or production environment vulnerabilities that aren't covered by the standard delivery procedure as bugs to the development backlog, and fix them in the following iteration (or as a special release, if necessary).

Although much less than in the usual procedure, there is still some manual vulnerability management work to be done.

Components that are at risk

What kind of vulnerabilities should you be concerned about? Imagine that your program is one of a stack of components, with the application on top and actual computers and resources at the bottom. Starting at the top of the stack, we will work our way down. Let's examine each of these layers in greater detail from the standpoint of vulnerability management.

Data access layer

In a cloud context, it is nearly always the customer's duty to decide how to allow access to the data in the application or service. The majority of data access layer vulnerabilities stem from issues with access management, such as leaving resources accessible to the *public*, maintaining access for those who no longer require it, or employing subpar credentials.

Application layer

When using a SaaS, the security of the application code will be the responsibility of your provider, but there may be *security-related configuration settings* that fall under your purview as the client. It is up to you to decide and set suitable options, such as two-factor authentication or virus scanning, if you're using a web email system, for instance. Additionally, you must monitor these configurations and make adjustments if they deviate from your specifications.

If you are not developing application code, whether it is hosted on virtual machines, in a PaaS, or in a serverless solution, you probably are. Your code will almost undoubtedly have some problems, regardless of how talented your team is, and at least some of those bugs will probably have an impact on security. You'll frequently use *frameworks*, *libraries*, and other *third-party code* in addition to your own, and these third-party pieces of code could be vulnerable. Since the same fundamental attack can be used against numerous apps, vulnerabilities in this inherited code are frequently more likely to be exploited by attackers.

Buffer overflows are a well-known illustration of an application vulnerability. Although buffer overflow attacks continue to occur, they are no longer the most common since many programs are now written in languages that make them challenging. OWASP's *Top 10* list of application vulnerabilities is shown in few of the examples that are provided as follows. If the application code contains these vulnerabilities in any of the following cases, *access controls*, *firewalls*, and other *security measures* are mostly useless at safeguarding the system:

- **Attacks by injection**: Your application receives some unreliable data from a malicious user and delivers it to an interpreter of some kind. An old-school illustration of this is **SQL injection** when the attacker transmits data that causes the query to return the entire table instead of just the data it was asked for.

- **External entity attacks on XML**: An attacker provides XML data that is processed unfavorably by one of your susceptible libraries.

- **Attack via cross-site scripting**: Your application is tricked by an attacker into delivering a user dangerous JavaScript.

- **Attack on deserialization**: Your application receives *packaged* items from an attacker that, when unpacked, have negative side effects.

Middleware

The middleware or platform elements your application code frequently makes use of include *databases, application servers, message queues*, and *middleware*. Attackers are attracted to these vulnerabilities because they allow them to exploit them across a variety of apps, frequently without even having to understand the programs themselves. As with dependent frameworks or libraries, these vulnerabilities can cause you serious difficulties.

You will need to keep an eye out for updates, test them out, and apply them if you're running these components yourself. Depending on how you've deployed your containers, these components may be operating directly on your virtual machines. Be aware that techniques for inventorying installed software on virtual machines typically fail to locate software deployed in containers. Your cloud provider will often be in charge of patching these components if they are offered as a service by your cloud provider. *The catch is that, though!* Occasionally, updates won't be sent to you automatically because they can disrupt your service. In some circumstances, you might still be in charge of testing before pressing a button to roll out the changes at a suitable moment.

Even in a PaaS environment, you still need to be concerned about applying fixes and middleware configuration. Examples of middleware/platform configuration errors that can result in a security incident or breach are shown as follows:

- The password file can be viewed, thanks to a web server that was unintentionally set up to allow it.

- If the database's authentication settings are incorrect, anyone can use them to log in as a database manager.

- A Java application server is set up to display debug information that, when a bug is discovered, reveals a password.

Operating system

When people think about managing vulnerabilities, they frequently think of operating system patches. *Operating system updates* are an essential component of managing vulnerabilities, but we need to move beyond *Patch Tuesday*, which is the standard patching schedule.

When launching the operating system instance and on a regular basis thereafter, you must carry out appropriate benchmarking. Additionally, operating systems frequently come pre-installed with a wide variety of extraneous parts that are not applicable to your situation. It's *crucial* to turn off anything that is not required because leaving these components in an instance that is running might be a major source of vulnerabilities due to defects or incorrect configuration. A few people refer to this as **hardening**.

You should get a system that is at least somewhat current when deploying because many cloud providers maintain a library of virtual machine images that are automatically updated. *Patches* should be applied as part of your deployment procedure even if the cloud provider doesn't do it automatically.

Hypervisors are typically handled by the cloud service provider. Hypervisors, on the other hand, are also included in this category if you're in charge of any of them because they essentially function as *special-purpose operating systems* created to house other operating systems. The majority of the time, hypervisors are already well-hardened, but they still need to be patched frequently and include configuration options that must be set up properly for your environment.

Virtual infrastructure

In an environment where infrastructure is provided as a service, your cloud provider will be in charge of managing the virtualized infrastructure (*virtual network, virtual computers,* and *storage*). On the other hand, in a *container-based environment,* you can be in charge of security for the virtualized platform or infrastructure that sits on top of the one provided by the cloud provider. For instance, vulnerabilities may result from incorrect configuration or a lack of patches for the orchestration layer, such as **Kubernetes**, or container runtime, such as **Docker**.

Physical infrastructure

Most of the time, your cloud provider is in charge of the physical infrastructure. However, there are a few circumstances in which you might be in charge of managing settings or vulnerabilities at the physical level. You might be responsible for maintaining some of the physical infrastructure if you are managing a *private cloud* or if you order *bare-metal computers* as a service. For instance, missing BIOS/microcode updates or inadequate security settings on the baseboard management controller, which enables remote management of the physical system, might lead to vulnerabilities.

Vulnerability scanners for networks

The second most well-known component of vulnerability management, after operating system patches, is network vulnerability scanning. This is for good reason—they're excellent at identifying specific types of vulnerabilities—but it's crucial to recognize their limitations. Scanners for network vulnerabilities do not examine software components. Simply said, they send out network queries to see what's available and look for susceptible settings or server application versions. Network vulnerability scanners cannot, of course, scan the entire internet or your cloud provider to determine which systems are under your control. You must give these programs lists of network addresses to scan, and if you exclude any addresses, you will have vulnerabilities that you are unaware of. This is where the discussed automated inventory management is *crucial*.

Your cycle time for inventorying internet-facing components, scanning them, and correcting any issues discovered needs to be as quick as possible since many cloud components are open to the internet and because attackers can swiftly exploit vulnerabilities that they identify in common components.

Even while network vulnerabilities on a section of a secured *virtual private cloud network* are less urgent than those on a component that is open to the internet, you should nonetheless find and address them. Attackers have a very annoying habit of finding themselves in areas of the network where they are not supposed to be.

You should whenever possible include a *network vulnerability scan* of the test environment in the deployment process, depending on how your deployment pipeline operates. Any discoveries made in the test environment should be recorded in a bug tracker, and if they are not classified as *false positives*, they should preferably prevent the deployment.

Cloud Service Provider (CSP) security management tools

Tools in this category are frequently exclusive to a single cloud provider. Typically, they either get that information from a third-party tool or collect configuration and vulnerability management data using agents or agentless techniques.

They are frequently promoted as a *one-stop dashboard* for various security operations on the part of the provider, such as *access control, configuration management*, and *vulnerability management*. As an incentive to use the tool for your whole infrastructure, these tools may also include the capability to manage infrastructure or apps not hosted by the cloud provider—either on-premises or hosted by another cloud provider.

Container scanner

Traditional agent and agentless scans are effective in virtual machine environments but frequently fall short in container systems. The deployment of an agent created for a virtual machine environment with each container can cause performance and scalability problems that can be fatal. Containers are intended to be very *lightweight operations*. Agentless scanners made for virtual machines will likewise fail if containers are used properly since they often do not provide a conventional network connection.

Although this field is still in its infancy, there are now two that are widely used. Scanners that disassemble container pictures and search through them for vulnerabilities constitute the first method. If an image is classified as insecure, you are aware not to deploy any new containers based on it and to replace any containers already deployed from it. The *advantage* of this is that no access to the production systems is needed, but the *disadvantage* is that if a susceptible image is discovered, you must have accurate inventory data on all of your active containers in order to make sure that all of the vulnerable ones are replaced.

The *second* strategy is to focus on the currently operating containers using an agent on each container host that checks the containers on that system and notifies which containers are *susceptible* so that they can be patched (or preferably, replaced). The advantage is that, if the agent is installed everywhere, you won't have any *forgotten* containers running a vulnerable image after you've built a fresh image with the update. Naturally, having an agent on each host is the main drawback. If you're utilizing a *Container-as-a-Service* offering, this may pose a performance issue and may not be supported by your supplier.

Some tools use both of these methods, which may not necessarily conflict. Make sure you have a method for scanning for vulnerabilities in running containers and/or running container images and feeding the results into an issue-tracking system if you use or plan to utilize containers soon.

Dynamic Application Security Testing (DAST)

While dynamic web application vulnerability scanners operate against specific URLs of live web apps or REST APIs, network vulnerability scanners operate against network addresses. By utilizing the application or API like a user would, **dynamic application security testing (DAST)** solutions can detect problems like *cross-site scripting* or *SQL injection vulnerabilities*. These scanners frequently require application credentials. Web application firewalls have the ability to block some of the vulnerabilities discovered by dynamic scanners. Although you should still address the problems reasonably promptly to provide security in depth, doing so may allow you to lessen the importance you place on them. If the application systems aren't set up correctly, a hacker could get past the WAF and target the application directly. When updates are made to the program or on a set schedule, dynamic scanners can typically be activated automatically. They can also transmit the results of their scans into an issue-tracking system.

Static Application Security Testing (SAST)

In contrast to dynamic application scanners, static application security testing solutions explicitly examine the code you've written. Due to their ability to offer quick feedback, they make a strong choice for executing as a component of the deployment pipeline as soon as the new code is committed. They can detect faults that are important for security, including *memory leaks* or *off-by-one errors*, which can be very challenging for humans to notice. You need to utilize a *scanner* created for the language you're using because they're analyzing the source code. Fortunately, scanners for a variety of widely used languages have been created and can be used as a service.

The largest issue with static scanners is that they frequently return false positive results, which can cause developers to get *security fatigued*. Make sure static code scanning will work with the language you're using and that you can quickly and effectively mask false positives before deploying it as a component of your deployment pipeline.

Software Composition Analysis Scanner (SCA)

Software composition analysis tools, which are arguably an extension of static code scanners, focus more on the *open-source dependencies* you utilize than the code you actually write. Open-source libraries and frameworks are widely used in today's applications, and their vulnerabilities can have serious effects. The open-source components and versions you are utilizing are automatically identified by SCA tools, which then cross-reference those versions with known vulnerabilities. Some can automatically suggest code updates that make use of more recent versions. In addition to managing vulnerabilities, some programs can check the licenses that are being used by open-source components to make sure you don't employ any with unfavorable licensing.

Interactive Application Scanning Test (IAST)

Interactive Application Security Testing (IAST) tools perform some static and some dynamic scanning. They may see how the code is written and observe it operating from within. This is accomplished by loading the IAST code alongside the application code and monitoring it while it is used by functional tests, a dynamic scanner, or actual users. Compared to SAST or DAST solutions, IAST solutions are frequently better at identifying issues and removing false positives.

The particular language and runtime you're using must be supported by the tool, just like with *static code scanners*. Performance in production scenarios may suffer as a result of this because it runs concurrently with the program, although with modern application architectures, this can typically be readily handled with horizontal scalability.

Runtime Application Self-Protection (RASP)

Runtime Application Self-Protection (RASP), despite sounding like a scanning technology like the ones previously mentioned, is not one. RASP functions similarly to IAST in that it deploys an agent alongside your application code, but RASP tools are intended to *thwart* rather than merely identify vulnerabilities (although a few products do both, identifying vulnerabilities while also thwarting attacks, making them both RASP and IAST products). Since more code is running in the production environment with RASP products than with IAST products in some circumstances, performance may suffer.

Given that they both prevent attacks in real-world settings, RASP systems provide some of the same security as a distributed WAF.

Code reviews

Even though they can be costly and time-consuming, manual code reviews can be more effective than application testing technologies at identifying various vulnerabilities. Additionally, rather than trying to comprehend the outcomes of automated tools, having someone else explain why a certain piece of code has a vulnerability can be a more effective method to learn.

In many *high-security environments*, code reviews are a common procedure. They may only be utilized in a lot of different contexts for programming with unique security-related functions, such as *access control* or *encryption*.

A few tools for vulnerability management

Most of the technologies mentioned in the preceding sections are compatible with cloud environments, and the majority of cloud service providers have exclusive partnerships with vendors or their own unique vulnerability management systems. It makes no sense to classify tools according to the categories mentioned before because so many of them deal with more than one. In the cloud vulnerability and configuration management arena, we have compiled a list of some typical solutions, along with a very brief description of each. The use of some of these tools is also related to *data asset management*, *inventory and asset management*, *access management*, *detection and response*, and *asset and inventory management*.

Please note that the intent here is not to endorse any specific OEM and partner but just to bring forward based on our understanding:

- An agent-based scanner called **Amazon Inspector** may check *Linux* and *Windows* computers for outdated configurations and missing updates.

- Configuration management is one of the many tasks that **Ansible**, an agentless automation engine, may be used for.

- **AWS Config** verifies the intricate configurations of your AWS resources and archives previous versions of those configurations. You may verify, for instance, that all of your security groups block access to SSH, all of your **Electric Block Store** (**EBS**) volumes are *encrypted*, and all of your **Relational Database Service** (**RDS**) instances are encrypted.

- AWS **Systems Manager** (**SSM**) is a *security management application* that handles a variety of tasks such as *patch management, configuration management,* and *inventory.* Both of these tasks are performed by an SSM agent installed on your instances: the **State Manager** component can be used to enforce *configurations,* and the **Patch Manager** component can be used to install *patches.*

- **AWS Trusted Advisor** conducts examinations in a number of areas, including *cost, performance, fault tolerance,* and *security*. Trusted Advisors can run some high-level configuration management for AWS resource checks, like determining whether an appropriate IAM password policy is in place or **CloudTrail** logging is turned on.

- **Azure Security Center** (now renamed as **Defender** for cloud) is a security management solution that can interface with partners like **Qualys** and **Rapid7** to get vulnerability data from their agents and consoles.

- Agent-based **Azure Update Management** may manage software inventory and configuration tasks in addition to managing operating system security patches.

- Dynamic web application scanning software is called **Burp Suite**.

- **Chef** is an agent-based automation technology that may be used for *configuration management,* and the **InSpec** project primarily focuses on *compliance and security-related settings.*

- Solutions for IAST and RASP are offered by **Contrast**.

- The **Google Cloud Security Command Center** is a *security management* *tool* that can collect data from the **Google Cloud Security Scanner** and other outside resources and also offers inventory management and network anomaly detection features.

- **Google App Engine** applications can use the DAST tool **Google Cloud Security Scanner**.

Network security

Since cloud providers exclude entire hosts or networks as access points, network controls are a crucial component of comprehensive security in both traditional and cloud systems. It is impossible to compromise a component that you can't even communicate with.

For many years, administrators relied largely on the network perimeter for security despite the cry that the *perimeter is dead!* System administrators occasionally rely only on network security as their primary form of protection. No environment, traditional or cloud, should use that model. The boundaries are frequently simple to define in an on-premises setting. In the simplest scenario, you draw a dotted line around your *internal network* and a DMZ (trust zone), and you carefully restrict what enters and exits the DMZ to your inside network.

The selection of what belongs inside your perimeter and how that perimeter is implemented in the cloud are frequently very different from those in an on-premises system. Your trust boundary is less clear; if you use a database as a service, *is that inside or outside of your perimeter? Are all of your installations inside the same perimeter or do you have various perimeters if you have deployments all over the world for latency and disaster recovery reasons?* Moving to the majority of cloud environments also makes building these perimeters less expensive, allowing you to rapidly and easily leverage other services like web application firewalls and have distinct network segments for each application.

The wide range of delivery methods you can choose from when developing your application is the most perplexing aspect of network controls in cloud environments. Depending on the delivery model, different things make sense. In the case of the following models, we must think about what a fair network security model entails:

- IaaS settings, including virtual machines and bare metal. These environments are the most similar to traditional ones, but they frequently benefit from per-application segmentation, which is not practical in the majority of on-premises systems.
- Container-based environments with orchestration, such as **Docker** and

Kubernetes. Greater network control inside each individual application is achievable if it is divided up into microservices.

- Application PaaS environments like **Elastic Beanstalk**, **Heroku**, and **Cloud Foundry**. The number of available network controls varies between these. Some may allow for *per-component isolation*, some may not offer any programmable firewall features, and some may allow the use of firewall features all the way down to the IaaS.

- *Serverless* or *function-as-a-service* platforms like **Google Cloud Functions**, **Open Whisk**, **Azure Functions**, and **AWS Lambda**. These work in a communal setting that might not provide network controls or might provide them solely on the front end.

- SaaS-based settings. While some SaaS solutions include basic network controls (such as limiting access to VPN connections or IP addresses on the whitelist), many don't.

Concepts and definitions

Although there are some novel notions introduced by cloud networking, many established terms and definitions are still applicable in these settings. They might be applied in slightly different ways, as explained in the subsections that follow.

Whitelists and blacklists

Whitelist is a set of items that are permitted while everything else is prohibited. A **blacklist** is a particular list of items to refuse while permitting everything else. A whitelist can be compared to a blacklist. Generally speaking, we want to be as *restrictive* as we can be without interfering with business operations, therefore we typically want to use whitelists and deny anything else. You have minimal control over the IP addresses given to your systems in many cloud settings, where computers are frequently produced and removed. Because of this, IP whitelist source or destination addresses may need to have a considerably wider scope than was previously permissible.

As network addresses can be changed quickly, IP whitelists are also losing their usefulness for some types of filtering with the emergence of **content delivery networks (CDNs)** and global server load balancers. CDN's addresses change *every week*, thus if you insist on using exact IP addresses for every rule, you will have a lot of connections mistakenly banned.

DMZ

A traditional network control idea called a **DMZ** works effectively in many cloud scenarios. Simply said, it's a place in the front of your application where you let the least-trusted traffic in. Your proxy, load balancer, or static content web server are examples of simpler, less-trusted components that you often install in the DMZ. It shouldn't give the attacker a significant advantage if that specific component is compromised. In some cloud systems, a separate DMZ region might not be necessary, or it might already be offered as a feature of the service model.

Proxies

Components that act as proxies are those that receive a request, forward it to another component for processing, and then return the completed request to the original sender. **Proxies** can be helpful for security needs as well as functional needs. They are frequently applied in either of *two* paradigms, both in traditional and cloud environments:

- **Forward proxies**: The proxy is sending requests on your behalf; the requester is one of your components. Most frequently, forward proxies are utilized to set restrictions on the type of network traffic that is permitted to pass through them.

- **Reverse proxies**: The proxy sends requests to your backend servers on behalf of your users.

SDN

The phrase **software-defined networking (SDN)** is overused a lot and refers to numerous virtualized networking technologies. Your cloud provider might implement the virtual networks that you utilize in this situation using SDN. The networks you see might really be encapsulated on top of another network, and the rules for handling their traffic might be governed centrally rather than at each individual switch or router.

Even while the implementation may be a centralized control plane coordinating numerous separate data plane devices to move traffic from one location to another, you can still handle the network as if you were using physical switches and routers.

Feature of the network virtualization

Network Features Virtualization (NFV), sometimes known as **virtual network functions (VNFs)**, reflects the idea that various network operations, such as *firewalling*, *routing*, or IDS/IPS, can now be carried out without a specialized hardware box. You can employ NFV appliances specifically in your design, and many cloud providers will offer you network *functions-as-a-service* using NFV. Instead of maintaining your own services, use the *as-a-service* functionalities whenever possible.

Encapsulation and overlay networks

On top of the network provided by your provider, you can build a virtual network called an **overlay network**. Regardless of the underlying provider network, overlay networks are frequently utilized to enable communication between your virtual systems as if they were on the same network. The most common method for achieving this is **encapsulation**, in which packets between your virtual systems are enclosed and transferred through your provider network.

Virtual Private Cloud (VPC)

Although **virtual private cloud (VPC)** rarely isolates virtual hosts to the same extent as a genuine private cloud, each cloud provider's definition may differ. Typically, *storage*, *network*, and *compute* resources are shared resources in cloud IaaS. Contrary to its name, a VPC often only addresses network isolation by enabling you to set up distinct virtual networks to keep your applications isolated from other customers or app usage. The best of all worlds, then, is what many businesses get with VPCs. VPCs allow you to have tight control over whatever parts of your application you choose to make available to the public while yet enjoying the cost and elasticity advantages of a highly shared environment. Through software-defined networking and/or overlay networks, cloud providers frequently build VPCs.

Network Address Translation (NAT)

NAT is widely utilized in cloud environments, especially in VPC settings where private range addresses are used for the systems inside the VPC. In contrast, NAT *rules in firewalls* typically do not need to be explicitly configured in cloud systems. The NAT function will typically be carried out automatically for you if you merely establish the rules using the portal or API. Please understand that NAT is not a security component or control. As you route IP packets, you just make a few changes when you perform NAT; it doesn't in and of itself offer any security.

Adoption path of network security components

Since we spoke about the basic components of the network security domain, let's take the next step and understand how these components should be adopted for your cloud landscape.

Encryption in motion

The most popular approach to protecting data *in motion* (passing between computers on a network) communication is **Transport Layer Security (TLS)**, formerly known as **SSL**. TLS is supported natively by many components. In cloud environments, we strongly advise employing TLS for all communications that pass via a *physical* or *virtual* network switch, not just at the front end. This also applies to communications that might in fact cross these boundaries in the future as components are relocated. Using TLS for communications between components that will always run on the same operating system, or between several containers in a Kubernetes pod, does not increase security.

However, simply enabling TLS is insufficient. Because it is relatively simple for an attacker to hijack a connection and carry out a *man-in-the-middle attack*, TLS loses the majority of its effectiveness if the other end of the connection is not likewise authenticated by certificate checking. It is possible to have a system start up automatically, authenticate itself with a *PKI provider*, and obtain a *key pair* and *certificate* that are trusted by other components in your environment when you combine an identity document with the capacity to automatically issue TLS certificates. You can be positive that you're speaking to the system you wanted to speak to and not to a man-in-the-middle attacker in this way. The cloud provider must be trusted, but you already have to because they create new instances and alter those that currently exist.

If properly set up, TLS is a very secure protocol. As of right now, only particular cipher suites should be permitted, and TLS 1.3 is the version of the protocol that should be used. Although authoritative sources for legitimate cipher suites exist, such as *NIST SP 800-52*, for the majority of users, an online test is the quickest way to determine whether a public-facing TLS interface is set up correctly. A proper configuration can then be copied to any TLS interfaces that are not public facing after you have confirmed your public interface. Tools for detecting network vulnerabilities might also point out encryption suites or protocols that are too *weak* for your systems. The following diagram will explain the TLS 1.3 *lifecycle*:

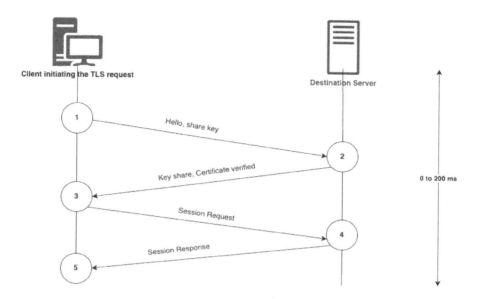

Figure 5.2: TLS 1.3 session lifecycle

As new *cipher suites* are released, you will need to remove the outdated cipher suites from your settings and add the new ones. As part of your vulnerability management procedures, you can assess secure cipher suites because network vulnerability scanners can identify outdated, insecure cipher suites. Fortunately, the rate of cipher suite compromises is substantially *lower* than that of other widely used programs, where flaws are frequently found. Additionally, it's critical to create fresh TLS private keys whenever you receive a new certificate or suspect that the old ones may have been hacked.

Segmenting the network with firewalls

Many people are familiar with firewalls as a network control. Once you have a strategy for protecting all of your communications, you can start segmenting your network into parts based on *trust zones* and installing *firewall restrictions*. **Network firewalls**, at their most basic, establish IP whitelists between two networks (each of which may contain a large number of hosts). A terminating VPN, IDS/IPS, or WAF are just a few of the additional tasks that firewall appliances may carry out. Firewalls are typically employed for *two* main reasons:

- **Perimeter control**, which isolates your systems from the outside world
- **Internal segmentation** to maintain the separation of groups of systems

Even while both tasks can be completed using the same technologies, there is a significant difference in what you need to focus on. *Alerts* from the perimeter are highly *noisy* because there are constantly people trying to attack you online. Any blocked connection attempts on internal segmentation firewalls are either caused by a misconfiguration or by an attacker seeking to migrate laterally.

The *three* most common firewall configurations in the cloud are:

- **Virtual firewall (VM series)**: This is essentially a *lift-and-shift model* from on-premises systems, while it is still suitable for some implementations. The majority of virtual firewall appliances are next-generation devices that integrate whitelisting with other features like WAF or IDS/IPS. Treat each of these distinct tasks as if they were a different device put in back-to-back while creating and implementing your network controls. Don't worry about building the higher-level controls until you have developed the perimeter and internal segmentation.

- **Network Access List (ACLs)**: Rather than maintaining your own firewall hardware, you merely set rules for each network regarding what is permitted to enter and leave that network.

- **Security groups**: Similar to network ACLs, security group rules are implemented as a service after being simply defined. Security groups now operate at a *per-OS* or *per-pod level* rather than a *per-network level*. The functionality that network ACLs offer, such as tracking of allowed and refused connections, may not be included in every implementation.

The following table talks about different controls available with the respective cloud service provider to offer this solution:

CSP	IP whitelisting feature
AWS	VPC, network ACLs, security groups, and virtual appliances (third party) from the marketplace.
Microsoft Azure	**Virtual Network (V-NET)**, **Network Security Group (NSG)**, virtual appliances.
GCP	VPC and firewall rules.
IBM Cloud	VPC with network ACLs, gateway appliances, and security groups.

Table 5.5: *Consumer identity services (CIAM) on different clouds*

Now, we will take a deep dive to understand how to create firewall controls in a cloud context.

Perimeter controls

You should construct some kind of perimeter as the first firewall control. In some cases, a firewall appliance may be used to do this, but more frequently, a network ACL will be added to a virtual private cloud. *Network ACL creation* is often possible for providers. In that situation, you won't have to give a damn about the firewall that lies beneath; all you have to do is set rules across security zones, and everything below that is abstracted from you. Each application should have its own *unique perimeter controls* in cloud environments. Even though it may seem like a lot of work, keep in mind that you are usually only supplying firewall rules for the cloud provider to follow. By defining the network perimeter rules independently for each application, you can manage the rules together with application settings and allow each application to modify its own perimeter rules without affecting other applications.

We would set up a VPC with a private subnet for the application servers and a public subnet for the web servers on AWS, *Google Cloud Platform*, and *IBM Cloud*, respectively. With the help of subnets, we would build virtual networks on *Azure*. Following that, we would designate which internet communications should be let into our VPC.

Internal segmentation

Now that we have a perimeter, we can position our sample application (in the form of a VPC) behind it to restrict access to only certain types of traffic. The implementation of network controls within our program is the following stage. The *web layer* (the DMZ), the *application layer*, and the *database layer* are only a few examples of the trust boundaries that the program is likely to have.

We may now apply network ACLs or network security groups once our subnets have been created (some of them may automatically be produced when you construct a VPC). Set the security groups to allow appropriate traffic now (like HTTPS towards inbound on a specific web application). This is fairly similar to traditional settings, with the exception that we can afford to have different subnets for each application and share none of them thanks to how quickly and easily we can construct them.

You can generally accomplish whatever you can on the portal by using a *command-line tool* or a REST API, according to the majority of cloud providers. This is crucial for automating deployments, even though in certain instances it necessitates a little more human plumbing work. In this scenario, we would set up a VPC with a *single public subnet* and *two private subnets, attach an internet gateway, direct traffic through the gateway,* and *only permit communication on port* **443** *to enter the DMZ subnet.* We suggest using an *infrastructure-as-code* solution like **HashiCorp Terraform**, **AWS Cloud Formation**, or **OpenStack**

Heat templates rather than writing a script from scratch. These kinds of tools enable you to specify the design of your network infrastructure, and they automatically issue the right orders to build or modify your cloud architecture to match.

The best resource is typically the online documentation provided by the cloud provider because cloud web consoles, command-line invocations, and APIs change over time. It's crucial to understand that most cloud platforms let you build a virtual private cloud with one or more subnets that can be used as trust zones.

Security groups

Why would we require additional IP whitelists at this time when we already have perimeter and firewall rules? The reason for this is that it's likely that our attacker gained a thin foothold within one of our subnets, putting her inaccessible to our current subnet controls. Her attempts to travel elsewhere within our program, including by hitting our administrative ports, would like to be stopped or detected. We'll employ per-system firewalls to achieve this.

Even though your operating system's local firewalls can undoubtedly be used, most cloud providers offer a way for the cloud architecture to filter traffic entering your virtual system before your operating system even notices it. Security groups are another name for this feature.

Similar to the on-premise firewall setup, you should set up your security groups to only permit traffic on the ports required for that kind of system. Allow only traffic on the application server port, for instance, when using an application server. Additionally, limit administrative access ports, such as SSH, to specific IP addresses that you know you will use for administration tasks, like your bastion host or company's IP range. For the majority of implementations, you have the option of allowing traffic from any instance that has a different security group specified in addition to specifying a specific IP source.

Network segmentation and firewall policies for container

In a container world, *what about restricting access?* The fundamentals are still largely the same, despite minor implementation differences. Here, we will talk specifically about Kubernetes, which is the most widely used container orchestration system at the time of this writing. However, you may also utilize Kubernetes network policies to implement local firewalls on the worker nodes. For a perimeter, you will normally leverage existing IaaS network controls like VPC or security groups, such as security groups or security groups. Any inbound traffic other than to the **NodePort**, ingress controller, or other mechanisms you're employing to accept traffic from the outside must be prevented in either situation. This could be an additional security measure to stop a poorly configured backend service from unintentionally becoming accessible via the internet.

You can separate pods for internal segmentation using Kubernetes network policies. For many use scenarios, the functional equivalent of security groups is already present. As part of the configuration for container networking, you can restrict access to only a few container-specific ports. This conducts a large portion of security group functionality at the container level. Furthermore, containers often only perform the precise operations that are required and have no extraneous services. Security groups serve as a *secondary line of defense* to block access to unwanted services, which is one of their main advantages.

Administrative access

Other systems or your administrators may require a way to go past your perimeter to maintain your application now that you have installed some walls around it and some internal tripwires to catch anyone who has gotten inside.

You have to go through a lot of trouble before you can even try to enter into the backend database since we require that all administrative access take place via a VPN or a bastion host. If you have a mechanism to execute commands on servers, or if your administrators are always able to identify issues from the logs flowing out and replace any component that's acting up with a new version, you might not even need to let them within the perimeter. Although it's ideal, many programs aren't made to allow you to carry out routine tasks without going outside the border. Now, when to utilize VPNs or bastion hosts is covered in this section as follows.

Jump servers (or bastion hosts)

Bastion hosts are *administrative access systems* that may be accessed from a less reliable network. They are also known as **jump hosts** (such as the internet). Because of the way the network is configured, all communication with the internal networks must go through a bastion host. The following valuable security attributes apply to a bastion host:

- Similar to a VPN, it decreases your attack surface because it serves as a *single-purpose protected host* behind which other machines can hide.

- It has a session recording feature that is highly helpful for sophisticated privileged user monitoring. The ability to *spot-check session recordings* allows for the detection of insider attacks, the use of stolen credentials, and the use of remote access *Trojans* by attackers to take over a legitimate administrator's workstation.

- A bastion host may sometimes carry out a protocol transition. The attacker must take over both the destination application and the bastion host, which can make things more challenging for attackers.

If session recording or protocol switches are useful in your environment or if a *client-to-site* VPN is not appropriate for some other reason, we advise employing bastion hosts. Otherwise, using client-to-site VPNs offered as a service for administrative access is what we advise since it will reduce your maintenance burden.

Virtual Private Network (VPN)

Making a VPN is similar to running a virtual connection from one place to another. In fact, connectivity is carried out using an encrypted session over an unreliable network, such as the internet. There are two main VPN functions, and they are significantly distinct from one another:

- **Site-to-site communications**: An encrypted tunnel is used to connect two different sets of systems through an unreliable network, like the *internet*. This could be used for one application to communicate with another application or for all users at a location to pass through the perimeter to access the application. Protecting administrative interfaces shouldn't be done with it.

- **Client-to-site communications**: An individual user virtually connects to a remote network via a workstation or mobile device. An administrator or end user could use this to access an application and work on its separate components.

Site-to-site communications

VPNs can bring more protection to site-to-site interactions, but they can also encourage bad security habits. Due to this, we no longer advise using a *site-to-site* VPN if all communication flows between the sites are encrypted using TLS and IP whitelisting is used wherever practical. The following points justify this:

- TLS requires less setup than a *site-to-site* VPN. In order to set up a VPN, *two* firewalls must be configured (or frequently *four*, because they are typically redundant pairs) with the correct routing information, parameters, and credentials.

- If a *site-to-site* VPN forces the usage of unsafe protocols, it may be less secure to utilize it. VPNs still leave data in motion unprotected on either end before entering the tunnel, making it possible for an attacker who succeeds to breach the perimeter to eavesdrop on that traffic.

- Site-to-site VPNs are too *coarse-grained* because they let everyone on one network (typically a big corporate network) access another network (such as your administrative interfaces). Access control should be handled at the administrative user level rather than the network level.

In addition, VPN and TLS connections inside the VPN can be used for added protection. The majority of the time, though, your efforts would be better spent somewhere else, thus *end-to-end encryption* with TLS should always come first. Hiding your communications' specifics from an attacker—like destination ports—can offer some minimal security benefits. If you do decide to utilize both TLS and a VPN, be sure to use a different protocol for your VPN, such as **IPsec**, or the same issue may arise.

Client-to-site communications

For your admins, this type of access might be a useful approach to learning more about how your cloud environment operates internally. (A **bastion host**, or **jump host**, as previously mentioned, is another effective method.) The reasons I advise a VPN for administrators rather than regular end users are that the backend connections they use are *riskier* (because there are more of them, making them harder to secure), and the cost is *lower* (because there are fewer administrators than end users), and there ought to be a sufficient number of administrators so that it's more difficult for an attacker to unintentionally gain access. Therefore, whereas end users rarely find value in VPN access, administrators often do.

The fact that VPNs support more protocols than bastion hosts has both *advantages* and *disadvantages*. Having access to more protocols can simplify things for administrators, but it can also make it simpler for a hacker using a compromised workstation to attack the live network. Higher-security environments frequently use bastion hosts because VPNs don't additionally provide session recording in these circumstances.

Client-to-site VPNs are typically simple to use, but they frequently call for the installation of some form of software on the administrator's workstation, which can raise questions in organizations that forbid software installation. To reduce the risk of easily guessable or stolen credentials, the majority of solutions offer the usage of sophisticated credentials (such as a *certificate* or a *key*) and *two-factor authentication*.

In the following table, many cloud platforms are listed with examples of client-to-site VPN connections:

CSP	IP whitelisting feature
AWS	Amazon Managed VPN
Microsoft Azure	VPN Gateway
GCP	Google Cloud VPN
IBM Cloud	IBM Cloud VPN

Table 5.6: VPN access with different cloud providers

Web Application Firewall (WAF)

A **web application firewall (WAF)** is an excellent approach to provide an additional layer of security against vulnerabilities in libraries or other dependencies you employ, as well as from typical programming faults in your application. A WAF is basically simply a *clever proxy*; it receives the request, examines it for various undesirable behaviors like *SQL injection attacks*, and then sends it to the backend system if it is safe to do so. Since TCP/IP traffic is completely valid and traditional firewalls don't consider the actual impacts on the application layer, WAFs can defend against attacks that regular firewalls can't.

WAFs can also speed up your response to a new vulnerability because it's frequently quicker to configure the WAF to block the exploit than to update all of your systems. The following diagram will provide a high-level understanding of WAF positioning between the *requester* and *destination* host:

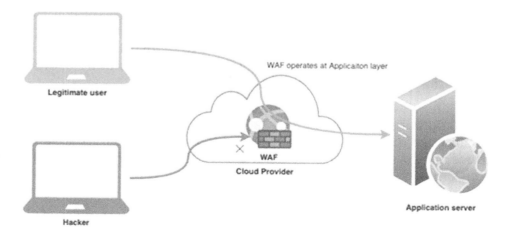

Figure 5.3: WAF positioning in the cloud

A WAF may be *distributed (host-based)* or provided as an *appliance* in cloud environments. You must make sure to confirm that all traffic truly goes through the WAF when using a WAF service or appliance. Since the list of IP addresses for requests originating from a cloud WAF solution can change over time, this frequently necessitates the usage of IP whitelists to block all traffic that isn't coming from the WAF. This can result in more maintenance.

Additionally, without creating a single point of failure, it can be challenging to route all traffic through your WAF appliance. You may make sure that your apps are always protected by a WAF by using services provided by some cloud providers, like **AWS Firewall Manager**. All traffic will be processed by the distributed WAF regardless in a *host-based paradigm*; hence, these issues are not present. Although it is necessary to have effective inventory management and deployment procedures (to make sure the WAF is installed on each system), this is frequently a simpler operation than making sure all traffic goes through a SaaS or appliance.

DDoS protection

DDoS attacks are a major issue for many businesses online. You can't supply services to legitimate requesters if you get too many bogus requests or too much pointless traffic. The additional safeguards we've described are generally advised; you shouldn't frequently take the chance of doing without them. Before spending too much on anti-DDoS measures, you should examine your threat model. To put it clearly, *how much of an issue is it for you if someone decides to remove you from the internet?* A DDoS attack will eventually come to a stop, unlike a data breach when it is impossible to erase all copies of the stolen material. You are undoubtedly a target for extortionists who will demand money in exchange for stopping an attack if you are operating any type of online retailing application, a large corporation's web presence, or any other application like a game service where downtime can obviously cost you money or cause embarrassment. You are also a clear target if you host any stuff that is content that is contentious. You should be aware that the entry barrier is very low; there are inexpensive *testing* services that can easily produce too much traffic for your site to handle, so it only takes one person with a few hundred bucks to destroy your day.

If you decide to utilize the *DDoS protection service*, we advise using a cloud provider. You'll need to fine-tune your rules, simulate an attack, and have a way of routing all of your traffic through that provider. *Anti-DDoS services* are offered by third-party suppliers and some IaaS companies.

Intrusion Detection System (IDS) and Intrusion Prevention System (IPS)

When traffic passing through an **intrusion detection system (IDS)** satisfies one of its rules, warnings are generated and sent out, which is common in the traditional IT sector. Traffic will be blocked in addition to notifying by an **intrusion prevention system (IPS)**. To identify and stop malicious traffic from reaching a host, an IDS/IPS agent can be deployed and centrally configured on each host. IDS and IPS are typically provided in the same product and are regarded as the same type of control. You'll configure a certain rule to block traffic rather than just notify if you're more certain that the traffic is malicious or if your risk tolerance is lower.

An IDS/IPS rule may be *signature-based* and *trigger based* on the content of the communication, such as seeing a specific stream of bytes in malware. To make this work, the IDS/IPS must be able to see the *clear-text communications*, which it frequently accomplishes by performing a sanctioned *man-in-the-middle attack* to decrypt all communications. This is a reasonable model, but it makes the IDS/IPS an attractive target for attackers. An attacker who obtains the signing certificates or private keys used by the IDS/IPS may be able to carry out attacks elsewhere on the network.

In addition to being triggered merely by network traffic information, IDS/IPS rules may also be based on behavior. You can create a rule that looks for situations where an attacker may be using a system that is starting connections to numerous network ports (port scanning), for instance. Even in situations when *end-to-end encryption* prevents the IDS/IPS from looking into communication, such rules can still be helpful. There is little difference in this control between traditional and cloud deployments. In cloud environments, the *blinky box model* will frequently use a virtual appliance instead of a physical box. To detect or prevent attacks, however, all traffic must pass through that virtual appliance. This can sometimes cause scalability issues because virtual appliances do not always have the capacity to handle as much traffic as a dedicated box with hardware optimizations. It can also be challenging to position an infrastructure IDS/IPS solution in such a way that all traffic flows through it.

In cloud context, *host-based IDS/IPS solutions* perform similarly to their conventional equivalents, albeit they are frequently easier to integrate into virtual machine images or container layers than into operating systems that have already been deployed. In cloud situations, where the systems being protected may be dispersed globally, including them in images may be a simpler paradigm to employ.

Despite various disagreements on the subject, if a WAF is used properly, an IDS/IPS may not provide much value as a component of perimeter control. The WAF shields the IDS/IPS from the majority of attacks, explaining why. To find an intruder who has already breached the perimeter, an IDS/IPS might be quite helpful. An *internal IDS/IPS* may be able to warn us of the threat if our attacker attempts to do reconnaissance by performing a port scan from one of our cloud instances. If you've already correctly implemented and tested the other controls in this section and want to add more security, we recommend baking a host-based IDS/IPS agent into each of your systems and having the agents report to a central logging server for analysis.

Egress traffic filtering

The restrictions we've mentioned have all been put in place, and now you want to make the environment even tighter. *Great!* Unquestionably, you must prepare for and repel outside threats. The possibility still exists that someone might seize possession of one of your parts. Limiting outward communications from parts that you ought to be able to trust is a good strategy as a result. Egress filtering may be carried out for the following reasons:

- An attacker may attempt to steal a copy of your data by transferring it to a location that is not under your control. Data exfiltration is the term for this. In the event of a successful attack, egress filtering can aid in reducing or slowing data exfiltration. However, in addition to limiting normal connections, you must also take precautions to prevent data exfiltration via **DNS tunneling**, **ICMP tunneling**, and **hijacking of existing allowed inbound connections**. If an attacker compromises a *web* or *application server*, for example, the system will happily serve up the data, bypassing any egress controls. Smaller amounts of data could be written down or screenshot instead.

- The simplest and least efficient method of traffic limitation is outbound port restrictions. For instance, you may determine that while you can enable TCP/**443** to any destination, you have no clear reason for any portion of your cloud deployment to communicate with anything other than over the standard HTTPS port, TCP/**443**. That might stop certain malware from calling home, but it's a rather flimsy defense in general. Similar to how it's done for the ingress controls previously covered, *port-based egress filtering* in a cloud deployment can be accomplished using security groups or network ACLs.

Outbound port restrictions are the simplest way to limit traffic, but they are also the least effective. For example, you may decide that there is no reason for any part of your cloud deployment to communicate with anything other than the default HTTPS port, TCP/**443**, but that you can allow TCP/**443** to any destination. This may prevent some types of malware from calling home, but it is a *very weak overall control*. In a cloud deployment, *port-based egress* filtering can be accomplished using security groups or network ACLs, similar to how ingress controls are accomplished.

With the emergence of CDNs and GSLBs, outgoing IP whitelisting is similarly losing its viability to inbound IP whitelisting. These are very significant tools for making material and services more quickly and consistently available, but they make IP-based controls useless because the content may be located at a variety of distinct, rapidly changing IP addresses throughout the globe.

Implementing efficient egress restrictions can be done in one of *two* ways:

- The first is done using an **explicit proxy**, which is implemented by configuring each component to use the proxy rather than directly connecting to the outside world. A proxy can be explicitly set up on the majority of operating systems. Even though not all operating system apps will use it, many of them will if it is set.

- The second option is to use a **transparent proxy**. In this case, the traffic is routed to the proxy by something on the network (such as an intelligent router). If the request meets the validation requirements, the proxy evaluates it (for example, to see if it is going to a whitelisted URL) and makes the request on behalf of the backend system. Only allowed traffic within a Kubernetes cluster can be transparently proxied by some newer technologies. Even though proxies are available for various protocols besides HTTP, HTTP is undoubtedly the most used. Please take note that for HTTPS connections, the source should use an X.509 *certificate* to verify that the destination is the right system. Without the transparent proxy's ability to mimic any site that is dangerous, this validation will fail.

A proxy might draw attackers' attention just like an IDS or IPS. Anybody with access to the proxy might launch a *man-in-the-middle attack*, listen to or alter any data passing through it, and easily compromise the entire program. Furthermore, until the certificate is removed from the trust stores of all components, an attacker who obtains the proxy's signing certificate can impersonate any website. This is *true* if the proxy has a signing certificate that is trusted by the components in your cloud deployment. If you decide to use a proxy for egress traffic, make sure it is protected at least as well as the other system components.

Unless preventing data exfiltration in the event of a breach is the main concern, we generally only advise *minimal egress controls* (such as port-level controls via network ACLs and security groups). *Strict egress controls* may be useful if you have plenty of valuable data and wish to allow yourself more time to react.

Data Loss Prevention (DLP)

Data Loss Prevention (DLP) keeps an eye out for confidential information that is poorly kept in the environment or escaping it. If you want, you can implement DLP controls in your environment yourself, or cloud companies may offer DLP services as an *add-on option* to other services.

DLP may be deployed as a component of egress controls in an IaaS/PaaS cloud environment. For instance, if a *web proxy* is used for outbound communications and credit card information is detected, DLP technology may be configured to alert an administrator or to stop the communication altogether. DLP can be carried out by a *stand-alone virtual appliance* that decrypts and inspects traffic, as well as by an IDS/IPS device or an IDS/IPS component. Direct integration of DLP is possible in a SaaS environment to either completely forbid the storage of specific data types or to automatically tag them. If available, this sort of DLP may be significantly more effective than *egress-based DLP controls*, but it is highly specialized to the SaaS.

You may need to implement DLP protections in your cloud environment if you have sensitive data, such as *payment* or *personal health information*. However, DLP may not be necessary for the bulk of cloud deployments. DLP will only give you a fictitious sense of security unless you are prepared to thoroughly *design the technology, monitor warnings*, and *handle false positives*.

Security incident response management

In recent years, there have been a lot of high-profile breaches. How long it took to realize what was happening and how well the victim reacted are frequently the defining characteristics between a *bad breach* and a *truly disastrous breach*. The average time to discover a breach was 197 *days*, according to a study of 477 *businesses*, and businesses that discovered a breach in less than 100 *days* were able to save more than $1 *million* compared to businesses that took more than 100 *days*. In light of this, let's investigate what we can do to identify problems and address them before they turn into tragedies.

Differences from traditional IT

Compared to on-premises environments, the rate of change in cloud environments is frequently significantly higher, and these ongoing changes may render obsolete more established vulnerability management procedures. To prevent missing new systems as they *go live*, you must use inventory from cloud APIs to input each system into your vulnerability management tool as it is produced.

In a conventional setting, you would have to be concerned about each of these levels. The good news about a cloud provider is that, like other *controls*, *intrusion detection*, and *response* are their responsibilities in the areas where they do so. You can be impacted by a breach at your provider, in which case you ought to be informed and might need to carry out response and recovery tasks unique to the services you're employing. All of your *detection*, *response*, and *recovery* efforts, however, will be concentrated in regions denoted as *consumer responsibility* in the great majority of situations. Although occasionally you can see activities the provider has taken on your behalf, such as obtaining your encryption keys, you rarely get to see any logs from the levels that are under the provider's control. However, there is a significant new source of privileged user logs in a cloud environment: you can monitor what your team did by using the provider's portals, APIs, and command-line interfaces.

In a cloud environment, you will not be permitted to touch the physical hardware. Many incident response teams use forensic laptops, hard drive duplicators, and other similar technology in a *jump bag*. Although such tools may still be required to deal with incidents involving non-cloud infrastructure (for example, malware infections on employee laptops), virtual, cloud-based equivalents of *jump bag* tools will be required for incident response in the cloud. This also implies that the forensic aspects of cloud incident response can be performed from anywhere, though there may still be significant advantages to being physically collocated with other people involved in the response.

What to monitor?

Any system of a moderate scale provides a dizzying array of logs and analytics, making it simple to become overwhelmed by information that is useless for security. It's crucial to choose what to watch. Unfortunately, as this will inevitably be unique to your environment and application, you need to consider your threat model, the assets you have, and the attackers that are most likely to target them, as well as the logs generated by the systems in your asset management pipeline.

If you have many terabytes of data, for instance, keeping an eye on metrics like the amount of network traffic and the number of connections could be quite helpful in spotting someone who is stealing it. However, those kinds of network traffic statistics won't be as helpful if you're disseminating software that you fear someone would try to hack with a backdoor. The amount of data transferred, the location, and the duration of the session wouldn't change in that situation, but the content would be tainted.

Once you've established a threat model and a good understanding of the components that comprise your environment, the following sidebar provides some good general starting points for what to look for. These are roughly in order of priority, though this will vary greatly depending on your environment.

Make sure the log entries for each of the following sorts of occurrences have enough information to be of value. This often denotes *when what,* and *who, that is, when the event occurred, what transpired,* and *who caused the occurrence.* The term *who* may occasionally refer to a system or other automatic instrument, such as when a system detects high CPU consumption.

Privileged user access

At all levels of their environments, almost everyone should be recording privileged user logins and at the very least occasionally monitoring them. Inquiries like *Why is that individual logging in at all? Didn't that person depart the company? Does anyone recognize this account?* might be sparked by keeping an eye on these and helping identify malicious activities.

Monitoring privileged user access does not imply that you do not trust your administrators. In an ideal world, you would not have to put your entire trust in any single person. Each task would end up with at least two people who were aware of the task being performed, necessitating collusion to complete tasks without being detected. That level of diligence is not required for all tasks in all organizations, but it should be considered for *high-value actions* such as money transfers or access to secret data stores. The main goal here is to detect an unauthorized person posing as an administrator. Since lost or stolen credentials are one of the most frequent reasons for security incidents, keeping an eye on what your administrators are doing will help you discover anyone posing as an *admin*.

Cloud providers can keep *good logs* of who logged in as one of your administrators and what they did using the cloud administrative interfaces (the web portal, APIs, or command-line interfaces), for example, *created an instance, created a database,* or *created an administrative user.* These logs may be collected by cloud services such as **AWS CloudTrail**, **Azure Activity Log**, **Google Stack Driver Logging**, and **IBM Cloud Activity Tracker**; however, in some cases, you must explicitly enable the logging feature, specify where and how long logs should be retained, and pay for storage.

Administrators frequently have *privileged access* to systems built in the cloud environment in addition to the privileged user logs that the cloud provider collects. For instance, you might have administrative accounts on databases, firewall appliances, or virtual machines. Using a protocol like **Syslog**, access to these may be reported. You might also have additional systems that administrators use, like a password vault to look for shared IDs. In general, any system that administrators utilize to carry out privileged tasks should log such actions for later review.

Defensive tool logging

You should be looking at the logs that these defensive instruments, such as *firewalls, web application firewalls, intrusion detection systems*, and *network monitoring tools*, produce. You can't be sure that those tools will always be successful in thwarting attacks. Sometimes the tools will stop one assault while allowing another to proceed, or they may just log that an attack occurred without stopping it. You risk losing a significant early-warning advantage if you don't gather and analyze the logs from these services.

The issue is that a number of these techniques are inherently noisy and generate a large *number of false positive alerts*. The possibility of false positives shouldn't be ignored! It's quite simple to teach yourself and your team to disregard signals that might be crucial. You need a feedback loop so that users who encounter false positives may either block out particular logs from processing altogether or adjust the system so that the tools don't generate false warnings as frequently. Naturally, this is an art since you run the risk of filtering or missing actual positives, but in most circumstances, you should be willing to take a very modest risk to avoid completely disregarding the alerts. In the same way that you should have many layers of defense, you should also have multiple layers of detection so that you are not reliant on a single tool to spot malicious behavior.

The majority of defensive tooling in cloud settings follows the same logging principles as on-premises environments. Let's look at the recommended approach for a couple of the defensive solutions:

- **DDoS protection**: Systems used to protect against *denial-of-service attacks* should be set up to alert on attacks since they may become more severe over time or signal a possible extortion attempt. Additionally, although the frequency of this varies, a DDoS attack may serve as a smokescreen to hide other breach-related activity.

- **Web Application Firewall (WAF) solution**: Attacks that were stopped or suspicious-looking requests can trigger alerts from both distributed and centralized WAF solutions. These notifications might help you determine when an attack on one of your web applications has been attempted.

- **Firewall and IDS/IPS**: Because systems exposed to the internet are constantly under *low-grade assault* (such as *port scans* and *password guessing*), internet-facing firewalls, and IDSs will need to be adjusted pretty low for alerting. However, when an occurrence is detected, the historical data offered by these systems may be helpful.

On the other hand, a firewall or IDS installed inside your perimeter should be set up to be fairly sensitive, as alarms received here are likely signs of a *misconfiguration* or *actual attack*. Nothing else should truly be scanning your internal network or producing lost connections, except various defensive tools that can be whitelisted so that they don't raise alarms.

- **Endpoint security (antivirus)**: Make sure you receive notifications if any in-scope systems in your asset management system aren't running antivirus software and if any malware is discovered.

It's important to keep in mind that the first thing an attacker does when they use a vulnerability to access your machine is typically to install malware. If the attacker is cunning, they'll make sure the malware they use is tailored enough not to trip any AV protection you may have in place. To ensure that their malware is *undetectable*, attackers can use services or even their labs to run it through all of the AV programs currently in use. Fortunately, not all attackers are that cunning, and these tools can still be quite effective in catching the less intelligent ones.

- **EDR: Endpoint Detection and Response (EDR)** software is more focused on enabling teams to investigate and respond to threats that have gotten beyond the initial line of defenses than standard anti-malware software, which primarily focuses on stopping malicious activities. The EDR software is comparable to the smoke detectors and sprinkler systems in a physical structure if AV is like the *flame-retardant materials* in that structure. EDR is typically performed by logging a large amount of information about the running systems, such as hash values for each executable or library that has run on the system, or a history of network connections attempted or made. While some of this data is available from the operating system or network logs, EDR software can easily compile it all in one place. It can then be linked to threat intelligence feeds, such as newly discovered *command-and-control servers* or newly reported malware signatures, to detect both current and historical activity. When an attack is detected, some EDR software can also be used to quarantine and investigate systems. While these features are frequently used interactively by the response team, EDR systems can deliver alerts when dangers are found in your environment, thus they partially overlap with antivirus software.

- **File Integrity Monitoring (FIM)**: There are some files that shouldn't change frequently, and if they do, that could be a sign of an attack. The configuration of the logging system, for instance, being changed by someone, raises suspicion. The majority of changes to the **/etc** directory tree on a Linux system should actually be viewed with some skepticism.

  Software called **file integrity monitoring** (FIM) can send you an alert when specified files are modified, and some products also let you receive an alert when specific Windows registry entries are altered. In their IaaS cloud management platform, certain cloud providers include FIM capability. The FIM products that you can install on your computers come in both free and paid editions. File integrity monitoring is explicitly required for *PCI DSS certification*, and some auditors may require it to cover not only flat files but also changes to the *Windows registry*.

Cloud service logs

Most cloud providers give helpful logs and data regarding their services in addition to documenting administrator actions. Look over the available logs and metrics for the cloud services you're utilizing and consider which ones might go wild in an attack or which ones might be helpful for determining how terrible things are after the fact. Consider these instances:

- **Statistics for CPU usage**: The presence of active crypto mining or ransomware encryption may be indicated by spikes in CPU utilization that are not explained by increased usage.

- **Metrics and logs for the network**: For instance, if you are using virtual private cloud subnets, many cloud providers can offer analytics on the data entering and leaving these subnets, in addition to flow logs displaying accepted and refused traffic. When traffic is denied from a component of your own, this may be a sign of an *attack* or a *misconfiguration* and has to be looked into. The onset of a *denial-of-service attack* or the active data theft of an attacker may be indicated by spikes in network traffic.

- **Input/output metrics for storage**: If an increase in I/O cannot be attributed to an increase in consumption, it may be a sign of active ransomware, a denial-of-service attack, or a data theft attempt.

- **Metrics for platform component queries to databases or messaging queues**: If your database begins to act erratically, that can be a sign that someone is trying to steal a lot of data. If your message queue starts acting strangely, there may be an attacker inside the system who is attempting to transmit messages to other parts of the system.

- **Logins and activity from end users on SaaS offerings**: It may be a sign that an account has been compromised if a user starts downloading enormous amounts of data from a cloud storage provider. If you're employing a **cloud access security broker (CASB)** to mediate access to a cloud service, it might also produce additional specific events related to user activity that you can watch.

- **Metrics and logs for platform services**: Each platform service might contain logs and metrics that are helpful for detection and reaction in addition to operational monitoring. You can enable auditing, for instance, if you're utilizing a platform for orchestration like Kubernetes.

Operating system logs

The security of the operating system, including gathering and examining logs, is often your responsibility if you are running *bare-metal* or *virtual computers* in the cloud. On-premise infrastructure is similar to this:

- For many various operating systems, products, and services that you might have in your environment, the CIS Benchmarks list provides a reasonable baseline collection of events to log.

- Microsoft offers some useful information regarding event IDs to monitor if you're using Windows.

- If you use Linux, a lot of Linux operating system providers offer instructions on how to enable audit logging to adhere to various industry and governmental standards. Even if you are not required to comply with those requirements, the instructions can be a good starting point for what to log and analyze in your environment.

- Metrics such as memory usage, CPU usage, and I/O can be very useful to both security and operations teams.

How to monitor?

We've discussed what events and metrics your environment might benefit from monitoring; now, let's look at how to efficiently gather and analyze these data to identify intrusions and take appropriate action. The various processes in this process are shown in the following-mentioned figure. A **SIEM** or other single product or service, or a group of products and services working together, may carry out each of these phases:

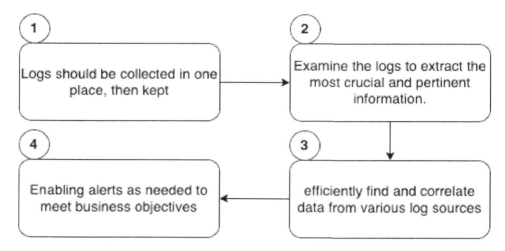

Figure 5.4: Log monitoring process flow

Now, we will do a deep dive into each of these steps to understand the same.

Aggregation and log retention

All of the logs mentioned before must be retained for at least a certain amount of time and stored somewhere. While allowing logs to accumulate across many systems is much preferable to having no logs at all, it's still *not* ideal. A *system attacker* who gains access can delete the logs to hide their traces. Individual system discs may become full, leading to loss of logs and operational issues. Additionally, logging into dozens of different systems to examine logs and compile a picture of what's happening can be quite slow and inconvenient.

Important logs used to frequently be printed on paper and delivered to a physically secure location. Even while that is a rather secure method of keeping things safe and rendering them inerasable by computer, the paper has some pretty significant *disadvantages*: it cannot be searched by *automation*, is *expensive, heavy,* and a *fire hazard.*

By placing your log aggregation service in a new cloud account with unique administrative credentials so that the logs can't be deleted by someone with access to the principal systems, you can achieve many of the same benefits much more quickly and easily in the cloud. You don't need to set up log aggregation from scratch because the majority of cloud providers offer services that can aggregate, store, and search logs.

Although you should save most logs for at least a year, longer retention times can occasionally be useful for analyzing security occurrences. Look at the specific retention requirements for those logs if you are bound by any industry or regulatory norms; otherwise, a year should be adequate.

Once you have all of your logs and alerts in one central, secure location with the appropriate retention period, you must deal with the challenges of searching through those logs to alert on suspicious behavior and of making sure the alerts reach the correct people, are *acknowledged*, and are *investigated*.

Parsing the logs

It's wonderful if you have your logs gathered in one secure location. Even if it may take some time, a determined individual may eventually go through all of those logs and obtain the necessary information. Handling data more quickly than humans can, however, was one of the main drivers behind the invention of computers. *Log parsers* extract particular pieces of data (fields) from various kinds of events. A few instances of log parsers in action are as follows:

- The parser will recognize the timestamp, the name of the system producing the event, and the event text for an operating system event. Some event types may undergo additional parsing; for instance, in the case of a failed login event, the parser can identify the IP address from which the login attempt was made.

- The parser for firewall logs will identify the timestamp, source IP address, destination IP address, and outcome of accepted/denied.

- For antivirus logs, the parser will identify the *timestamp*, *hostname*, and *event data* like a failed update or the finding of infection.

Unfortunately, there are thousands of different log formats. However, there are a few *standard event log formats* that make parsing a little easier. Many tools can parse logs in these formats into specific fields, but this does not always imply that the fields are useful. Here are some examples:

- **Syslog** is a standard format for long messages, though the term *format* is a little broad. A Syslog record will typically include a *timestamp*, the *name of the system generating the message*, the *type of process sending the message*, *a severity level*, and a *mostly free-form message*. It's often up to the parser to figure out what generated the free-form message and parse it further.

- Web servers primarily use **Common Log Format (CLF)** and **Extended Log Format (ELF)** to log requests.

- The **Common Event Format (CEF)** is an extension of the Syslog format that is primarily used by traditional SIEM platforms such as **MicroFocus ArcSight**. It adds structured fields to the Syslog format.

Investigating and correlating the logs

You can search using the parsed fields and correlate events amongst various systems after the logs have been gathered and processed. For instance, you may look for all instances of unsuccessful login attempts over a specific time frame, all instances of the same person successfully logging in without a VPN connection or all instances of malware detection followed by a *successful login*. Quick searches across numerous different data sources and log kinds can be quite helpful when responding to an occurrence. Before you find yourself in the middle of a security incident, test the system's capacity to handle numerous searches by a large number of panicked people.

Alerting and response

An *automated system* may issue an alarm (sometimes referred to as an *offense*) when it detects anything that should be reviewed by a human. In some instances, the system may then automatically take action by blocking access to or shutting down a component. Alerts may be based on specific occurrences, correlations of occurrences, or the achievement of specific thresholds.

The art of log analysis actually resides here. All of the alerts will be swiftly disregarded if the system is calibrated so delicately that your security team is consistently receiving erroneous alarms. However, if you aren't receiving at least some warnings on a regular basis, you're probably not following through on some things that you ought to be. A *feedback loop* is required for each type of false alert to determine whether it is appropriate to filter out those types of events, raise thresholds, or take other actions to reduce false alerts. Consider running periodic tests that you know will generate alerts to ensure that they are not ignored. Some alerts should almost always be followed up on. Multiple login failures for privileged users, malware discovered on systems, and other alerts that may be precursors to a security incident should be investigated, even if they are usually false alarms.

In theory, the automated reaction is a terrific idea, but in practice, it could seriously harm your company's operations. *Automated response systems* can be intentionally utilized by attackers to cause disruptions in addition to faulty responses or overreactions produced by them. The operational and security risks need to be balanced more carefully in most environments because some environments have such high-security requirements that you're willing to suffer an outage rather than accept even a small risk of allowing a potential attack to continue until a human can investigate.

Alerting shouldn't be something you do once and then forget about. Nobody wants to be on call all the time, so you frequently need a mechanism to switch people in and out, and you also need a way to make sure that an alert is noticed within a particular time frame or escalated to another person to handle. *Alerting* is just one of a wide range of services available in the cloud. Typically, one system can be utilized for both operational and security response tasks. Larger organizations will typically build a system or contract with a **managed security service provider** (**MSSP**) to monitor and respond to alerts *24 hours a day, 7 days a week*. A room with many screens displaying important-looking graphics is *optional*, but it looks impressive to your *C-suite management* and *customers*, and it can help present important information quickly in an emergency. In many cases, organizations employ a hybrid model in which an MSSP handles some of the lower-level monitoring and alerting while in-house staff handles the more critical alerts.

Incident response

Usually, you accomplish *a security incident response* by employing a mix of a system shutdown or quarantining, password changes, access revocation, and network connection blocking. At the same time, you should contact the incident response business for assistance and take a few moments here and there to make notes on what you need to remember so that you will be more prepared in the future. In the event of a *real security incident*, your response will be largely determined by what the attacker is doing and your threat model, but there are a few guidelines that will help. First, assign at least some of your team to triage. You don't want to wake up *30 people* for a malware infection that appears to be completely contained after a *few minutes of investigation*. It's easy to overreact or underreact, so having some predefined severity levels and response guidelines for each level can help.

Now, carry out the strategies you've put in place while attempting to predict what the attacker's goals will likely be based on a kill chain or an attack chain.

Cloud forensic

It's critical to create copies in a *documented, replicable* manner so that you can consistently show that you have a reliable copy of the original data that hasn't been altered. To demonstrate that you have a copy of the uncorrupted data, this typically entails creating a verification string (cryptographic hash). A **cryptographic hash**, like SHA-256, is made to be quick to calculate yet nearly impossible to use to make another piece of data with the same hash.

Conclusion

You must determine what data you have, including both the obvious and obscure components, before developing your cloud strategy. Sort the different types of data based on how much it would affect you if an attacker read, changed, or deleted it. Use the *tagging features* provided by your cloud provider to tag resources that include data. Agree on the tags to be used across the company in a *tag dictionary*.

To avoid difficulty changing your mind later, choose your encryption strategy before you launch storage instances. In most circumstances, you should use your cloud provider's key management system to maintain the encryption keys and, if available, employ the storage services' built-in encryption, even though doing so comes with the risk that the storage service may be compromised. If you must encrypt the data manually before storing it, only utilize secure algorithm implementations that have undergone thorough testing.

In cloud environments, IAM is *crucial*. Although the basics are the same for deployments in the cloud and on-premises, there are new technologies and cloud services that enhance security and simplify the task.

In many aspects, managing vulnerabilities in cloud settings is analogous to managing vulnerabilities on-premises. However, the rapid deployment of new features is frequently given more business priority as a result of cloud computing. This creates a need for vulnerability management procedures that can keep up with infrastructure changes that happen quickly.

For your cloud environment, *network controls* are a crucial layer of security. The finest protection for your efforts can be obtained even though there are many technically challenging controls available.

In the next chapter, we will talk about various regulatory compliance requirements which are important for cloud adoption. We will cover regulatory compliance understanding, risk management, disaster recovery, and best practices to consider for your cloud security.

Questions

1. Define different classification levels of data.
2. Define the importance of tagging in the cloud landscape.
3. Explain in detail the different ways to keep data secure in the cloud by leveraging native cloud services.
4. Please explain the difference between SAML and OIDC.

5. What is the recommended approach to handle SSO functionality for legacy applications?

6. Explain container scanning and how it is different from traditional application scanning.

7. What all components are considered in the operating system vulnerability assessment?

8. Explain SAST and DAST from a cloud perspective.

9. What are the various native tools of a cloud ecosystem that contribute to the vulnerability management process?

10. What is the difference between whitelisting and blacklisting and how does it happen on the cloud landscape?

11. How is encryption in motion controlled in the cloud landscape?

12. How do you segment the network in the cloud? Please explain the different ways you configure the native firewall services on the cloud.

13. How do you differentiate perimeter controls and internal networks and which one plays the crucial role?

14. Why are security groups important in the cloud and also called the last line of defense from a network security perspective?

15. Why are jump servers important and what are the other alternatives in case you don't have jump servers for administrative purposes in the cloud?

16. Explain how DDoS protections work in cloud.

17. Explain how IDS and IPS operate in a cloud.

CHAPTER 6

Examine Regulatory Compliance and Adoption path for Cloud

Introduction

This chapter will focus on the regulatory compliance requirements for cloud adoption. While our earlier chapters were focused on architecture and building blocks, in this chapter, we will learn the importance of compliance requirements in the cloud and its adoption path. This chapter will help us understand the requirement, mapping of controls with technology and business, adoptions path, and best practices. Last but not the least, this chapter will also provide a brief on auditing exercises and checklists along with a risk management approach that should be adopted for the cloud segment.

At the end of the chapter, you will have a complete understanding of how compliance requirements are aligned with overall cloud security and how to adopt the same in your landscape.

Structure

In this chapter, we will discuss the following topics associated with cloud security:

- Navigating regulatory compliance
- Compliance framework for cloud landscape
- Importance of automated and continuous monitoring
- Cloud auditing and compliance
- Risk management and disaster recovery in cloud
- Best practices and recommendations

Overview and concept understanding

Regulatory compliance is the discipline and process of ensuring that a company follows the laws enforced by governing bodies in their geography or the rules required by voluntarily adopted industry standards. People and processes monitor corporate systems to detect and prevent violations of policies and procedures established by these governing laws, regulations, and standards for IT regulatory compliance. This, in turn, applies to a wide range of monitoring and enforcement processes. These processes can become lengthy and complex depending on the industry and geography.

Compliance is challenging for multinational corporations, particularly in highly regulated industries such as *healthcare* and *finance*. Standards and regulations abound, and in some cases, they frequently change, making it difficult for businesses to keep up with changing international electronic data handling laws.

Organizations should understand the division of *responsibilities* for regulatory compliance in the cloud, just as they do for security controls. Cloud providers work hard to ensure that their platforms and services are compliant. Organizations must also confirm that their applications, the infrastructure on which those applications rely, and third-party services are all compliant.

The following are descriptions of a couple of compliance regulations in various industries and geographies:

- **HIPAA**: A healthcare application that processes **protected health information (PHI)** is subject to both the privacy rule and the security rule contained in the **Health Insurance Portability and Accountability Act (HIPAA)**. At the very least, HIPAA may require that a healthcare organization receive written assurances from the cloud provider that any PHI received or created will be protected.

- **PCI**: The **Payment Card Industry Data Security Standard (PCI DSS)** is a proprietary information security standard for organizations that deal with branded credit cards from major card payment systems such as *Visa, MasterCard, American Express, Discover,* and *JCB*. The *Payment Card Industry Security Standards Council* enforces the PCI standard, which is mandated by card brands. The standard was developed to tighten controls on cardholder data to reduce credit card fraud. Compliance is validated on an annual basis, either by an external **qualified security assessor (QSA)** or a firm-specific **internal security assessor (ISA)**, who generates a **report on compliance (ROC)** for organizations handling high volumes of transactions or by a **self-assessment questionnaire (SAQ)** for businesses.

- **Personal data**: Personal data is information that can be used to identify a consumer, employee, partner, or any other living or legal entity. Many new laws, particularly those concerning privacy and personal data, require businesses to comply and report on compliance and any breaches that occur.

- **GDPR**: The **General Data Protection Regulation (GDPR)**, designed to strengthen data protection for individuals in the *European Union*, is one of the most significant developments in this area. Individual data must be kept on servers within the EU and not transferred outside of it, according to GDPR. It also requires businesses to notify individuals of any data breaches and to have a **data protection officer (DPO)**. Similar regulations exist or are being developed in other countries.

Frameworks for compliance

These frameworks especially address the need for *cloud compliance*. Customers and cloud vendors should be knowledgeable about the intricacies of these frameworks. The technique and structure offered by these frameworks can assist prevent damaging security incidents:

- **Cloud Security Alliance (CSA) controls**: By providing a fundamental framework for security suppliers, this foundational set of security controls strengthens security control environments and makes audits easier. The risk profile of potential cloud vendors is also evaluated by possible consumers using this methodology.

- **FedRAMP**: Any corporation wishing to conduct business with a *Federal* agency must comply with this set of data security standards related to the cloud. The goal of *FedRAMP* is to guarantee that all cloud deployments utilized by the federal government have the bare minimum of necessary protection for data and applications.

- **Sarbanes-Oxley (SOX)**: A system of regulations governing how publicly traded corporations report financial data to safeguard clients from fraudulent or inaccurate reporting. Even though SOX standards don't specifically address security, many IT security measures are covered by them because they promote data integrity.

- **ISO 27001**: Created by the *International Organization for Standards*, this collection of requirements for information security management systems proves that your company follows industry best practices for information security and values data protection.

- **NIST cybersecurity framework**: This fundamental guideline for policies and practices for businesses evaluates how well they can manage and counteract cyber-attacks. This framework aids in comprehending and managing risk and serves as a best practice guide for security professionals.

- **CIS rules**: Developed by the *Center for Internet Security*, this framework offers practical defense techniques based on a list of 20 *Critical Security Controls* that are concentrated on enforcing access controls, strengthening defense systems, and continuously monitoring surroundings.

Auditing and compliance – overview and importance

Audit and compliance refer to the internal and external processes that a company uses to:

- Determine whether the requirements must be driven by business objectives, laws, regulations, customer contracts, internal corporate policies, standards, or other factors.

- Implement policies, procedures, processes, and systems to meet such requirements.

- Check to see if such policies, procedures, and processes are consistently followed.

Traditional outsourcing relationships have always placed a premium on audit and compliance functions. However, given the dynamic nature of **software- as-a-service (SaaS)**, **infrastructure-as-a-service (IaaS)**, and **platform-as-a- service (PaaS)** environments, these functions take on increased importance in the cloud. **Cloud Service Providers (CSPs)** are challenged to *implement*, *monitor*, and *demonstrate* ongoing compliance with a set of controls that meet the business and regulatory requirements of their customers. Separate compliance efforts for various regulations or standards are not sustainable. *Internal policy compliance, regulatory compliance*, and *external auditing* are all part of a practical approach to cloud audit and compliance.

CSP policy compliance

Cloud Service Providers must develop processes, policies, and procedures for managing their IT systems that are appropriate for the nature of the service offering, can be operationalized in the organization's culture, and meet relevant external requirements. CSPs must consider the following when developing their service offerings and supporting processes:

- Consider their current and prospective customers' needs.

- Establish a strong control foundation that will substantially meet customer requirements, reducing the need for infrastructure customization, which could reduce efficiencies and reduce the value proposition of the CSP's services.

- Set a high enough standard to meet those requirements.

- Establish standardized processes to increase efficiency.

A life cycle approach for *determining, implementing, operating,* and *monitoring* controls over a CSP is depicted in the following figure (*Figure 6.1*):

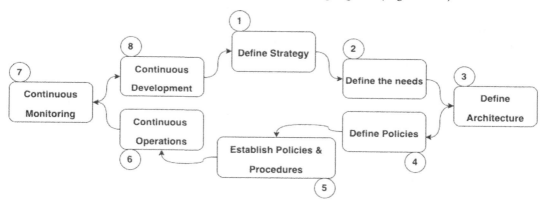

Figure 6.1: *Cloud Service Provider's life cycle approach for policy compliance*

Now, we will do a deep dive to understand each step:

1. **Define strategy**: As CSP expands or revamps its service offerings, it should clearly define its business strategy and risk management philosophy. *What market segments or industries will the CSP serve?*

   This strategic decision will determine how high the CSP needs to *set the bar* for its controls. Setting it too low will make it challenging to meet the needs of new customers while setting it too high will make it difficult for customers to implement and difficult to sustain cost-effectively for the CSP. A clear strategy will allow the CSP to meet its customers' baseline requirements in the short term while also allowing for the flexibility to incorporate necessary changes while avoiding unnecessary or potentially unprofitable customization.

2. **Define the needs**: The CSP must define the requirements for providing services to that client base after defining its strategy and target client base. *What are the specific regulatory or industry requirements? Is there a range of requirements for various types of clients?*

The CSP must determine the bare minimum of requirements to serve its client base, as well as any additional industry-specific requirements. For example, the CSP must decide whether it will support all of those requirements as part of a base product offering or offer incremental product offerings with additional capabilities at a premium, either now or in the future.

3. **Define architecture**: The CSP must now determine how to architect and structure its services to address customer requirements and support planned growth, guided by its strategy and requirements. For example, as part of the design, the CSP must determine which controls are implemented by default as part of the service and which controls (for example, *configuration settings*, *selected platforms*, or *workflows*) are defined and managed by the customer.

4. **Define policies**: The CSP must translate its requirements into policies. The CSP should draw on applicable industry standards to define such policies, as discussed in the sections that follow. The CSP will also need to examine its staffing model to ensure that it is in line with policy requirements.

5. **Establish appropriate procedures**: Using applicable industry standards and leading practices guidance, the CSP must then translate its policy requirements into *defined*, *repeatable processes*, and *procedures*. To facilitate scalability and monitoring, controls should be automated to the greatest extent possible.

6. **Continuous operations**: After defining its processes and procedures, the CSP must implement and execute those processes, ensuring that its staffing model meets the needs of the business.

7. **Continuous monitoring**: The CSP should continually assess the effectiveness of its key control activities, with instances of non-compliance reported and addressed. A strong monitoring program should result in compliance with relevant internal and external requirements.

8. **Continuous development**: As issues and opportunities for improvement are identified, the CSP should ensure that a feedback loop is established to ensure that *processes* and *controls* are continually improved as the organization matures and customer requirements evolve.

Understanding of audit objectives

Cloud compliance refers to meeting the requirements or criteria required to obtain a specific type of certification or framework. Compliance may be required by the *industry*, *request for proposal*, *client*, and so on. The type of cloud security and compliance requirements will aid in determining the appropriate cloud compliance for an organization.

It is critical to understand the audit objectives during the planning and execution stages of cloud security and compliance audit. Companies should strive to align their business goals with audit goals. This ensures that the time and resources spent will contribute to a strong internal control environment and reduce the risk of a qualified opinion.

Auditors use objectives to conclude the evidence they collect. A sample list of cloud computing objectives for auditors and businesses alike is provided as follows:

- **Develop a strategic IT plan**: IT resources should be used following the company's business strategies. Some key considerations when defining this objective should be whether IT investments are supported by a strong business case and what education will be required during the rollout of new IT investments.

- **Define information architecture**: The information architecture encompasses the *network*, *system*, and *security requirements* required to protect the integrity and security of information. Regardless of whether the data is at rest, in transit, or being processed.

- **Define IT processes, organizations, and relationships**: Creating processes that are *documented*, *standardized*, and *repeatable* results in a more stable IT environment. Businesses should concentrate on developing policies and procedures that address organizational structure, roles and responsibilities, system ownership, risk management, information security, segregation of duties, change management, incident management, and disaster recovery.

- **Communicate management goals and directions**: Management should ensure that its *policies*, *mission*, and *objectives* are communicated throughout the organization.

- **Assess and manage IT risks**: Management should document any risks that may jeopardize the company's objectives. These could include *security flaws, laws and regulations, access to customers or other sensitive information*, and so on.

- **Identify vendor management security controls**: Because businesses rely on *third-party* vendors such as AWS to host their infrastructure or ADP for payroll processing, they must identify risks that could jeopardize the *reliability*, *accuracy*, and *security* of sensitive information.

Defined scope for compliance audit

A cloud computing audit will include procedures specific to the subject of the audit. It will also include IT general controls for organization and administration, communication, risk assessment, monitoring activities, logical and physical access, system operations, and change management.

The *auditor* is free to review and request evidence for any of the controls identified in these areas to gain the necessary assurance that controls are designed and operate effectively. It is also important to note that the controls maintained by the vendor are not included in the scope of the cloud computing audit.

Defined role and audits criteria

An auditor's role is to provide an objective opinion based on facts and evidence that a company has controls in place to meet a *specific objective, criteria,* or *requirement.* In many cases, the auditor will also provide an opinion on whether or not those controls were operational over some time. Auditing the cloud for compliance is no different. In cases where the audit requires cloud compliance to satisfy the criteria, the auditor will request evidence that controls are enabled (that is, *security groups, encryption,* and so on). This will allow the cloud auditor to provide an opinion on whether controls were in place and, if applicable, how long they were operational.

As previously stated, auditors collect evidence through various procedures such as inquiry, physical inspection, observation, confirmation, analytics procedures, and/or re-performance. These test procedures will be used in conjunction to gather evidence for an opinion on the service being audited. The following table talks about a few examples of tests performed for each of the IT general control areas mentioned as follows:

Requirements	Control
Organizational requirements	• Examine the company's organizational structure. • Examine job positions for employee roles and responsibilities. • Examine interviews to see if the company's test technical competencies are adequate. • Examine evidence of completed background checks.

Communication	<ul><li>Examine policies and procedures.</li><li>Examine evidence that policies and procedures are accessible to all employees for reference.</li><li>Examine the company's *Terms of Service* or *Privacy Policies* to see whether or not they identify responsibilities and commitments</li><li>Inquire with management about their commitment to ethical values.</li></ul>
Risk analysis	<ul><li>Examine the company's risk assessment documentation.</li><li>Examine the risk assessment to see if the necessary mitigation activities have been identified.</li></ul>
Activity monitoring	<ul><li>Examine documentation that identifies system flaws.</li><li>Examine system configurations to see if notifications are sent when vulnerabilities or failures are discovered.</li><li>Examine evidence that identified vulnerabilities have been addressed.</li></ul>
Physical and logical access	<ul><li>Keep in mind that entering the office requires a badge.</li><li>Examine evidence that individuals with *administrator-level* access are authorized.</li><li>Examine the password policy used to gain access to the network.</li></ul>
System management	<ul><li>Examine monitoring tools that are used to monitor traffic and alert on unusual activity.</li><li>Examine evidence that the tools send alerts as needed.</li><li>Examine evidence that notifications are followed up on and, if necessary, corrected.</li></ul>
Change management	Inspect evidence to ensure that changes have been defined and documented, that they have been approved for development, that they have been tested, and that they have been approved for implementation.

Table 6.1: *Sample checklist for the auditor to perform the assessment*

Governance, Risk, and Compliance (GRC)

CSPs are typically challenged to meet the needs of a diverse client base. To build a sustainable model, the CSP must first establish a solid foundation of controls that can be applied to all of its clients. In this regard, the CSP can employ the GRC concept, which has been adopted by several leading traditional outsourced service providers and CSPs. GRC recognizes that compliance is not a *one-time event*, but rather an ongoing process that necessitates a formal compliance program. The following illustration (*Figure 6.2*) depicts a programmatic approach to compliance:

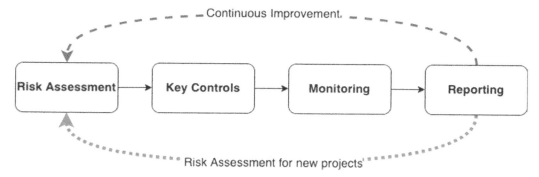

Figure 6.2: *Programmatic approach to meet compliance*

The key components of this approach are as follows:

- **Risk assessment**: This approach starts with an assessment of the risks that the CSP faces, followed by the identification of the specific compliance regimes/requirements that apply to the CSP's services. Risks associated with key areas such as appropriate user authentication mechanisms for cloud access, encryption of sensitive data and associated key management controls, logical separation of customers' data, and CSP administrative access should be addressed by the CSP.

- **Important controls**: The identified risks and compliance requirements are then addressed by identifying and documenting key controls. These key controls are captured in a unified control set that is intended to meet the needs of the CSP's *customers* as well as other *external* needs. Instead of disparate sets of externally generated compliance requirements, the CSP drives compliance activities based on its key controls.

- **Monitoring**: For important controls, *monitoring* and *testing* processes are defined and implemented on an ongoing basis. Remediation gaps are identified, and progress on remediation is tracked. The outcome of ongoing monitoring activities may also be used to support any necessary external audits.

- **Reporting**: Ongoing metrics and **key performance indicators (KPIs)** are defined and reported. CSP management and external customers, as appropriate, receive reports on control effectiveness and trends.

- **Continuous development**: Management continuously improves its controls, acting quickly to address any significant gaps discovered during monitoring and seizing opportunities to improve processes and controls.

- **Risk assessment for new IT projects and systems**: As new IT projects, systems, and services are developed, the CSP performs a risk assessment to identify new risks and requirements, assess the impact on the CSP's current controls, and determine whether additional or modified controls and monitoring processes are required. When considering entering a new industry or market, or taking on a large new client with unique control requirements, the CSP also conducts an assessment.

GRC advantages for CSPs

CSPs must comply with a number of IT process control requirements, including both *external* and *internal* requirements. We discover numerous points of intersection as we examine these requirements. Increased efficiencies and compliance can be achieved by combining compliance efforts to address all of these requirements and taking a more uniform and strategic approach. Rather than performing separate control reviews and testing cycles, control language, and testing can be structured to meet the needs of multiple sets of requirements. To meet the demands of multiple sets of requirements, control review and testing must be completed only once.

Because control language is defined more efficiently to support many compliance needs, this strategic approach results in less effort to meet control requirements and increased compliance.

CSPs frequently struggle to meet the numerous compliance demands. These efforts are frequently *fragmented, unstructured*, and *reactive*. Repeatedly non-compliant controls are discovered during an audit or as a result of a security incident. Significant advantages can be gained by implementing a structured compliance program and organization. Achieving periodic compliance silos, primarily through *third-party reviews*, will be replaced by a continuous focus on compliance to increase overall IT process compliance more efficiently.

KPIs and risk assessments based on compliance will provide valuable insight into areas of IT control weakness. Improved visibility into IT control flaws can significantly improve decision-making for new investments, directing scarce resources to where they are most needed. *Continuous control monitoring* will be carried out to transition from a detective approach of discovering compliance failures to a more preventive approach of regularly reviewing control effectiveness and thus avoiding compliance failures before they occur. Control changes caused by the introduction of new regulations, threats, and IT systems can be more smoothly managed and integrated into the control environment with proactive compliance management performed by control and compliance subject matter professionals.

Automation can be used more effectively to improve control compliance, extending compliance benefits even further. In a nutshell, the GRC approach will help CSPs to:

- Use a structured risk management approach and reducing risks.

- Increase IT compliance monitoring.

- Increase security.

- Make compliance requirements and control assessment processes more rational.

- Reduce the workload associated with compliance monitoring and testing.

GRC implementation path

Several major scope elements must be developed, approved, and put in place before a GRC program can be implemented. The major work components have been divided into the following work streams: *governance*, *risk management*, *compliance*, and *continuous improvement*. The following diagram will depict a detailed process layout to implement a unified IT compliance program:

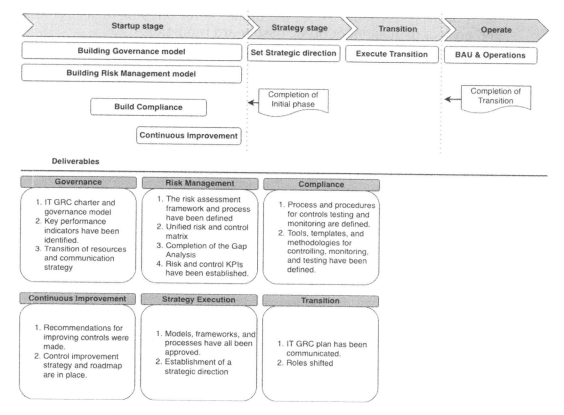

Figure 6.3: *Unified IT compliance program implementation plan*

Starting up entails creating all of the major work components required to define and run the program. The *GRC team* is usually in charge of this, with guidance and input from IT management. The following will be included:

- **Building governance model**: The GRC team's operating scope/charter, procedures, and governance mechanisms will be created. Organizational change management and transition plans will be developed to help the organization communicate how the GRC team will integrate with the CSP overall.

- **Building a risk management model**: Using existing methodologies, a *risk assessment framework* will be developed. This framework will be customized to the CSP's processes and will be supported by a risk assessment process definition. The CSP's compliance requirements will be rationalized to support the development of the unified control matrix. A *unified control matrix* will be created and mapped against current control processes to identify gaps. KPIs will be defined to monitor progress and serve as a foundation for ongoing measurement and project management office dashboard reporting.

- **Build compliance**: Testing/monitoring processes and procedures, tools, templates, and methodologies will be developed to support effective compliance in a standardized and efficient manner.

- **Continuous improvement**: Recommendations for control improvement will be *developed*, *risk-rated*, and *prioritized*.

- **Strategy stage**: The GRC team will present the program as a whole to the GRC oversight group during the *set-strategy phase*, gaining consensus and approval for the program strategy and approach.

- **Transition**: The *transition period* will include a brief period of communicating the new GRC roles and introducing resources and activities to the rest of the organization.

- **Operate**: The *operation phase* is when the program's ongoing services are made operational and the charter, strategy, and approach that were defined and approved in previous phases are carried out.

Compliance frameworks for cloud landscape

Organizations that use public cloud **Infrastructure-as-a-Service (IaaS)** can benefit from the cloud's ease of deployment and management uniquely. This *incredible speed* and *power* brings with it its own set of challenges, one of which is security, and compliance is a subset of that.

Cloud compliance is required as soon as you begin building on the cloud. Given our shared responsibility for cloud security, we must comprehend the regulatory frameworks that we must be aware of in light of the cloud landscape. As an organization that benefits from the cloud, the shared responsibility of security in the cloud means that you are only responsible for *managing data*, *classifying assets*, *managing access*, and *cloud configurations*, while the **Cloud Service Provider (CSP)** manages the hardware and operations ancillary to their data centers.

Choosing the right cybersecurity framework from the available frameworks necessitates a thorough understanding of your business's areas of jurisdiction and business requirements. Frameworks are classified into *three* broad categories and we will have a quick discussion on all these three categories:

- Industry and location-specific regulations
- Frameworks focused on security, and
- Cloud-well-architected frameworks

Industry and location-specific regulations

The laws within an organization's geographical jurisdiction and the industries in which it operates should be at the top of its compliance priority list. Non-compliance with these laws can have *serious consequences*, such as a loss of reputation, hefty fines, and the loss of business licenses.

Payments by credit card: PCI DSS

The **Payment Card Industry Data Security Standard** (**PCI DSS**) is a set of *security requirements* that apply to all merchants who accept credit or debit card payments. This set of guidelines is intended to protect cardholders from credit card fraud and identity theft.

Some of the things enterprises must do to comply with PCI DSS are as follows:

- Utilizing of anti-virus software
- Setting up firewalls
- Performing regular vulnerability assessments

If your organization stores and manages such *sensitive credit card information* in the cloud, it is your responsibility to provide your IT team with the specialized cloud expertise needed to securely design and maintain your cloud environment. Failure to follow the *PCI DSS cloud Computing Guidelines* could result in your organization losing the ability to process credit card payments.

HIPAA in healthcare

The **Health Insurance Portability and Accountability Act (HIPAA)** was enacted by the *United States Congress* to protect individuals' health-related information, and it includes sections that directly relate to information security.

HIPAA-regulated organizations must conduct risk assessments and develop risk management policies to address threats to the *confidentiality*, *integrity*, and *availability* of critical health data. If your organization uses cloud-based services (SaaS, IaaS, and PaaS) to manage and transmit this data, it is your responsibility to ensure that the service provider is HIPAA-compliant and that you have followed best practices in cloud configuration management.

MAS-TRM in Singapore

To regulate IT systems within *Singapore's* **Financial Institutions (FIs)**, the **Monetary Authority of Singapore (MAS)** first published the MAS-TRM (*Technology Risk Management*) *guidelines* in 2013. In 2019, MAS issued a consultation paper outlining changes to better reflect the state of IT systems in *Singapore*-based FIs. Among these modifications are:

- Specific Agile and DevOps guidelines

- Assistance with emerging technologies such as the **Internet of Things (IoT)**

- Increased focus on cyber resilience and security monitoring

While the majority of the MAS-TRM guidelines are not legally binding, MAS later issued a legally binding subset of the guidelines known as the *MAS Cyber Hygiene Notices*, which govern the entire range of FIs on cloud control items such as password policies, **Multi-Factor Authentication (MFA)**, and access controls.

BNM-RMiT in Malaysia

Risk Management in Technology (RMiT) guidelines issued by **Bank Negara Malaysia (BNM)** went into effect on *January 1, 2020*. The guidelines apply to *Malaysian* companies that fall into the following categories:

- Licensed financial institutions

- Investment banks that are licensed

- Islamic banks that are licensed

- Professional reinsurers are licensed insurers

- Professional *retakaful* operators, as well as licensed *takaful* operators

- Development financial institutions

- Electronic money approved issuers

- Owners and operators of a specific payment system

Since there were no clear regulations governing secure cloud operations in Malaysia previously, BNM-RMiT now provides a mix of legally binding regulations and best practices that include (but are not limited to):

- The inherent risk of using cloud computing technology is highlighted.

- Prior to migrating all infrastructure and assets to the cloud, conduct a risk assessment.

- Cloud service usage requirements.

APRA Prudential Practice Guide CPG 234 in Australia

The *Prudential Practice Guide* of the **Australian Prudential Regulation Authority (APRA)** identifies *Information Security* flaws within *Australian* financial institutions. They hope to assist *Australian* organizations in becoming more resilient to various threats.

On emerging technologies such as cloud computing, CPG 234 operates under the *zero-trust assumption*. The burden of demonstrating that your compliance posture is in line with industry best practices falls on you as a cloud-based organization operating in *Australia*.

GDPR in the Europe region

The **General Data Protection Regulation (GDPR)**, widely regarded as one of the most stringent data privacy laws in the world, seeks to protect the personal data of all individuals and entities within the **European Union (EU)**.

The GDPR applies to all organizations that conduct business in the EU, process data from EU citizens or residents, or provide goods and services to EU citizens or residents. GDPR is based on *eight* fundamental rights that individuals have over their personal data:

- **The right to know**: What information is collected and how it is processed
- **The right to information**: To request that the organization be completely open about data processing
- **The right to rectification**: Entails the ability to correct any incomplete or incorrect personal data
- **The ability to limit processing**: To put a stop to the processing of personal data
- **The right to be forgotten**: The right to have personal data erased at any time for any reason
- **Data portability**: The ability to transfer data from one service to another
- **The right to object**: The right to object to data being used for certain purposes, such as marketing research
- **The right to be notified**: Any personal data breach must be reported within *72 hours*

Non-compliance with the GDPR can result in severe penalties, including fines of up to €20 *million* or 4% of the organization's global annual revenue, whichever is greater. Even with these fundamental rights in mind, your organization must take concrete steps to ensure that you have the right cloud processes and technology in place to protect the personal information entrusted to you by the customer.

Frameworks focused on security

Security-centric frameworks are independent of legal and financial regulations, but they are strong guidelines that your organization can use to meet regulatory requirements.

ISO27001

ISO 27001 is one of the foundational standards in information security and compliance. The standard was created by ISO to assist organizations in protecting their information in accordance with best practices.

Compliance with ISO27001, as a CSP-*neutral international standard*, is globally recognized and can be a difficult requirement for companies to become approved third-party vendors. ISO 27001 governs everything from asset management and access control to cryptography and operational security in the cloud.

NIST cybersecurity framework

The **National Institute of Standards and Technology (NIST)** is a *United States* government agency responsible for developing standards and metrics that promote competition in the United States' science and technology industries.

NIST created its *Cybersecurity Framework* with U.S. standards like the **Health Insurance Portability and Accountability Act (HIPAA)** and the **Federal Information Security Management Act (FISMA)** in mind. They place a special emphasis on asset classification and asset security. NIST *Special Publication 800-53 - Security and Privacy Controls for Federal Information Systems and Organizations* and NIST *800-144 - Guidelines on Security and Privacy in Public Cloud Computing* are two relevant NIST cloud standards. These publications describe various security controls that organizations can use to secure their systems.

Center of Internet Security (CIS) controls

The **Center of Internet Security (CIS)** controls are a set of *open-source, consensus-based* guidelines that aid in the security of organizations' systems. All controls are subjected to a thorough review by a panel of experts until a consensus is reached. Each CIS control is classified into one of *two* groups:

- **Level 1**: Controls at *Level 1* help to reduce an organization's attack surface while maintaining functionality.

- **Level 2**: Comprehensive controls aimed at organizations that require stricter security measures.

To quickly access a set of cloud controls, your organization can consult the relevant CIS Benchmarks, which have been tailored to specific CSPs, such as CIS-AWS, a set of controls designed for **Amazon Web Services (AWS)** workloads.

CSA STAR

Security Trust and Risk Assurance (STAR) by the **Cloud Security Alliance (CSA)** is a comprehensive program for cloud security assurance. CSA STAR, which has controls mapped to *PCI DSS, ISO 27001, NIST,* and *ISACA COBIT,* stores documentation of major CSPs' security and privacy controls.

Your organization validates its security posture and can demonstrate proof of secure cloud controls by adhering to the STAR framework applicable to your CSP.

Cloud-Well-Architected frameworks

Today's major CSPs have their own **Well-Architected Frameworks (WAFs)** that are best practices in terms of not only security but also efficiency and cost.

AWS Well-Architected framework

The AWS *Well-Architected* framework guides AWS users in effectively architecting cloud solutions. It provides architects and evaluators with a consistent benchmark for evaluating cloud systems on AWS:

- **Operational excellence**: Adding value to the business
- **Security**: Safeguarding assets, systems, and information in the cloud
- **Reliability**: Recovering from disruptions and meeting demand
- **Performance efficiency**: Making efficient use of resources as they change
- **Cost optimization**: Reducing or eliminating unneeded expenses

Google Cloud Architecture framework

Google has provided the *Google Cloud Architecture* framework as a counterpart framework for organizations with workloads on the **Google Cloud Platform (GCP)**. They designed the framework so that organizations can highlight the parts of the framework that are most relevant to their needs. This structure is made up of *four* pillars:

- **Operational excellence**: Provides guidelines for increasing efficiency in areas such as *monitoring*, *disaster recovery*, and *automation*.

- **Security, privacy, and compliance**: A collection of security controls and which ones are best suited to specific use cases.

- **Reliability**: Suggestions for ensuring high *availability* and *reliability*.

- **Performance cost optimization**: Advice on how to strike a balance between performance and cost.

Microsoft Azure Well-Architected framework

If you're using *Microsoft Azure*, the *Azure Architecture* framework can help. It, like other architecture frameworks, is divided into *several* pillars:

- **Cost**: Providing the most value for the least amount of money

- **DevOps**: Keeping systems operational in production environments

- **Resiliency**: The ability to recover gracefully from failures

- **Scalability**: Adapting to changes in load, whether increasing or decreasing

- **Security**: Defending your data and applications against security threats

An automated approach to cloud security and compliance

Whether you are securely IT, IT security, DevOps, or regulatory compliance, chances are public cloud services are a growing part of your portfolio. This can be beneficial to the business by allowing for *lower costs*, *greater agility*, and *faster time to market*. However, this may present new and difficult challenges in ensuring security and compliance. The public cloud is a completely different world. If you believe that traditional methods of securing the data center or firewalling the perimeter will keep your data and applications safe, you may be in for a rude awakening. The fundamental problem with legacy approaches is that they were not designed for the cloud era, which means they do not support or leverage the public cloud's *API-centric infrastructure*.

The right cloud security platform can help the entire organization reduce risk and eliminate the human element from critical processes. Automation enables complete and continuous visibility across your cloud deployments, allowing for consistent duplication between usage environments such as *development*, *staging*, and *production*.

All put together – automation, security, cloud, and compliance

Cloud deployments move too quickly and are subject to too much rapid change for organizations to rely on manual resources. The problem is that most organizations still use legacy tools, technologies, and practices to manage cloud security and compliance.

Fortunately, new *cloud-native solutions* are now available, providing an agentless platform designed specifically for modern public clouds. These solutions take advantage of the cloud's API architecture to provide tremendous flexibility in scaling and managing cloud security and compliance. The following steps describe how a modern automated approach to continuous cloud security and compliance works:

- **Step 1: Monitor the cloud environment**: The cloud environment is constantly changing. These changes could be normal, routine activities of your DevOps or IT teams, or they could be the work of people who would harm your business. As changes are made across all *clouds*, *regions*, and *services*, the cloud security platform monitors infrastructure configurations to ensure that it adheres to security and compliance best practices.

- **Step 2: The security platform**: Collects data about your cloud services securely and continuously compares it to a set of best security practices. It also validates any pre-defined custom signatures. These checks determine whether or not there are any potentially exploitable vulnerabilities continuously.

- **Step 3: Deep analysis**: The platform then analyses the misconfigurations and exposures to determine whether they are classified as *high*, *medium*, or *low* risk.

- **Step 4: Automated remediation**: The results of the analysis are displayed on a *dashboard* and can be sent to integrated systems to initiate *auto-remediation workflows*.

- **Step 5: Robust reporting**: Detailed reports are made available so that your teams can see information about the risks, including *user attribution* and *affected resources*.

- **Step 6: Remediation**: The teams can then use simple remediation steps to restore the infrastructure to a secure state.

Continuous Security Monitoring (CSM)

CSM can help an organization improve its *threat detection* and *response*. The increased visibility provided by continuous monitoring enables businesses to quickly launch investigations into potential security incidents.

The CSM program is defined by *automation* and provides *end-to-end, real-time visibility* into an organization's security environment. It is constantly scanning the network for threats, vulnerabilities, and misconfigurations to notify security teams of potential breaches.

Continuous monitoring is gaining traction with regulators. If continuous monitoring programs are not in place, the *New York Department of Financial Services 23 NYCRR 500 standard* requires penetration tests and vulnerability assessments. This is not to dismiss pen tests or vulnerability management. Instead, this demonstrates the state's attempt to make the regulatory case for continuous monitoring as an essential component of cybersecurity.

Creating a program for continuous security monitoring

Continuous monitoring is used to improve processes that are constantly in motion. To begin, when developing your program, consider your risk tolerance. It will be especially difficult to define processes to avoid threats if an organization does not have a consistent understanding of the risks to its environment or where its critical assets are located. The first step in developing any security program is to identify the specific *risks* to your environment. The same is true for efforts to maintain continuous monitoring. Define the alerting process and how threat intelligence will be escalated based on *criticality*, *exposure*, and *risk*. This enables organizations to devise a game plan in the event of an incident. Otherwise, the focus is driven by the tool or analyst, who has little context or understanding of the overall strategy being implemented.

All programs for continuous security monitoring necessitate the use of tools and technology. It makes no difference whether a company uses *open-source*, *proprietary software*, or a *combination of the two*. What matters is how data is collected from these tools to apply to your risk profile, and then how it is *alerted*, *escalated*, and *reported*. SIEM, *vulnerability scanners*, *patch management*, *asset discovery*, and *network security* tools are common tools used in these data governance processes.

The goal is to collect security data from all aspects of the environment to be managed and monitored by *analysts* and *administrators*. When automated alerts and incident prioritization generate a pool of data within these systems, a continuous security monitoring program takes shape.

Decisions are left open to human interpretation and misinterpretation unless analysts can make quick decisions based on a tuned, correlated, and orchestrated technology stack that has been refined with your risk posture. CSM systems do the heavy lifting, allowing skilled analysts to *search*, *query*, and *hunt* through these programs and make informed decisions. A continuous security monitoring program is not a replacement for a trained analyst; rather, it is a tool that allows professionals to perform their jobs more effectively.

Procedures for escalation

The next stage in a continuous security monitoring program is **escalation**. Escalation procedures for management and required resources must be pre-configured. Security personnel on the front lines are frequently not called upon to take action. When using automation, a *security team* can make specific decisions to isolate and contain an incident, but this may necessitate escalation to other departments or roles.

The policy defining the continuous monitoring program should specify which company roles are notified in the event of a security incident. *Runbooks* and *tabletop exercises* are excellent tools for supplementing best practice processes with employees. To remain as agile and dynamic as possible, continuous security monitoring programs constantly adjust and tune their *technology*, *procedures*, and *risk posture*. Because attacks are *fluid*, monitoring programs must be as polished and adaptable in response.

Operating model for cloud security monitoring

Typically, Cloud Service Providers include native cloud security monitoring tools as part of their infrastructure. You can also supplement your cloud environment with a *third-party monitoring solution*. You can also monitor your cloud environment with on-premise security management solutions.

Log data from multiple servers, instances, and containers are consolidated by cloud monitoring tools. A sophisticated cloud monitoring solution correlates and analyses collected data to detect anomalous activity and notify the incident response team. The following capabilities are typically provided by cloud security monitoring solutions:

- **Continuous monitoring**: A cloud monitoring solution should continuously monitor all cloud activity, allowing you to detect and mitigate suspicious behavior in real-time.

- **Visibility**: When you migrate to the cloud, you lose visibility across your organization's infrastructure. A *cloud monitoring tool* can centralize monitoring and provide a unified view of the user, file, and application behavior.

- **Auditing**: Strong monitoring and auditing capabilities can assist you in staying in compliance with the regulations that apply to your organization.

- **Scalability**: A cloud security monitoring tool that can monitor large amounts of data distributed across multiple locations.

- **Integration**: For maximum visibility, the monitoring solution should ideally integrate with your existing tools and services. Choose a *solution* that can integrate with your existing productivity suites, endpoint security solutions, identity verification, and authentication services.

Advantages of cloud security monitoring

Cloud security monitoring encompasses several processes that enable organizations to *review*, *manage*, and *observe* operational workflows in a cloud environment.

Cloud security monitoring combines manual and automated processes to track and assess the security of servers, applications, software platforms, and websites.

Cloud security experts constantly monitor and assess the data stored in the cloud. They detect suspicious behavior and mitigate cloud-based security threats. If they discover an existing threat or vulnerability, they can recommend solutions to address the problem quickly and prevent further damage. Cloud security monitoring provides the following advantages:

- **Maintain compliance**: The majority of major regulations, such as *PCI DSS* and *HIPAA*, necessitate monitoring. To comply with these regulations and avoid penalties, organizations that use cloud platforms should use observation tools.

- **Discover vulnerabilities**: To identify vulnerabilities, it is critical to maintain visibility over your cloud environment. An automated observation tool can help your IT and security teams identify suspicious behavior patterns and indicators of compromise by sending alerts to them quickly.

- **Avoiding business disruptions**: Security incidents can disrupt business operations or force you to shut them down entirely. Disruptions and data breaches can have an impact on customer trust and satisfaction, so it is critical to monitor your cloud environment to ensure business continuity, data security, and business continuity.

- **Protect sensitive data**: You can perform regular audits and keep your data secure by utilizing a cloud security monitoring solution. You can monitor the health of your security systems and receive recommendations for implementing security measures.

Best practices and recommendations

In this section, we will go in sequential order to list down a few best practices which you should be adopting for your landscape. We will start with cloud security monitoring.

Best practices around cloud security monitoring

These best practices for cloud security monitoring will assist you in being strategic, gaining visibility into your environment, and providing layers of security that will protect against threats:

- **Perform a thorough evaluation of cloud service providers**: In terms of security, the big *three* cloud service providers (*Google*, *Amazon*, and *Microsoft*) are fairly comparable. Organizations should evaluate levels of compliance and data/network availability regardless of the vendor to ensure that it meets their needs.

- **Conduct cloud infrastructure inventory**: To understand potential risks like shadow IT, security teams should conduct a deep dive into their existing cloud infrastructure. Organizations should conduct regular audits and understand what changes were made within their cloud environments to help identify the root causes of misconfigurations.

- **Take a layered approach to cloud security**: Setting up layers of security can assist organizations in gaining the most visibility into their tech stack. Native cloud monitoring tools like **AWS GuardDuty** can help, but it's also important to bring in specialized tools to address different components of the tech stack, from physical hardware to orchestration.

Best practices of cloud compliance

Let's take a look at some of the best cloud compliance practices to follow:

- **Inventory your possessions**: Only what you can see can be protected. However, gradual cloud adoption and the spinning up of environments within the cloud make it easy to lose track of data. Creating a catalog of your assets will make it easier to find them. As a result, you will be able to apply the necessary compliances based on the data they store and thus protect them more easily.

- **Set a baseline**: The compliance you must meet will depend on your industry and location. Companies in the *United States* that handle **Personally Identifiable Information** (**PII**) may choose to use the framework developed by the **National Institute of Standards and Technology** (**NIST**). Furthermore, if you accept card payments from customers anywhere in the world, you must comply with the **Payment Card Industry Data Security Standard** (**PCI DSS**). Being compliant, however, is not the same as being recognized as compliant. For example, the PCI DSS requires you to complete a *self-assessment*, but they may then conduct their audit and report. A catalog of your assets is especially useful in situations like this.

- **Controls must be used**: Even if you use a cloud vendor to run your applications and store your data, the security of these assets is not their responsibility. And achieving compliance becomes even more difficult if you use multiple clouds or operate a hybrid cloud model.

  Cloud security controls will allow you to approach cybersecurity and compliance in a structured manner. This includes measures such as implementing access controls and monitoring your systems for IOCs.

  Financial controls will also give you more control over your expanding environment. This can be accomplished by implementing an authorization process for cloud service purchases.

- **Make use of automation**: When something suspicious is detected, *firewalls*, *anti-virus software*, and *vulnerability scanning tools* all generate alerts. As a result, the sheer volume of alerts can be exhausting. Furthermore, an event can go undetected until it is too late.

  Responses to specific alerts will be triggered by automated workflows, deploying applications to investigate. This reduces the time it takes to detect real threats and makes it easier to meet compliance policies. You can also incorporate these into your continuous integration/continuous delivery pipeline to automate security throughout the development process.

  You can also automate auditing and reporting to gain more intelligent insights into your posture. You can even use triggers to create new environments to aid in your threat investigation. And because your compliance standards are likely to evolve as your company grows, you can use automated operational controls to enforce compliance at scale. However, regulations are constantly evolving to address new technologies and vulnerabilities. As a result, you must regularly review the frameworks that are relevant to you.

Disaster Recovery (DR) in cloud

Cloud **Disaster Recovery (DR)** is a collection of *strategies* and *services* designed to backup data, applications, and other resources to public clouds or dedicated service providers. When a disaster occurs, the affected data, applications, and other resources can be restored to the local data center – or a cloud provider – and the enterprise can resume normal operations. The goal of cloud DR is nearly identical to that of traditional DR: to protect valuable business resources, and ensure that protected resources can be accessed, and recovered to continue normal business operations. DR is an essential component of any **business continuity (BC)** strategy. Before the advent of cloud connectivity and self-service technologies, traditional DR options were limited to local DR and second-site implementations. **Local DR** did not always protect against disasters such as fires, floods, and earthquakes. **Off-site DR** provided far better protection against physical disasters but imposed significant business costs for implementing and maintaining a second data center.

With the advent of cloud technologies, public cloud and managed service providers may be able to establish a dedicated facility to provide a wide range of effective backup and disaster recovery services and capabilities. Businesses gain continuous access to highly automated, highly scalable, self-driven off-site DR services without the expense of a second data center and without the need to select, install, and maintain DR tools.

Choosing the right partner for your DR strategy

When choosing a cloud disaster recovery provider, *five* factors must be considered: *location*, *reliability*, *scalability*, *security*, and *compliance*.

First, a company must consider the physical distance and latency of the cloud DR provide by putting DR too close, which increases the risk of shared physical disaster, but putting DR too far away increases latency and network congestion, making it more difficult to access DR content. While DR content must be accessible from multiple global business locations, location can be especially challenging. Consider the dependability of the cloud DR provider. Even the cloud experiences downtime, and service outages during recovery can be equally damaging to the business.

Consider the cloud DR offering's scalability as well. It must be able to protect specific data, applications, and other resources, but it must also be able to accommodate additional resources as needed and provide adequate performance as other global customers use the services. Understand DR content's security requirements and ensure that the provider can provide authentication, **virtual private networks** (**VPNs**), encryption, and other tools needed to protect the company's valuable resources. Examine compliance requirements and ensure that the provider is certified to meet business-related compliance standards such as ISO 27001, SOC 2, and SOC 3, and the **Payment Card Industry Data Security Standard** (**PCI DSS**).

Finally, think about how the DR platform should be designed. The *three* basic approaches to DR are *cold*, *warm*, and *hot*. These terms refer to how easily a system can be recovered:

- **Cold DR**: Cold disaster recovery typically entails storing data or **virtual machine** (**VM**) images. These resources are generally inaccessible unless additional work is performed, such as downloading stored data or loading images into a virtual machine. Cold DR is typically the simplest (often simply storage) and least expensive approach, but it takes the longest to recover, leaving the business with the most downtime in the event of a disaster.

- **Warm DR**: Warm DR is a standby approach in which duplicate data and applications are placed with a *cloud DR provider* and kept up to date with data and applications in the primary data center. However, the duplicate resources are doing nothing. When a disaster strikes, the warm DR can be brought online to resume operations from the DR provider, which is often as simple as starting a VM and redirecting IP addresses and traffic to the DR resources. Recovery time can be quite short, but it still results in some downtime for the protected workloads.

- **Hot DR**: Hot DR is typically a live parallel deployment of data and workloads running concurrently. That is, both the primary data center and the DR site run the same workload and data in synchronization, with both sites sharing a portion of the overall application traffic. When a disaster strikes one site, the remaining site continues to handle the work without interruption. Users should be completely unaware of the disruption. Hot DR has no downtime but is the most *expensive* and complicated approach. Higher-priority workloads can use a *hot approach*, while lower-priority workloads or data sets can use a *warm* or even *cold* approach. Organizations must, however, determine the best approach for each workload or resource and find a cloud DR provider that can adequately support the desired approaches.

Advantages of leveraging Cloud DR

When compared to more traditional DR strategies, cloud DR offers several significant advantages:

- **Pay-as-you-go options are available**: Organizations that deployed **do-it-yourself (DIY)** DR facilities incurred significant capital costs, whereas engaging managed colocation providers for *off-site DR services* frequently entailed long-term service agreements. The *pay-as-you-go* paradigm of cloud services allows organizations to pay a recurring monthly charge only for the resources and services that are used. Payments change as resources are added or removed.

  In effect, the cloud model of service delivery converts *one-time capital costs* into recurring operational expenses. However, cloud providers frequently offer discounts for long-term resource commitments, which can be more appealing to larger organizations with static DR needs.

- **Scalability and adaptability**: Traditional disaster recovery approaches, which were typically implemented in local or remote data centers, frequently imposed constraints on flexibility and scalability. The company had to purchase the servers, storage, network equipment, and software tools required for DR as well as *design*, *test*, and *maintain* the infrastructure required to handle DR operations – significantly more if the DR was directed to a second data center. This was usually a significant capital and recurring expense for the company.

  Cloud DR options, such as public cloud services and **disaster recovery as a service (DRaaS)** providers, can deliver massive amounts of *resources on-demand*, allow businesses to engage as many resources as needed – usually through a self-service portal – and then adjust those resources as business demands change, such as when new workloads are added or old workloads and data are retired.

- **High dependability and geographic redundancy**: A global footprint, ensuring multiple data centers to support users across major global geopolitical regions, is an essential feature of a cloud provider. This is used by cloud providers to improve service reliability and redundancy. Businesses can easily use *geo-redundancy* to locate disaster recovery resources in another region – or even multiple regions – to maximize availability. The traditional off-site disaster recovery scenario is a natural feature of the cloud.

- **Testing is simple, and recovery is quick**: Cloud workloads are frequently run as **virtual machines (VMs)**, making it simple to copy VM image files to *in-house test* servers to validate workload availability without interfering with production workloads. Furthermore, businesses can choose high bandwidth and fast disc **input/output (I/O)** options to optimize data transfer speeds in order to meet **recovery time objective (RTO)** requirements. However, data transfers from cloud providers incur costs, so testing should take these costs into account.

Cloud DR and business continuity

Disaster recovery, which includes *cloud-based* DR, is part of a broader BC umbrella. **Business Continuity (BC)** basically refers to the plans and technologies put in place to ensure that business operations can resume with minimal delay and difficulty following the onset of an incident that could disrupt the business.

According to this definition, BC is a broad topic area that includes a variety of subjects such as security, business governance, and compliance, risk assessment and management, change management, and disaster preparedness/recovery. For example, BC efforts could consider and plan for a wide range of disasters such as epidemics — loss of skilled personnel — earthquakes, floods, fires, service outages, physical or cyber-attacks, theft, sabotage, and other potential incidents.

BC planning typically begins with risk identification and assessment: *What risks is the company planning for, and how likely are those risks?* Once a risk has been identified, business leaders can devise a strategy to address and mitigate the risk. The plan has been budgeted, procured, and implemented. Once implemented, the plan can be *tested, maintained,* and *adjusted* as needed.

Disaster recoveries such as floods, earthquakes, and cyber-attacks, is typically central to many aspects of BC planning. For example, if the business is located on a known *earthquake fault*, the risk of earthquake damage would be assessed in order to develop a mitigation strategy. As part of the *mitigation strategy,* cloud DR in the form of a second hot site in an earthquake-free region could be implemented.

As a result, the BC plan would rely on the cloud DR service's redundancy to seamlessly continue operations if the primary data center became unavailable – continuing business operations. In this case, DR would be a minor component of the BC plan, with additional planning detailing corresponding changes in workflows and job responsibilities to maintain normal operations – such as taking orders, shipping products, and handling billing – as well as work to restore the affected resources.

Given the importance of DR in many aspects of BC, the two terms are frequently used interchangeably, even though this is technically incorrect, and BC necessitates a separate and more detailed discussion.

Creating a disaster recovery plan based on the cloud

Creating a cloud disaster recovery plan is almost identical to creating a more traditional local or off-site disaster recovery plan. The use of cloud technologies and DRaaS to support appropriate implementation is the primary difference between cloud DR and more traditional DR approaches. *Cloud-based* DR, for example, would back up an important data set to a cloud resource such as an Amazon **Simple Storage Service (S3)** bucket rather than a different disc in another local server. As another example, rather than running an important server as a warm VM in a colocation facility, the warm VM could be run in Microsoft Azure or any number of different DRaaS providers. As a result, cloud DR does not alter the fundamental need for or steps to implement DR, but rather provides a new set of convenient tools and platforms for DR targets. *Analysis, implementation,* and *testing* are the *three* main components:

- **Analysis**: Any disaster recovery plan begins with a detailed risk assessment and impact analysis, which examines the current IT infrastructure and workflows and then considers the potential disasters that a business is likely to face. The goal here is to identify potential vulnerabilities and disasters ranging from intrusion vulnerabilities and theft to earthquakes and floods, and then assess whether the IT infrastructure is up to the task.

  An analysis can assist organizations in identifying the most critical business functions and IT elements, as well as forecasting the potential financial consequences of a disaster event. Analysis can also aid in determining RPOs and RTOs for infrastructure and workloads. Based on these findings, a company can make more informed decisions about which workloads to protect, how those workloads should be protected, and where more investment is required to achieve those goals.

- **Implementation**: Typically, the analysis is followed by a careful implementation that details steps for *prevention, preparedness, response,* and *recovery*. Prevention is an effort made to reduce *potential threats* and *eliminate vulnerabilities*. This could include social engineering training for employees as well as regular **operating system (OS)** updates to maintain *security* and *stability*. Preparedness entails outlining the necessary response – who does what in the event of a disaster. This is fundamentally a documentation issue. The response outlines the technologies and strategies to be used in the event of a disaster. Recovery outlines the success conditions for the response as well as steps to help mitigate any potential business damage.

  The goal here is to determine how to address a specific disaster should it occur, and the plan is matched with the implementation of technologies and services designed to handle the specific circumstances. The plan in this case includes *cloud-based technologies and services*.

- **Testing**: Finally, any DR plan must be tested and updated on a regular basis to ensure that IT staff members are capable of successfully and timely implementing the appropriate response and recovery and that recovery occurs within an acceptable timeframe for the business. Testing can reveal gaps or inconsistencies in implementation, allowing organizations to correct and update their disaster recovery plan before a real disaster strikes.

Risk management in the cloud ecosystem

Because of its ubiquity and widespread use, cloud computing is the leading technology disrupting enterprise and consumer markets all over the world. Cloud computing has accelerated in adoption in a relatively short period of time, becoming a critical component of IT and business strategy.

Cloud computing will continue to enable the integration of emerging technologies and the formation of new business models as a strategic advantage in the near future.

Service offerings have rapidly expanded as the industry matures. There is some risk gradient across the various service models, but the deployment model is where the risks vary greatly. However, while cloud computing offers numerous advantages, it also introduces significant risks on several critical fronts that must be governed and managed by user organizations. To maximize the value of their cloud computing initiatives, well-managed organizations must understand and mitigate these risks. The following are *five* major risks and the same has been depicted in the following diagram also:

- Data security and regulatory compliance
- Operational
- Technology
- Vendor
- Financial

Figure 6.4: *Key risks in the cloud landscape*

Let's take a look at *five* different types of risks and how they apply or differ depending on the cloud deployment model.

Data security and regulatory compliance

Data loss, leakage, or *unavailability* can be associated with data security and regulatory risk. This can result in business interruption, revenue loss, reputation damage, or regulatory noncompliance.

Noncompliance with various national/geographic regulations, industry, or service-specific legal and regulatory requirements, such as the **Gramm-Leach-Bliley Act (GLBA)**, the **Sarbanes-Oxley Act (SOX)**, the **Health Insurance Portability and Accountability Act (HIPAA)**, or the **European Union (EU)** *Data Protection Directive*, is associated with regulatory risk. One of the most significant new regulatory schemes is the EU **General Data Protection Regulation (GDPR)**, which was recently adopted by the *European Parliament* and imposes stringent requirements on any organization doing business in *Europe* or storing data about EU residents. This necessitates a new level of tracking data and consent, both of which necessitate special considerations when using cloud computing. Non-compliance carries severe penalties, including fines of up to 4% of global annual turnover/revenues or €20 *million*, whichever is greater.

According to the *Cloud Security Alliance's Cloud Adoption* survey, data protection is the most important security concern for the financial sector as it moves to the cloud. Data protection standards and relevant laws were particularly *top of mind* for survey respondents. Compliance is driven by industry regulation, which requires financial institutions to implement specific security measures before considering cloud services. *Data protection (75%), corporate governance (68%),* PCI-DSS (54%), and *national regulations (47%)* topped the list.

According to the *Cloud Security Alliance* survey *The Cloud Balancing Act for IT: Between Promise and Peril,* the ability to enforce corporate security policies was cited as the main barrier to moving systems of record to the cloud by 67.8% of companies. When it comes to moving their systems of record to the cloud, 61.2% of companies see regulatory compliance as a major barrier.

The data risks for a private cloud are similar to those for traditional computing because organizations have better control and understanding of how various *government rules, laws,* and *regulations* apply to them. Furthermore, there is no data sharing between cloud users. However, there are additional risks associated with private external cloud computing:

- Inadequate visibility into controls over transaction initiation, authorization, recording, processing, and reporting.

- Unauthorized data access by a service provider and/or less control over who sees what data—for example, the service provider may use contractors or *third parties*.

The data risks associated with a private external cloud apply to a public cloud. Furthermore, the following dangers exist:

- Risk of data leakage or access due to multi-tenancy/shared infrastructure between organizations.

- Inflexibility in data protection mechanisms such as encryption and the implementation of specific controls based on the data type. Different organizations may have varying encryption and control requirements, and a public cloud provider may be unable to customize their infrastructure or provide customers with encryption key control. This is especially true for solutions delivered via SaaS and PaaS models.

Risk associated with technology

Technology risk is associated with constantly evolving technologies and a lack of standardization in how they integrate or interoperate. Technology risks could result in costly re-architecture efforts to adopt or integrate new technology. A technological risk for a private cloud could be:

- A constantly changing technological landscape may necessitate the organization upgrading or redesigning its computing resources and retraining its technical support staff.

- The possibility of human error due to the number of configurable points and frequency of deployments.

The evolving technology risk for a public cloud may be lower because service providers must worry about upgrading/rearchitecting their computing resources and retraining their support staff. Other technological risks, such as:

- Technology features are constantly evolving, and the organization may need to redesign its cloud applications much more frequently than mature technologies.

- We have observed several instances where the organization's cloud architecture was defined prior to the introduction of advanced security and control features, and management had not updated the cloud architecture to take advantage of these advanced capabilities provided by the vendor for free or at a low cost.

- Restrictions on what and how much an organization can customize (*infrastructure*, *platform*, or *applications*) based on the service model used.

- CSP dashboards for cloud management may provide limited visibility due to the use of multiple cloud providers and potentially hundreds to thousands of server instances in the cloud. Each vendor of public cloud solutions typically provides its own administration console. Due to the lack of a single/consolidated management dashboard, this is becoming an increasingly difficult task as the number of SaaS solutions in use at organizations grows.

Risk related to operations

The execution of IT services and tasks on which the business relies can pose an operational risk.

Migration to the cloud has also highlighted a new approach known as **DevOps**, in which development and operations responsibilities are merged. Deployment times can now be reduced to days rather than weeks or months. It may have an impact on IT operations, and development teams will need to be trained in cloud deployment and cloud-based systems management, though it will be less about managing IT hardware and networks.

Some operational risks for a private cloud are:

- Suboptimal service reliability and uptime because it may be cost-prohibitive for an organization to employ leading cloud computing technology that could provide better service reliability and uptime.

Some operational risks for a public cloud include:

- A lack of customized service levels for various IT services , which may necessitate the organization to select a proximate acceptable service level, such as those related to application availability and disaster recovery.

- Less control over service quality.

- Less control over critical application availability and disaster recovery.

Risk associated with vendors

Vendor risk arises as a result of vendor leverage or association. Unexpected vendor circumstances, such as bankruptcy, lawsuits, SEC investigations, or any other act of defamation for the vendor, could significantly harm an organization's reputation and goodwill. Due to the association with and reliance on the service provider, this risk applies to both *private external cloud* and *public cloud* computing scenarios(s).

Because of the ease of access to IaaS, there has been a proliferation of innovative SaaS start-ups, some with novel solutions that address the needs that traditional vendors have overlooked. Some of these vendors may not be viable options for large organizations looking to exchange increasing amounts of data while adhering to stringent control requirements.

Financial risk

Overspending and revenue loss can pose financial risks. According to one of the surveys, the cost of cloud services is three times more likely to be a concern today than it was *five* years ago. The following are the financial risks associated with a private cloud:

- Underestimating the initial cost of establishing a private cloud
- Maintaining capital expenditures for hardware and software

The financial risks of a public cloud are primarily related to the variable nature of costs, that is, running up the cost of using a public cloud due to poor planning and business requirements. Consider electricity as an analogy. During the winter, a consumer may use an electric heater all day without realizing the cost until the electric bill arrives at the end of the month. Managing cloud costs necessitates a level of focus, skill, and tools that were previously unavailable.

Cloud security assessment checklist

Organizations should think about how to mitigate the *five* major risks in order to reap the many benefits of cloud computing. Consider the following issues for your company:

Step 1: Policies and procedures

The responsibility for a secure system falls on both the cloud provider and you, the client.

Gartner estimates that *through 2022, at least 95% of cloud security failures will be the customer's fault.* Comprehensive policies and procedures in place and followed will help to eliminate this threat:

- *Has the cloud been incorporated into all security policies and procedures?*
- *Are there security procedures in place for onboarding employees?*
- *Are there procedures in place for when employees leave or change roles?*
- *Do you have procedures in place to deal with any security violations?*

Step 2: Access control

Identity and access management are crucial and foundation steps for any cloud landscape. *Does this determine how users are identified and authenticated as well as who has the authority to assign access rights?*

- *How many people have access to your system? Have they been properly vetted?*

- *Is security awareness training provided to all of your employees?*

- *Do you employ two-factor authentication? Before granting access, use at least two forms of authentication to ensure that the person requesting access is who they say they are.*

- *Is your visitor access restricted? Guest access can lead to security flaws. Make sure their permissions are restricted and only enable them when necessary.*

Step 3: Network

When using a *cloud-based environment*, the cloud provider assumes much of the responsibility for network security. You must inquire as follows:

- *Are there any gateway security measures in place to protect against malware injection? Hackers may be able to intercept and steal sensitive data by injecting malicious code into cloud services.*

- *Are network-based attacks protected by security measures?*

- *Restricting internet SSH and SQL Server access and disabling RDP from the internet will help prevent brute force attacks on VMs.*

- *Is all sensitive data encrypted when it travels over less-trustworthy networks?*

Step 4: Backup and data recovery

Data can be lost due to a number of factors such as *hardware failure, natural disasters,* or *malicious action.* A recovery plan is essential for avoiding catastrophic data loss:

- *Does your cloud provider address backup and data recovery adequately with detailed plans and procedures?* This includes physical storage locations, physical access to server facilities, and disaster recovery plans.

- *Do you conduct regular testing to ensure the success of the restoration?* Checking your backup and restoration procedures on a regular basis will ensure a smooth recovery if the worst happens.

Step 5: Security patches and updates

Keeping your systems up to date with the latest security patches is a critical step in maintaining a secure environment. Consider this:

- *Have you installed the most recent security patches?*
- *Can you show me which patches you have installed?*
- *Do you test security patches in a development environment before deploying them to live servers?*
- *Do you scan your environment for critical system vulnerabilities on a periodic basis?*

Step 6: Monitoring and logging

A security breach can take a company six months or more to discover. As a result, it's critical to ensure that your system activity is logged and saved for future analysis:

- *For how long do you keep your logs?*
- *Do you keep track of when applications interact with sensitive data?*
- *Do you keep track of changes to policy assignments, network security groups, and security policies?*
- *Do you keep an eye on your system for potential security breaches?*

Step 7: Data encryption

Encryption ensures that even if your data is compromised, the hacker is rendered ineffective as long as the keys are secure. The more sensitive the information, the more critical encryption is:

- *Is all sensitive information stored on servers and in transit encrypted?*
- *Have you secured all private and public keys for certificates?*

Conclusion

The public cloud is here to stay. Quite the contrary. According to *Forrester Research*, the public cloud services market will exceed $230 *billion* by the end of the decade. As the cloud becomes more important to your organization's success, it is critical that you focus on security and compliance, regardless of your role in IT, *security, compliance, DevOps,* or *corporate management.*

By embracing a continuous security model, your organization will be able to automate many processes that would otherwise overwhelm your teams and systems. It not only provides enhanced security and compliance protections, but also reduces the burden on your staff, improves security for DevOps and other teams, and lowers the cost and risk of cloud security and compliance.

Cloud computing audits have become commonplace as users become aware of the risks associated with having their data hosted by other organizations. To combat this, they are requesting various types of cloud computing audits in order to gain assurance and reduce the risk of their data being lost or hacked.

SOC 1 and SOC 2 *reporting*, HITRUST, PCI, and *FedRAMP* are all examples of cloud computing audits. One of these should meet your audit requirements, depending on your needs.

The use of cloud services provides tremendous opportunities for businesses to accelerate and grow. Though cloud services provide numerous benefits, they also expose organizations to security risks. Appropriate cloud security controls must be in place to mitigate such risks. While migrating data or applications to the cloud, organizations should be aware of the risks and vulnerabilities they face. A comprehensive and holistic approach to cloud risk management is required, which includes developing a cloud security strategy, roadmaps, and policies and procedures.

In the next chapter, we will try to understand security policy adoption and various approaches to adopt the right culture. It will be more focused on policy and culture which need to be adopted by enterprise for cloud security.

References

- **PCI DSS Cloud Computing Guidelines**:

  https://listings.pcisecuritystandards.org/pdfs/PCI_SSC_Cloud_Guidelines_v3.pdf

- **HIPAA Guidelines**:

  https://www.hhs.gov/hipaa/for-professionals/special-topics/health-information-technology/cloud-computing/index.html

- **NIST cybersecurity framework**:

  https://www.nist.gov/cyberframework

- **AWS Well-Architected**:

  https://aws.amazon.com/architecture/well-architected/

- **Microsoft Azure Well-Architected Framework**:
  https://docs.microsoft.com/en-us/azure/architecture/framework/

Questions

1. Explain the policy compliance approach and life cycle for CSP.
2. Why is defining the scope of an audit important?
3. Give a few examples to explain the audit criteria.
4. Why is continuous improvement important in the overall approach to compliance?
5. What are the different benefits CSP will get by adopting GRC practice?
6. Could you please explain the implementation path for the compliance program with the help of a diagram?
7. What are the industry and geo-specific regulations you should be aware of?
8. What do you mean by Cloud Well-Architect framework? Please explain the examples.
9. Define **Continuous Security Monitoring (CSM)**.
10. Explain in detail the operating model of Cloud Security Monitoring.
11. What advantages can you think of by leveraging cloud security monitoring?
12. What are the different best practices around cloud compliance?
13. Why choosing the right partner for your DR strategy is critical?
14. What DR options can you think of considering the cloud landscape?
15. What are the different key risks in the cloud?

CHAPTER 7

Creating and Enforcing Effective Security Policies

Introduction

This chapter will focus on security policy adoption and an approach to adopting the required culture. *Policy and culture* plays a vital role in the long run and we must understand the importance of the same and how we should create and adapt it for our organizations. We will focus on understanding various roles and responsibilities and how each of these contributes to a desired cultural state to adopt security as a shared responsibility. We will also talk about how you should inject the training and awareness session with a few examples and recommendations. We will also talk about various security policies like data protection, encryption, and many others.

At the end of the chapter, you will have a complete understanding of how security policies are adopted in the cloud ecosystem and to create an effective cybersecurity team.

Structure

In this chapter, we will discuss the following topics associated with cloud security:

- Cloud security policy adoption
- Cloud security policy templates
- Operating in a shared-responsibility environment
- Creating **Data Loss Prevention (DLP)** policies
- Protecting sensitive data with encryption

- Enforcing your policies
- Educate your users on the cloud security policy
- Creating an effective cybersecurity team

Cloud adoption

Cloud computing is quickly becoming a mainstay for many businesses today due to its superior *flexibility*, *accessibility*, and *capacity* when compared to traditional computing and storage methods. However, cloud computing, like traditional storage and data sharing methods, has its own set of data security concerns. Concerns about cloud security risks can stifle cloud adoption in some cases, and rob organizations of the numerous benefits provided by the cloud. Indeed, according to a recent *RightScale* report, *security* is the top cloud concern among IT professionals. While cloud adoption may appear daunting, beginning with a thorough plan and taking a pragmatic, *data-centric approach* to implementing cloud security measures will make the process manageable and achievable for security teams. This section will discuss a framework that organizations can use to create an effective cloud security program.

Due diligence

Conduct due diligence before choosing a cloud service provider to understand:

- *What types of data will be uploaded to the cloud, and how sensitive will that data be?* (as well as if any of that data is subject to specific regulations like *PCI, HIPAA, HITECH*, and so on).

- The provider's security measures. Secure cloud providers should provide:

  - Data encryption at rest and in transit – providers should be FIPS 140-2 certified for data in storage and use HTTPS for data in transit.

  - Access control mechanisms that are secure, such as *two-factor/ multi-factor authentication*.

  - Findings from independent security audits to validate the adequacy of the provider's security measures.

  - Monitoring and logging functionality including but not limited to security monitoring, configuration monitoring, incident monitoring, and other critical parameters health check.

- Compliance certifications such as HIPAA/HITECH, PCI-DSS, *Cloud Security Alliance Cloud Controls Matrix*, and *Safe Harbor*. If asked for, should share the audit report (under NDA).

- The provider's privacy, data ownership, customer support, compliance with any applicable regulations, and policies for data breach liability, notification, and response.

- How will the cloud alter or impact current business processes?

There are several *reputable, industry-standard resources* that businesses can use to assess the efficacy of cloud providers' security. Use frameworks such as ISO 27002 or the *Cloud Security Alliance's Cloud Controls Matrix* to validate your own findings and obtain an authoritative evaluation of cloud vendor security.

Securing endpoints when accessing the cloud

Cloud applications exist outside of your IT environment, beyond the scope of many *networks-* or *perimeter-based* security technologies. It is critical to secure the devices that will be used to access the cloud before using cloud storage or services. Controls for *data exfiltration, end-to-end encryption,* and *secure access* should be implemented at these endpoints. This prevents unauthorized uploads of sensitive data to the cloud, or at the very least ensures that data is encrypted prior to upload. Data should be encrypted in the cloud and decrypted only when it reaches the device of an authorized user. Once information enters the cloud, it is no longer directly under your control; so it is essential to encrypt it or forbid the upload of certain data types to keep it away from hackers.

Monitoring data and access to the cloud

Visibility into data access and usage is essential for effective data security. In addition to securing the endpoints used to access cloud data, ensure that you have visibility into who is accessing the cloud and what data they are uploading or downloading from the cloud.

Your endpoint security controls will be more effective thanks to this visibility, which will also help your security team quickly identify and address any risky cloud data behavior, whether it originates from insiders like employees or from outsiders who have broken into your systems and gained access.

Adopting API for data protection in the cloud

If your organization is going to allow the use of *cloud-based email* or *storage services*, use the APIs of the providers to extend existing data protection measures to those platforms. This can improve visibility over cloud data access and enable better control - such as encryption or access control - over data stored in the cloud. Many network security appliances provide cloud integrations via APIs, so ask your providers which cloud platforms they integrate with and take advantage of these features where available.

Securing cloud applications

Aside from *endpoints* and *networks*, cloud security is also dependent on the security of cloud-based applications. Far too often, security takes a back seat to form and function in cloud application development, especially when single developers or small teams are involved.

Test your own cloud applications for commonly exploited security vulnerabilities, and require *third-party cloud application providers* to share the results of their own application security testing (such as static or dynamic analysis or penetration testing). Any vulnerabilities found during the application testing process should be patched securely before the applications are used.

Security and controls to protect Bring Your Own Device (BYOD)

If you are going to allow access to cloud data via employee-owned mobile devices (laptops, smartphones, or tablets), you must first create a **Bring Your Own Device (BYOD)** policy and implement controls to enforce proper data access and usage by these users.

Consider using *two-factor authentication, end-to-end encryption*, and **mobile device management (MDM)** software to secure BYOD in the cloud. *Two-factor authentication* helps prevent unauthorized access, while encryption ensures that any sensitive cloud data accessed by BYOD users is only viewable by authorized parties. MDM software is a good last line of defense if a device is lost or stolen, as it allows IT departments to restrict BYOD access or remotely wipe a device if necessary.

Data backup

Companies must prepare for the *worst-case scenario*, which is the permanent loss of cloud-stored data, as cloud providers and applications are increasingly targeted in cyber-attacks. While regular data backups will not protect you from many of the costs of a data breach, such as *financial losses*, *brand damage*, or *regulatory penalties*, they will ensure that any critical data is lost in a cloud data breach, ransomware attack, or destructive malware infection can be recovered. Prior to moving to the cloud, make data backups a regular and routine process.

Training and awareness

Your endpoints, applications, and network connections are only as secure as the users who use them. Social engineering techniques, such as **spear phishing**, continue to be among the most *common*, *simple*, and *effective* methods cybercriminals use. Ongoing security training is essential to ensuring that employees can recognize and avoid social engineering attacks, as well as develop secure web habits. Simulated social engineering attacks should be conducted on a regular basis to assess your employees' ability to detect and avoid them.

Cloud security policy template

We all understand and agree that developing a cloud security policy must be highly recommended. This *policy*, an essential component of your cloud security strategy, assists your organization in properly storing and protecting its critical data assets. It identifies who is in charge of each aspect of cyber security, explains your approach to cloud services, and provides written proof of your commitment to protecting enterprise data. Furthermore, some compliance regulations require the creation of a documented cloud security policy document.

A *cloud security policy* does not exist in isolation. It must be linked to other security policies established within your organization, such as data security and privacy policies. The following cloud security policy template provided (*Table 7.1*) is a roadmap of recommended key sections, complete with descriptions and examples. Adapt it to your organization's specific legal and regulatory needs:

Controls/ require- ments	Description	Example
Objective	The reasons for developing and maintaining the policy are detailed in the purpose section.	This policy protects the *confidentiality, integrity,* and *availability* of data stored, accessed, and altered using cloud computing services. It establishes a framework of responsibility and actions necessary to meet regulatory requirements and cloud computing security guidelines.
Scope	This section defines the policy's scope. It may contain sections highlighting specific groups, services, or locations.	This policy applies to data handling systems. This policy will apply to all cloud services that fall into this category. As a result, it applies to any server, database, or other information technology system that handles such data, including any device that is regularly used for email, web access, or other work-related tasks. These specifications apply to both new and existing installations. This policy applies to any user who interacts with the company's IT services. Security controls are product agnostic and apply to all approved cloud systems.

Controls/ requirements	Description	Example
Information category	Please provide a list of the types of information covered by this policy. Use best practices for data classification to label the data that your organization stores and processes.	This policy applies to all your customer data, personal data, and other organizational data classified as sensitive in accordance with the company's data classification policy. This policy applies to the following sensitive data types: **Data on identity and authentication**: • Cryptographic private keys • Passwords • Tables of hashes **Financial information**: • Receipts • Payroll information • Revenue figures • Accounts receivable information **Personal data**: • Names and addresses • Social security numbers • State-issued driver's license number • Identification card number issued by the government • Financial account numbers, including the security code, access code, or password that allows access to the account • Medical and/or health insurance information

Controls/ requirements	Description	Example
Responsibility and ownership	List all roles related to cloud security actions, controls, and procedures in this section. Cloud security administrators, data owners, users, and cloud providers are a few examples. Describe each role and the responsibilities that come with it for safe cloud usage and security upkeep.	Consider the following questions when putting together this list: • *Who is making use of the cloud?* • *Who is in charge of cloud service maintenance on both the organizational and provider levels?* • *Who is accountable for cloud security?* • *Who is in charge of choosing new cloud solutions?* • *Who is in charge of major decisions?*
Use of cloud computing services in a secure manner	This section defines the conditions for using cloud services in an acceptable manner.	Prior to purchase and deployment, all cloud-based services must be approved. The following steps must be taken to ensure secure adoption and use of cloud services: • The organization's needs and priorities should be identified. • Define internal and external service users. • Decide on the type of cloud service to use, including physical and operational characteristics for SaaS, PaaS, and IaaS solutions. • Specify the data types that will be saved. • Identify the security solutions and configurations required for encryption, monitoring, backups, and other functions. • Compile a list of previous security incidents that have involved this cloud provider.

Controls/ require- ments	Description	Example
		<ul><li>Request any security certifications that are available.</li><li>Obtain copies of all agreements, including SLAs, with the provider.</li></ul>
Risk analysis	In this section, you will integrate your cloud security policy with the risk assessment policy of your organization. Define the scope of the risk assessment and the timeline.	Data from the *sensitive* tier of the *data classification policy* must be accessible for discovery and audit at all times, according to regulations. These compliance requirements must be followed by the cloud providers. At the following times, the *Cloud Security Administrator* and the IT *Security* team shall conduct a risk assessment:<ul><li>Following the deployment of a new cloud service</li><li>Following significant enhancements or updates to an existing cloud service</li><li>After any changes to the cloud service's configuration</li><li>In the aftermath of a security event or incident</li><li>Every quarter for all current cloud services</li></ul>The following must be included in the cloud security risk assessment:<ul><li>Internal and external audit outcomes</li><li>Risk and vulnerability assessment</li><li>Observance of regulations</li></ul>

Controls/ require- ments	Description	Example
Security measures	The *cloud security policy* specifies the various security components available to and used by the organization. It should include both internal controls and cloud service provider security controls, as well as specific groups of requirements such as technical and control requirements, mobile security r e q u i r e m e n t s , physical security requirements, and security, and controls assurance practices.	The *Cloud Security Administrator* shall review each *service-level agreement*, as well as request and analyze the cloud provider's security audits, at the time of cloud service implementation and quarterly thereafter. **Prerequisites for technical security controls** <ul><li>Audit attempts to access any device on the company network</li><li>Permissions for files and folders in Windows NTFS</li><li>Access model based on roles</li><li>Access to the server</li><li>Firewall access rights</li><li>Network zone and VLAN access control list</li><li>Web authentication rights</li><li>Database access rights and ACLs</li><li>Rest and in-flight encryption</li><li>Segregation of networks</li></ul> **Security requirements for mobile devices** Mobile security controls to prevent malware infection on company mobile devices and privately owned devices used to access the organization's cloud services must be included in cloud security. Any device discovered to be lacking anti-malware protection will be quarantined.

Controls/ require- ments	Description	Example
		Requirements for physical security The data center's interior temperature must be monitored by the company. Make sure the owner of physical security is notified right away if the temperature deviates more than 5 *degrees* from the baseline.
Recovering from a secu- rity incident	This section establishes priorities for cloud service and data recovery and contains rules for determining the areas for assessment in the event of a security incident.	The *IT Security Department* or the *Incident Response Team* must produce and manage daily incident reports. The IT *Security Department* shall produce weekly reports detailing all incidents and deliver them to the IT *Manager* or *Director*. High-priority incidents discovered by the *IT Security Department* must be escalated immediately and the IT *Manager* contacted as soon as possible. In addition, the IT *Security Department* must produce a monthly report detailing the number of IT *security incidents* and the percentage of them that were resolved.
Awareness	This section specifies how frequently the organization should conduct security training, who must pass the training, and who is in charge of conducting the training.	All cloud service users must receive quarterly security training from the *IT Security Management* office. To maintain permission and access to cloud services, all users must complete security training.
Enforce- ment	This section describes the policy violations' penalties and how they will be enforced.	Employees who attempt to use unauthorized services will have their access privileges revoked until they complete security training.

Controls/ require- ments	Description	Example
Reference documents	This section contains a list of all documents pertaining to cloud security policies and procedures.	<ul><li>Data security policy</li><li>Policy for data classification</li><li>Security policy</li><li>Policy on risk assessment</li><li>Security policy</li><li>Policy on workstation security</li><li>Policy on incident response</li><li>Data processing agreement</li></ul>

Table 7.1*: Cloud security policy template*

Shared responsibility model

Cloud service providers use a *shared security responsibility model*, which means that your security team retains some security responsibilities as you migrate *applications, data, containers,* and *workloads* to the cloud, while the provider assumes some, but not all, of the responsibility. To reduce the risk of introducing vulnerabilities into your *public, hybrid,* and *multi-cloud environments,* it is critical to define the line between your responsibilities and those of your providers.

In a traditional data center model, you are in charge of security throughout your entire operating environment, including applications, physical servers, user controls, and even physical building security. Your cloud provider provides valuable relief to your teams in a cloud environment by sharing many operational burdens, including security. Security ownership must be clearly defined in this shared responsibility model, with each party maintaining complete control over the *assets, processes,* and *functions* that they own. You can maintain a secure environment with less operational overhead by collaborating with your cloud provider and sharing portions of the security responsibilities.

Defining a thin line of responsibility

Understanding where your provider's responsibility ends and yours begins is critical to a successful security implementation in a cloud environment. The answer isn't always obvious, and definitions of the shared responsibility security model vary depending on the service provider and whether you're using **infrastructure-as-a-service (IaaS)** or **platform-as-a-service (PaaS)**:

- AWS claims responsibility for *protecting the hardware, software, networking, and facilities that run AWS cloud services* under the AWS *Shared Security model*. The reference URL is mentioned in the *References* section.

- Microsoft Azure claims physical host, network, and data center security ownership. Both AWS and *Azure* state that the services you choose will determine your retained security responsibilities. The reference URL is mentioned in the *References* section.

While the language is similar, shared responsibility agreements leave a lot of room for debate and interpretation. However, some aspects of security are clearly owned by the provider, while others are always retained by you. Security responsibilities differ depending on the cloud provider and service type for the services, applications, and controls that exist between those ownership layers. These variations in ownership introduce complexity and risk in a multi-cloud environment. For security assessment and monitoring, each environment, application, and service necessitates a distinct approach. Your overall security posture, however, is defined by your weakest link. If there is a coverage gap in any one system, it increases vulnerability across the entire stack and out to any connected systems.

Your contribution to cloud security responsibilities

You are always responsible for securing what is under your direct control, whether in the data center or via a SaaS, IaaS, or PaaS cloud service:

- **Control over information and data**: By keeping control over information and data, you can control how and when your data is used. Your provider has no access to your data and all data access is intended to be controlled by you.

- **Application logic and code**: No matter how you spin up cloud resources, your proprietary applications are yours to secure and control throughout the application lifecycle. This includes protecting your code repositories from malicious misuse or intrusion, performing application build testing throughout the development and integration process, ensuring secure production access, and ensuring the security of any connected systems.

- **Identity and access**: You are in charge of all aspects of **identity and access management (IAM)**, such as *authentication* and *authorization mechanisms*, **single sign-on (SSO)**, **multi-factor authentication (MFA)**, *access keys, certificates, user creation processes*, and *password management*.

- **Platform and resource configuration**: You control the operating environment when you spin up cloud environments. Controlling those environments differs depending on whether they are server-based or serverless. A *server-based instance* necessitates more hands-on security controls, such as OS *and application hardening*, OS *and application patch management*, and so on. In essence, your cloud-based server instances behave similarly to physical servers and serve as an extension of your data center.

You are also responsible for securing everything in your organization that connects to the cloud, including your on-premises infrastructure stack and user devices, owned networks and applications, and the communication layers that connect your internal and external users to the cloud and to each other. You'll also need to set up your own monitoring and alerting for security threats, incidents, and responses to domains that you still have control over. These are your responsibilities whether you're using AWS, Azure, or another public cloud provider's systems.

Understanding the shared responsibility model's grey zones

Depending on whether you're running an IaaS or PaaS implementation, you may have additional security responsibilities, or your provider may relieve you of some of those responsibilities. The distinction between your responsibilities and those of your cloud vendor is determined by the services you choose and the terms of those services.

When it comes to *server-based instances*, you frequently take full responsibility for:

- **Identity and directory infrastructure**: Whether you use OS-level identity directories, such as *Microsoft Active Directory* or *LDAP* on Linux, or a third-party identity directory solution, the security configuration and monitoring of that system are under your control in an IaaS cloud implementation.

- **Applications**: Just like on-premises hosts, server-based cloud environments are a blank slate for installing and maintaining applications and workloads. Running PaaS applications on your cloud servers may relieve you of some of the security burdens. Any application or workload that you migrate from your data center to a server-based instance in the cloud, on the other hand, is entirely your responsibility to secure.

- **Network controls**: Your provider is only responsible for the network under their direct control. All networking above the virtualization layer requires your security configuration and monitoring, whether physical or *infrastructure-as-code*.

- **Operating system**: You can select your operating system and patch levels with server-based instances. While this gives you more flexibility, it also means more responsibility for security. To keep your server-based cloud resources secure, you'll need to stay current on vulnerabilities, security patches, and environment hardening exercises.

A shared responsibility model in operation

When discussing *shared responsibility*, keep in mind that you and your cloud provider will never share responsibility for a single aspect of security operations. The areas of ownership that you control are solely yours, and your provider has no say in how you secure your systems. Similarly, you have no say in how the provider secures their portions of the application and infrastructure stack. You do, however, have the ability and right to view your cloud vendor's audit reports in order to ensure that their systems are secure and that they are following your terms of service. Cloud providers publish these reports on a *regular* and *free* basis, and the most recent reports are always available.

Shared responsibility with the development team

Cloud services provide easy, automated environment provisioning, allowing developers and test teams to spin up servers via self-service processes. These environments, while beneficial in terms of innovation, are frequently linked to your production assets and can pose significant security risks if not properly configured. While the cloud is inherently secure from the perspective of the provider, a secure cloud necessitates proper configuration and vigilant access management. According to *Gartner*, misconfiguration is to blame for 99% of cloud security failures. Cloud development and testing environments that are not set up with proper security policies can serve as a gateway into your production systems or proprietary code storage for would-be hackers. This means that identity and access management, as well as environment configuration management, must be closely monitored, sometimes at the expense of unrestricted convenience. The success of your cloud security implementation depends on centralized, automated access management and policy-driven environment creation.

Cloud applications, powered by an automated *CI/CD pipeline* and driven by a **DevOps** organization, accelerate the rate at which your company delivers new applications and features. Unfortunately, this means that without proper consideration and management, your DevOps pipeline may inadvertently and rapidly introduce security vulnerabilities. In a *shared responsibility model*, you are responsible for securing your code as well as the tools you use to deliver applications to the cloud. The servers and serverless assets that comprise your DevOps tool chain must be secured, including *code repositories, Docker image registries, Jenkins orchestration tools*, and so on. Beyond securing your CI/CD pipeline, you can and should use *CI/CD automation processes* to shift security left by integrating security into the code and making it part of the build. In order to find new vulnerabilities and fix them before they are merged into the main code tree or added to the production service, the term *shifting left* refers to automating testing against well-defined security requirements early and frequently in the development process.

Automating the shared responsibility model

Effective cloud management consolidates your security responsibilities on a single platform, providing shared responsibility model automation controls and compliance across all of your servers, containers, IaaS, and PaaS in any *public, private, hybrid*, or *multi-cloud environment*. In order to provide *complete, effective*, and *efficient security*, your security solution should include the eight key features listed as follows:

- **Unified**: Traditional security tools frequently fail to meet the diverse and unique requirements of a complex, shared-responsibility cloud security environment. You end up tying together several different tools without a unified security solution, which can lead to operational complexity, unnecessary redundancy, and potential coverage gaps.

  A unified cloud security platform streamlines operational processes for continuous monitoring, automatic detection of cloud compromise, and network traffic visualization, and automates compliance management across IaaS services, virtual and bare-metal servers, containers, and Kubernetes environments. A *cloud security platform* designed specifically for the cloud provides a comprehensive set of configurable tools as well as the flexibility required to close gaps, improve security posture, and adapt as your infrastructure grows and changes.

- **Automated**: As your environment grows in size and complexity, keeping track of all the various moving parts becomes increasingly difficult. Automation based on the shared responsibility model provides *consistent speed* and *consistency* while freeing up staff time to focus on strategic goals rather than repetitive tasks. When a new service, environment, or application is created, your cloud security automation platform should automate asset discovery and monitor and deploy sensors automatically.

  You'll also need integration with your DevOps tools to automatically fail builds when new vulnerabilities are introduced, assign new issues automatically, and monitor the development pipeline for remediation.

With a comprehensive, shared responsibility model automation in place, you can centralize and simplify your cloud security integration and operations across systems and solutions with varying security concerns. Cloud security automation effectively allows security to shift left into the development process, enabling the adoption of a **DevSecOps** culture.

- **Movable**: With the rate of change in technology, saying *no* to a better solution when it comes along is no longer an option. Everything in your application infrastructure must be portable, from the code you write to the containers you configure to security. When you move a workload or application stack from one cloud to another, your share of the shared responsibilities may change. Your security solution must operate seamlessly across any *public, private, hybrid,* or *multi-cloud environment*, with as few changes as possible required during lift-and-shift operations and when switching from one cloud service provider to another.

  Some cloud security platforms automate and integrate via bi-directional REST APIs, ensuring that security sensors and the policy checks they perform migrate seamlessly with workloads during cloud or on-premises architecture migration. Your policies are enforced throughout your CI/CD workflows through automation, and compliance is enforced based on pre-established rules and standards, regardless of the intended production environment. These controls enable you to identify and address potential vulnerabilities before they become security holes.

- **Comprehensive**: Your contribution to the shared responsibility model includes a wide range of requirements, such as *asset discovery, inventory, assessment, remediation, threat detection, micro-segmentation, traffic discovery,* and *continuous compliance*. If you have separate tools for each of those security domains, you risk operational headaches and, worse, the very real possibility of introducing blind spots and gaps.

  To reduce operational burdens, comprehensive cloud security should address all of these requirements and automate as much of the security management as possible. You should be able to quickly and efficiently deploy security controls across all of your *cloud servers, environments,* and *containers*. You can better monitor and evaluate security across your public and private clouds, and even across your data center infrastructure, with comprehensive cloud security that includes the right sensors, registry connectors, and APIs that work together, and unify security management while decreasing operational complexity.

- **Automation and optimization**: Everything about the cloud is about making things *simple, automated, quick,* and practically *optimizing* the overall landscape. The demand for fast, integrated security grows as CI/CD pipelines deliver microservices and features to the cloud in *real-time*. Your security processes must not become a bottleneck in your development team's delivery schedule. Instead, you must provide high-speed deployment, telemetry, and analytics that keep up with the speed of DevOps.

When properly designed, automated, distributed security offloads processing and accelerates security control, allowing you to ensure compliance without affecting system performance or deployment cadence. *Security automation* built for the cloud is designed to maintain security coverage even as infrastructure and workload scale. Once you've defined your security policies, you should be able to quickly add or remove assets without any additional, hands-on configuration.

- **Integrated**: The issue with legacy security solutions is that they *bolt on* to cloud environments rather than working in tandem with your cloud infrastructure and workloads. These *non-cloud-based solutions* increase manual tasks and complicate monitoring. Cloud security integrates directly with cloud infrastructure and ensures consistency and compliance without the need for manual intervention.

  Integrating security into your DevOps processes and workflows via APIs enables you to auto-scale your security implementation up and out as needed and in parallel with your growth without becoming a bottleneck for the CI/CD pipeline. You can enforce security coverage for your code repositories, build and test processes, production deployment, and remediation processes with the right SDK and integrations with popular CI/CD tools like **Jenkins**, **Jira**, and **ServiceNow**. This early detection and intervention via security automation gives you feedback on *alerts* and allows you to address potential vulnerabilities and misconfigurations before they become production security events.

- **Scalable**: While nothing is truly *infinite*, cloud resources come close. When you reach the limits of your current cloud infrastructure, unlike in a bare-metal data center, you simply ask for more, and it is provided. That means your security solution must scale automatically and instantly to keep up with the rapid and dynamic changes in the cloud.

  However, scaling up is not always possible. Cloud resources also offer a valuable opportunity to use resources only when they are needed and then release them when demand declines. This elasticity should be reflected in your cloud security so that you only use what you need in real-time, and your security implementation should always match your cloud footprint.

DLP solution in cloud

Data Loss Prevention (DLP) is a method of reducing the likelihood of data theft or unauthorized exposure by protecting sensitive data at rest, in transit, and on endpoints. DLP solutions aim to keep *sensitive* data and *confidential* information safe from unauthorized storage, use, or transfer.

Cloud DLP solutions, in particular, protect organizations that have adopted cloud storage by ensuring that sensitive data does not enter the cloud without first being encrypted and that it is only sent to authorized cloud applications. Most cloud DLP solutions remove or alter classified or sensitive data before sharing files to the cloud to ensure data security while in transit and storage.

The following image (*Figure 7.1*) will give you a quick brief understanding of how DLP scans and blocks sensitive information:

Figure 7.1: *DLP positioning and working model*

Cloud DLP protects an organization's sensitive or critical information from cyber-attacks, insider threats, and accidental exposure. Cloud DLP solutions provide *visibility* and protection for *sensitive* data in SaaS and IaaS applications. Please note that the primary capability of a **Cloud Access Security Broker (CASB)** is cloud DLP.

Challenges without cloud DLP

Organizations that do not use a cloud DLP solution leave cloud data protection to their cloud storage providers. However, issues can arise when those providers fail to implement security measures commensurate with the organizations' data protection requirements, such as *not providing cloud encryption, multi-factor authentication,* or *strict access controls.* Furthermore, a breach at a cloud storage provider can result in a breach of an organization's data if the organization did not take precautions to secure it before sending it to the cloud.

There are enough challenges associated with cloud storage providers handling cloud data protection that many organizations prefer to be proactive in protecting their data in the cloud by implementing a cloud DLP solution to secure their sensitive and confidential information, rather than relying on cloud services providers that their DLP and other security measures are adequate for meeting company security requirements and compliance standards.

Benefits of cloud DLP

Data is being jeopardized today as organizations migrate to the cloud and employees work from various locations, accessing corporate files from anywhere and at any time. Employees use the cloud to collaborate, but they may use unapproved services and cloud storage apps. As a result, organizations must safeguard sensitive data not only on their own networks and devices but also in the cloud.

The following are some of the key benefits of leading cloud DLP solutions:

- Work with cloud storage providers to scan servers, identify sensitive data, and encrypt it before sharing it in the cloud.
- Scan existing cloud data and audit it at any time.
- Discover sensitive data in the cloud with precision.
- Constantly review uploaded files.
- Apply controls to sensitive data automatically (*prompt, block, encrypt*) in accordance with enterprise policies.
- Notify appropriate administrators and data owners immediately when data is compromised.
- Maintain the necessary visibility and control to comply with privacy and data protection regulations.

Protecting sensitive data through encryption

The process of encoding and transforming data prior to transferring it to the cloud is referred to as **cloud encryption**. Using mathematical algorithms, this process converts plaintext data into cipher text, rendering the data unreadable to unauthorized and potentially malicious users.

Cloud encryption is a simple yet effective method for preventing unauthorized access to sensitive cloud data in the event of a breach. Even if the data is *stolen*, cybercriminals are unable to read the encrypted files' contents. Many experts consider encryption to be a successful and effective method of ensuring strong data security.

Simply put, encryption scrambles the content of business databases, systems, and files so that *deciphering* it without the correct decryption key is impossible. Cloud storage is quickly becoming the most popular method of storing enterprise data while ensuring maximum availability and redundancy. By combining encryption and cloud storage, businesses can secure encryption keys while maintaining complete control over sensitive data access.

The fact that encrypted cloud data is unreadable without proper authorization is perhaps its most significant advantage. This means that it is ineffective unless the party with unauthorized access also possesses the correct decryption key.

Simply put, encryption scrambles the content of business databases, systems, and files so that deciphering it without the correct decryption key is impossible. Cloud storage is quickly becoming the most popular method of storing enterprise data while ensuring maximum availability and redundancy. By combining encryption and cloud storage, businesses can secure encryption keys while maintaining complete control over sensitive data access.

The fact that encrypted cloud data is unreadable without proper authorization is perhaps its most significant advantage. This means that it is ineffective unless the party with unauthorized access also possesses the correct decryption key. Cloud encryption solutions typically have multiple applications. These are some examples:

- Encrypting *cloud-to-endpoint* connections
- Restricted encryption of sensitive data
- Encrypting all data from inception to storage from beginning to end

To facilitate safe data decryption, all models typically involve cloud storage vendors encrypting information upon receipt and transmitting the encryption keys to clients.

Cloud encryption can be a simple process if done correctly. Cloud encryption can help organizations improve data privacy, enable remote work flexibility, and ensure regulatory compliance. Let's look at some of the advantages of cloud encryption:

- **Ensures continuous data protection**: In general, enterprise data is most vulnerable when it is transferred or stored in a *third-party environment*, such as a cloud server. Cloud encryption protects both data at rest and data in transit. As workflow structures become more flexible and employees stretch their shifts and shuffle their devices or locations, data must be protected around the clock. If not, there is a good chance that it will be accessed by unscrupulous elements looking to cause harm to the enterprise.

- **Insider threat is reduced**: External factors are not the only risk factor for an organization's data security, particularly during remote work when scrutiny is stretched thin and monitoring is not always effective.

Employees, business partners, and contractors with malicious intent can wreak even more havoc than a non-affiliated cybercriminal if they choose to do so. However, it is not always on purpose. An employee who is not well-versed in technology may make unintentional mistakes that expose the organization's data to unauthorized access and cause harm to the enterprise.

While cloud encryption is not a substitute for carelessness or a lack of training, it does aid in the transfer of enterprise data to an experienced and trustworthy cloud service provider. This adds another layer of security and helps to keep employees from causing harm to the company.

- **Keeps the organization's integrity**: We have seen an increase in the frequency of cyber-attacks in recent years, particularly in the *healthcare, banking and finance, education*, and *government sectors*. This is due to a shift toward storing data in the cloud rather than on local databases, which can no longer be accessed by employees working remotely. Cloud databases use wired and wireless technologies to connect and provide a simple way to store large amounts of data, such as employee, customer, sales, and financial records. However, the growing popularity of remote workplaces has provided cybercriminals with a plethora of new opportunities to exploit the shortcomings of cloud computing platforms.

Unencrypted cloud data is vulnerable to unauthorized access because hackers disguise malicious packets as local traffic and illegally introduce them into organizational cloud databases. Furthermore, cybercriminals can benefit from data modification in order to commit fraud. When cloud data is encrypted, however, stealing or modifying it becomes nearly impossible.

Cloud encryption methods

Cloud encryption solutions *encrypt* and *decrypt* data using two methods: **symmetric** and **asymmetric**. These methods, also known as **encryption algorithms**, are described further as follows.

Symmetric algorithm

As the symmetric algorithm cloud encryption method employs the same keys for encryption and decryption, it is ideal for *closed* organizational systems. This technique, also referred to as the **secret key algorithm method**, secures all forms of communication using keys. This method is best suited for data encryption in bulk. The main benefits of this method are its quick and simple hardware implementation and faster encryption. Any employee with access to the secret key, on the other hand, can decrypt encrypted sensitive data using that same key, even if the data is not intended for them.

Figure 7.2 depicts the methodology of the symmetric method:

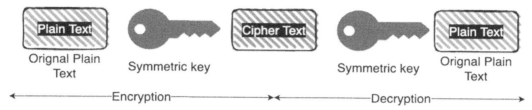

Figure **7.2**: *Symmetric method of encryption*

Asymmetric algorithm

The asymmetric algorithm method employs two mathematically linked keys, one *private* and the other *public*. As the name implies, the keys in this method are *asymmetric* — they are not the same even though they are paired with each other. These private keys are only shared by cloud encryption solutions with relevant authorities within the organization, often via a *secure communication channel*.

These keys must be kept secret because they can be used to decrypt all encrypted data. However, public keys are shared with all relevant stakeholders, both inside and outside the organization, to enable data encryption before transmission. The following diagram (*Figure* 7.3) explains the methodology of asymmetric encryption:

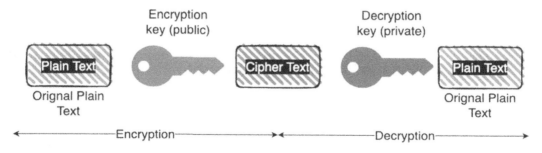

Figure **7.3**: *Asymmetric method of encryption*

Best practices for encryption management in the cloud

Data protection has always been a top priority for businesses, and as remote work becomes more popular in the coming year (2021), more efficient methods to safeguard sensitive enterprise data are required. *Figure* 7.4 will give you a quick glimpse of the benefits one can get while adopting encryption solutions to the landscape:

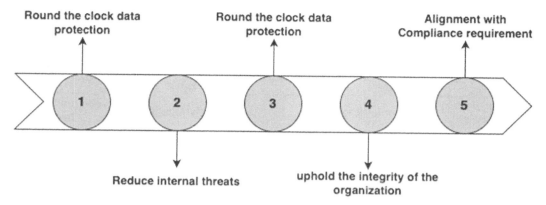

Figure 7.4: *Benefits of adopting an encryption solution*

The following best practices for cloud data encryption help ensure strengthened *privacy* and *security* at all levels within and outside an organization, as well as that the company's information is secure on the cloud:

- **Determine security requirements for cloud deployment**: Begin by identifying the organizational data that requires encryption and developing a strategy for prioritizing databases that are more *sensitive*. This plan should ideally be detailed enough to be shared and discussed with the chosen cloud encryption service provider.

  When evaluating the various features provided by cloud encryption providers, look for service interface access that is restricted to authenticated and authorized personnel only. The provider must provide authentication and identity features such as *username, password*, TLS *client certificates, two-factor authentication*, and *identity federation* with the enterprise's current identity provider.

  Assure the ability to restrict access to a *dedicated enterprise, line*, or *community network*. To avoid encryption keys falling into the wrong hands, it is critical to avoid vendors who use insecure authentication practices. Failure to do so exposes company systems to cybercriminals looking to steal data, modify information, or launch denial-of-service attacks.

  Since email, phone, and HTTP are vulnerable to social engineering attacks and the interception of authentication or identity credentials, the cloud encryption vendor should not rely on them for authentication. To ensure complete security, a genuine cloud encryption vendor will provide authentication through secure channels such as **HTTPS**.

- **Before selecting a CSP, deep dive analysis of their services**: Reading the user agreement usually allows the client company to understand the specifics of the plan offered by the **cloud service provider (CSP)**. Ensure that this agreement is reviewed by knowledgeable personnel from multiple departments and that adequate time is allowed for input and questions to be shared. If any information is omitted from the user agreement, ensure that clarification is sought regarding details, particularly *when*, *how*, and *where* data will be stored, especially in the case of public cloud services. Any aspect of the user agreement that may end up violating the enterprise's privacy policy or the regulations to which it is subject should be highlighted immediately.

  Examining the contracts and SLAs of potential cloud encryption providers is an essential part of cybersecurity. These two elements provide the strongest guarantees of recourse in the event of adversity. A cloud encryption contract's terms, conditions, appendices, and annexes can have a significant impact on a company's cybersecurity.

  Examining the contracts and SLAs of potential cloud encryption providers is an essential part of cybersecurity. These two elements provide the strongest guarantees of recourse in the event of adversity. A cloud encryption contract's terms, conditions, appendices, and annexes can have a significant impact on a company's cybersecurity.

- **To ensure access, use cloud cryptography**: Cloud cryptography solutions safeguard an enterprise's cloud architecture and provide a layer of encryption based on the *Quantum Direct Key system*, allowing secure access to shared cloud users. Cloud cryptography provides enhanced privacy and data security by utilizing cryptographic keys.

- **Leveraging CASB to protect data in transit and at rest**: Through API connectors and proxies, a **cloud access security broker (CASB)** facilitates *secure* connections between users and cloud applications. CASBs enable businesses to gain greater control over cloud data encryption, encryption keys, visibility, and access to cloud-based applications. CASB solutions act as a *go-between* for the enterprise and its CSPs, providing visibility into the cloud environment, effectively implementing data safety policies, ensuring effective threat detection and protection, and ensuring regulatory compliance. CASBs are quickly becoming a best practice in cloud security.

- **Choose a CSP that offers comprehensive encryption**: Some cloud encryption providers also offer local encryption, which adds an extra layer of security during data creation and transfer. When selecting a cloud encryption service provider, make sure it protects data in transit from the end-user level. Simultaneously, ensure the implementation of network protection that prevents data interception at the corporate level. It is always preferable to use a cloud vendor that provides encryption in transit and at rest from the moment data is created.

Policy enforcement in cloud

Defining organizational policy is useless unless implemented throughout your organization. A critical component of any cloud migration strategy is determining how to best combine the cloud platform's tools with your existing IT processes to maximize policy compliance across your entire cloud estate.

As your cloud estate expands, so will the need to maintain and enforce policy across a wider range of resources and subscriptions. As your estate grows and your organization's policy requirements become more stringent, the scope of your policy enforcement processes must broaden to ensure consistent policy adherence and rapid violation detection.

For smaller cloud estates, platform-provided policy enforcement mechanisms at the *resource* or *subscription* level are usually sufficient. Larger deployments require a broader enforcement scope and may necessitate more sophisticated enforcement mechanisms such as *deployment standards*, *resource grouping*, *organization*, and *integration policy enforcement* with your logging and reporting systems.

Your organization's cloud governance requirements, the size and nature of your cloud estate, and how your organization is represented in your subscription design are the primary factors in determining the scope of your policy enforcement processes. An increase in enforcement scope may be justified by an increase in the size of your estate or a greater need to manage policy enforcement centrally.

Policy enforcement in the multi-cloud landscape

Almost every process necessitates some kind of policy to explain the desired outcome. This is especially true in computing, where policies define what we want systems and people to do. Policies can be designed to govern data, business processes, or both, and must comply with *internal* and *external* regulations. For example, data scientists working on clinical drug trials may be restricted to only seeing data related to the projects to which they are currently assigned as a business policy, as well as to meet various industry-specific compliance requirements.

One of the primary policy challenges in the cloud landscape is *translating natural language* into a *coherent machine policy* that can be executed by a system. This is frequently a time-consuming process that begins with collaboration among various departments and stakeholders within the organization, including business owners, information security staff, application developers, auditors, and even legal representation. The final step is typically performed by someone with technical expertise who can translate the roles and policies from English into machine language.

Meanwhile, enforcing the policies is particularly difficult because they span all *four* planes of the IT stack: *business applications*, *platforms (on-premises and cloud)*, *data systems*, and the *network*. They must also be updated and modified over time. Some policies will be fairly stable, while others may change every day or several times per day.

In centralized IT environments, this process is difficult enough. When an organization uses a distributed infrastructure, such as multiple clouds, policies must sync with both on-premises and cloud identity systems, which each speak a different language. Here are a few things to think about when implementing consistent policies in multi-cloud environments:

- **Abstraction** is used to decouple applications from their underlying cloud platforms. This removes the need to write policies in the proprietary language of each platform's identity management system.

- Take policies from each identity management system and summarize them. This will enable policies to be managed independently of the enforcement platform. Policies, for example, can be created and modified in a single administrative function.

- Use an orchestration platform to distribute policies, update them as needed, and provide audit capabilities. These platforms employ an abstraction layer to connect your distributed identity and access components into the fabric of services that can be configured and managed centrally. Identity orchestration ensures that all of the various steps of identity management take place in the most efficient order possible by utilizing elements from the abstraction layer to perform specific operations in a specific order.

Policy enforcement has always presented unique challenges for businesses. However, the widespread adoption of *cloud*, *multi-cloud*, and *hybrid cloud* environments has added layers of complexity and interoperability barriers that cannot be easily addressed using traditional, centralized approaches.

Using a distributed approach to policy management and enforcement, along with new interoperability standards, not only bridges the gap between old and new identity systems but also supports the unification of multiple cloud platforms.

User awareness of cloud policies

Cloud Computing Services for Awareness and Training are formal methods of informing employees and stakeholders. Read the *blog* for more information on these terms. Cloud security is now required to prevent cyber-attacks. Web-based systems are used by businesses to send messages and share information. Businesses have begun to use cloud security to reduce operational risks. Furthermore, cloud computing services have altered how services are managed. To gain access to cloud data, hackers employ a variety of techniques. To avoid such problems, you should understand how cloud security works. Let's talk about some cloud security facts.

Cloud security training

Employees are educated about computer system security through cloud security awareness. You can protect data from criminals by using cloud computing services. Furthermore, it is a method of providing a high-level overview of policies that explain how cloud security works. Businesses should implement effective security awareness and training programs. To reach more employees, businesses must employ novel methods. Furthermore, cloud security protects the digital system. Avoiding security risks will aid in the development of a solid brand reputation.

Important elements

Cyber security awareness programs should effectively reach workers. The cloud security strategy has four components. Let's examine them more closely:

- **Follow-up messages**: This messaging serves as a reminder to employers about cybersecurity policies. Furthermore, it is a way to refresh the information on how to avoid and identify security risks. As a result, you will be able to handle potential security issues and alerts using messaging.

- **Content variety**: A variety of educational content is one of the four components of the cloud. The content should range from written materials to online learning. Furthermore, educational content should include lessons with varying degrees of difficulty. Workers have access to audio and visual information. Employees will benefit from easier access to the most relevant information.

- **Reporting and measuring**: One of the four components of a cloud is measuring and reporting worker participation in training. Furthermore, it would be useful for increasing organizational awareness and training. You will be able to identify and strengthen program flaws.

- **Testing**: Testing is a method of assessing the performance of the enterprise workforce. With proper cloud computing service testing, you can address a variety of security issues.

Best practices around awareness and training in the cloud landscape

Security should be a top priority in the cloud, especially since data breaches are on the rise and risks can be exacerbated by inexperience. The public cloud pushes businesses toward self-service, and this includes security.

It is the responsibility of the entire IT staff to protect an organization and its data. It takes time and investment to build a security plan, support continuous education, and implement processes and frameworks to grow and mature in-house security. Prepare your IT staff, including non-experts, by using these cloud security best practices.

Employees must be educated and trained

If your company intends to migrate to the cloud, you must establish a cloud-education standard for both technical and business users.

This can be accomplished through a combination of on-site and online training. It's also beneficial to provide access to various resources, such as webinars and conferences, to keep up with ever-changing security threats. For all of your employees involved in the migration, start with entry-level cloud certifications like **AWS Cloud Practitioner**. The best cloud security comes from an educated user base, and these certifications are a good place to start.

The next step, depending on your staffing makeup, is to consider more technical cloud security training for experienced developers and operations staff. With the **AWS Solutions Architect** certificates, as well as the **CompTIA Cloud+** and **Certified Cloud Security Professional exams**, we have seen clients successfully transfer skills to the cloud.

Staff should be educated on internal cloud security best practices and management processes. Ensure that all security documentation is accessible to employees via a centralized repository.

Finally, and most importantly, include your cloud-savvy employees in any discussions with your provider as you plan your migration. They understand the *company's technical debt, which is and isn't documented*, and *have participated in compliance audits*. These are people who are intimately familiar with your operational realities.

Make your staff cloud-ready

When an enterprise moves to the cloud, the roles of IT staff change, and teams must be able to translate their responsibilities to their new environments so that security does not fall through the cracks. *Database administrators*, for example, must implement new data backup processes and tools. They should keep secure, offsite backups of their company's data. It must be easily retrievable in the event that its cloud storage is held for ransom, compromised, or destroyed.

Changes will also be required for software developers' tasks. They may need to modify their application design process to emphasize a security-first mindset; integrate cloud-based identity access management into their applications from the start, and incorporate automated security testing into the development processes.

Finally, you must devise a strategy for your developers to start implementing DevOps practices in order to best support your cloud application development, operations, and maintenance efforts.

Your associates can either become your strongest line of defence... or your weakest link, the choice is yours.

Building an effective cybersecurity team

Today's businesses must give top priority to cyber security. In the past, most businesses only required a physical security team, but in the modern, technologically advanced world, they now require much more. Today, a weak cybersecurity team could easily expose an organization's assets to risk without the need for criminals to enter the company's property. Effective cybersecurity teams have the potential to safeguard company assets and keep up with cybercriminals.

It's difficult to create and run an efficient cybersecurity team. Team members must be able to collaborate on frequently challenging and intricate tasks that could have an impact on the entire organization. It can be difficult to put together a *resilient*, *effective*, and *knowledgeable* cybersecurity team, but once you do, the team will be very powerful.

Putting together an effective cybersecurity team

Successful cybersecurity teams require proactive action and can be built from the ground up or reconfigured from existing teams to be more beneficial and effective to your company. Of course, technical abilities are essential. Fortunately, if you already have a team in place, you will have a good idea of each professional's current level of expertise. Professional certifications are a great way for those who are building from the ground up to determine the proficiency of potential team members. When forming a team, technical ability isn't the only factor to consider.

Here are some additional, equally important steps to consider:

- **Define key team roles**: When forming or reorganizing a cybersecurity team, the first step is to define the roles that will be required and create a clear separation of responsibilities for each. Some of these roles may already exist on your team. If this is the case, make certain that each member's responsibilities have been properly identified.

- **Decide on a training program and a career**: Members of your cybersecurity team need to have career development funding. This entails determining training paths that will enable your team to stay current on the most recent threats, instruments, and methodologies. Because cyber threats are intricate and dynamic, your team must keep their skills current.

  The best cybersecurity talent will be easier to recruit and keep on staff if you have development plans for your team. When you let your best employees know that their future matters to you, they are more likely to stay with you. Continuous professional learning, in the opinion of many cybersecurity experts, is essential for career advancement.

- **First, look within**: Don't be too quick to post a job advertisement for new cybersecurity employees. Instead, examine your internal options carefully. Current employees are frequently *underutilized* and *undervalued* assets when it comes to new job opportunities. Individual employees may experience very different results when incorporating existing team members into your new structure. Some may be well suited to their current role, while others may be better suited to other roles on the team. Some current team members may require additional training to update or refresh their skills, while others may wish to explore opportunities within an organization that is not related to the cybersecurity team. Additionally, employees from other departments may want to move to cybersecurity.

- **Take note of non-technical abilities**: Those with a variety of backgrounds and skill sets make up the most effective cybersecurity teams. To effectively address the complexities of cyber threats and attacks, you need people with unique perspectives. Look for professionals with abilities that go beyond technical; these include the ability to think critically and analytically, solve problems creatively, and work both independently and collaboratively.

- **Ascertain that the mission is understood**: Creating and communicating a clear organizational culture and purpose unites employees in pursuit of a common goal. Leaders of cybersecurity teams should instill the same values in their teams by focusing on the company's mission and objectives. Keeping members of the cybersecurity team informed improves working relationships with other departments and management. This ensures that everyone in the organization is working toward the same goals.

- **Consider the future**: Finally, it is critical to consider the long term. When putting together an effective and resilient cybersecurity team, you must be patient. Putting together a team that looks good on paper and works well together may require some trial and error.

Once your team is assembled

Once your team is put together, there are a few things to remember to ensure their utmost productivity. Talented security professionals seek employment with companies that will support them in honing their skills and advancing their careers. As a result, it's crucial to establish a positive and inspiring environment. You can keep your security team inspired and productive by using the following examples:

- **Understand the objectives of your team**: *Do you know what cybersecurity positions each member of your team is pursuing? Do they need to take a particular career path? Do they require additional education or certifications to accomplish their professional objectives?* It takes dialogue to provide answers to these questions. A successful team must have effective communication. You should communicate with your staff on a regular basis about both daily operations and their long-term aspirations and objectives. Such assistance demonstrates your appreciation for each team member and will boost morale and output. Schedule *one-on-one meetings* where you can ask employees to describe their potential career paths within your organization. This enables them to visualize their professional development within the organization and informs you of the best ways to support them as they progress along their chosen paths.

- **Encourage mentoring among employees**: Set up a mentoring program at your company if there isn't one already. One of the most encouraging and motivating things you can do for your team may be this. Both your team and the rest of the organization can benefit from mentoring. In a *mentoring program*, a more seasoned team member typically imparts knowledge and insights to a less experienced employee. This might appear in the IT department as a more seasoned worker assisting a less experienced one in getting ready for professional certification exams, promotions, and the like.

- **Acknowledge achievements**: It's crucial to give feedback, especially positive feedback, to cybersecurity team members. It shows the company is aware of the excellent work team members are doing and encourages them to feel confident and valued. You're not required to limit yourself to yearly performance reviews. Get used to praising and recognizing your valuable team members whenever a project is completed successfully when someone receives a promotion or new certification when a breach is avoided, or in any other circumstances.

- **Encourage industry training, conferences, exhibitions, and workshops to be attended**: It's also a good idea, if your budget allows, to pay for certification classes and exams for your team members. As previously stated, cybersecurity professionals prefer to work for organizations that prioritize training. Organizations should also encourage cybersecurity professionals to participate in *industry conferences, exhibitions,* and *workshops*. Every year, hundreds of these events take place all over the world, covering everything from ethical hacking to cloud computing to new trends and innovations in cybersecurity. Attendees will learn the most up-to-date information on current cybersecurity topics and will be able to apply them in the workplace. It benefits both the employee and the company.

Conclusion

You can create a solid cloud security policy for your organization using this cloud computing security policy, allowing you to protect sensitive data. Make the policy strong and feasible, and ensure that it is accessible, concise, and simple to understand at all levels of the organization.

When your cloud provider assumes some of the security responsibilities, your organization has one less thing to worry about. Clear shared responsibilities allow you to concentrate your efforts on your application delivery strategy without overburdening your teams with day-to-day operational concerns in the physical layer. A security platform that unifies and automates security controls across the data center and cloud simplifies security management and reduces risk. Centralized control and configuration provided by CSP which includes but not limited to hosting and container orchestration plays vital role in improving the overall security coverage for your environment.

End users or business staff can be the most effective line of defense in securing an organization's cloud environment if they are made aware of the risks. A thorough understanding of security practices and how to apply them could mean the difference between a secure enterprise network and one that is a prime target for cyber-attacks.

Every size company is susceptible to cybercriminals. Building a cybersecurity team that effectively safeguards the data and assets of your company is therefore essential. The professionals you've hired will be better able to mitigate situations when cyber threats and attacks are imminent if you follow the above advice for creating and inspiring your team.

In the next chapter, we will talk about various security services which are offered by different CSPs and MSPs in a SaaS format. We will also talk about the framework which is important for the Cloud SaaS stack.

Questions

1. Why is performing due diligence important before selecting a cloud service provider?

2. What are the critical due diligence parameters you should consider?

3. Define the importance of shared responsibility in the cloud landscape.

4. Why should you automate shared responsibility?

5. Explain the major key considerations while adopting an automated shared responsibility model.

6. Explain the working principle of DLP and its importance in cloud.

7. What is the difference between symmetric and asymmetric encryption?

8. What are the benefits of encryption solutions for your landscape?

9. Describe a few of the best practices for encryption management in the cloud.

10. How do you enforce policy to a multi-cloud setup?

11. Why is training and user awareness important to maintain a matured cloud ecosystem?

References

- https://aws.amazon.com/compliance/shared-responsibility-model/
- https://learn.microsoft.com/en-us/azure/security/fundamentals/shared-responsibility

Maturity Path

This section will include the following topics:

- Predicting security challenges in the Cloud
- Cloud security recommendations
- Checklist, Cloud audit, and compliance
- Security-as-a-service in Cloud

CHAPTER 8

Leveraging Cloud-based Security Solutions for Security-as-a-Service

Introduction

In this chapter, we will talk about different security services which can be offered from the cloud in a SaaS format. Here, we will talk about a framework for *evaluating* and *delivering cloud-based security services* to *businesses* in this section. First, we'll go through the framework's components in depth. Then we'll show you how to utilize this framework to evaluate and adopt security services through a detailed lifecycle approach. We will also cover a few examples and their adoption path which you can consider for your ecosystem.

At the end of the chapter, you will be able to choose the right security solutions which should be adopted as a service for your cloud transformation journey.

Structure

In this chapter, we will discuss the following topics associated with cloud security:

- Overview and concept understanding
- Key considerations towards SECaaS adoption
- SECaaS principle, framework, and lifecycle
- Potential benefits and concerns
- Major categories and feature sets as offering
- Security and governance for SECaaS
- Best practices and recommendations

Overview and concept understanding

With the introduction of the cloud, there is no aspect of your IT infrastructure that other individuals or businesses cannot handle for you. To obtain the necessary processing and storage resources to power their websites and applications, more and more businesses are turning to services like **Amazon AWS**. Others purchase an entire platform from a *third-party supplier* that includes operating systems, middleware, servers, and databases, depending on hypervisors and other technologies to obtain high-level APIs from internet services.

Others, however, depend on third-party suppliers of software and programs. Without having to construct their infrastructure or make investments in *creating*, *developing*, and *maintaining* these resources, firms may now more quickly, easily, and affordably meet their IT demands. Almost everything has been made available over time, from backends to *content*, *logging*, *disaster recovery*, and *storage*. Even security can now be provided as a service.

Defining and understanding Security-as-a-Service (SECaaS)

Using an external entity to handle and manage your security is known as **Security-as-a-Service** or **SECaaS**.

With security as a service, security solutions are no longer provided locally, where your IT department installs virus protection software, spam filtering software, and other security tools on each machine, as well as on the company network and server, and maintains the software's up-to-date status or instructs users on how to use it. The traditional method of doing things is also expensive; you must pay upfront fees for the necessary gear and ongoing costs for the software licenses. Instead, security as a service makes it simple and economical to employ the same capabilities with just a web browser.

The easiest way to characterize SECaaS is as a paradigm for outsourcing cybersecurity services that are delivered via the cloud. SECaaS offers security services via subscriptions hosted by cloud providers, much like *software as a service*. To reduce the workload on the internal security team, scale security requirements as the company expands, and avoid the expenses, and maintenance of on-premises alternatives, security as service solutions have grown in popularity for corporate infrastructure.

The most straightforward illustration of security as a service is the use of anti-virus software over the internet. With SECaaS, businesses can outsource cybersecurity management to a *third party*. Outsourced security solutions include functions including *intrusion detection, antivirus administration,* and *data loss prevention*. Companies that use SECaaS vendors gain access to the knowledge and creativity of a devoted cybersecurity staff that specializes in the intricate details of preventing intrusions in a cloud computing environment.

Defining SECaaS on cloud

A third-party remedy for cybersecurity problems is cloud security as a service. These service providers assist app developers in managing their risks in several ways. DevOps best practices are some of the most significant ones. A strict quality assurance process is also beneficial. Numerous software-related risks can be reduced by making sure that **Continuous Integration** (**CI**) and **Continuous Deployment** (**CD**) operations are carried out correctly.

Implementing an intrusion management system is another crucial cloud security solution that many cloud security providers supply. Using **intrusion detection systems** (**IDS**) and **intrusion prevention systems** (**IPS**), it is possible to determine in real-time who has access to your network. Security threats can be managed with the use of clear knowledge about the system's offender. To recognize and stop cyber-attacks, these technologies are highly helpful. As *Microsoft's* attack demonstrates, cyber threats are growing more prevalent.

Risks and challenges of adopting SECaaS

Adopting any solution is like accepting both sides of the coin. While there are many benefits associated, there are a few risks and challenges also and one should be aware of the same. There are various challenges to consider with an outsourced security solution, such as the following. We will talk briefly under the potential benefits and concerns within the SECaaS section:

- You are not completely in charge of security activities.
- You can encounter flaws in common technology.
- Data leaking is a possibility.

Companies can reduce the risks associated with outsourced security solutions by implementing and enforcing rules that address risks to cloud security. According to *Gartner*, customers, not service providers, will be responsible for 99% of cloud security failures through 2025. Hence, you must have a mature and comprehensive process to evaluate the right partner for SECaaS. We should be talking about the same in the subsequent section.

A few examples of cloud SECaaS

The most comprehensive level of protection is presently offered by a wide selection of cloud-based security (SECaaS) services. A few instances are:

- **Data Loss Prevention (DLP)**: Data loss may create serious disruptions to businesses and organizations of all kinds. This is why data loss prevention is important. To preserve data and avoid potential issues, data loss prevention frequently entails installing software and establishing a set of rules that everyone agrees upon. The security and ongoing monitoring of data protection will also be maintained.

- **Business Continuity and Disaster Recovery (BC/DR)**: Cloud-based BC / DR makes use of the cloud's flexibility to reduce costs and increase advantages.

- **Email security**: Email servers that are hosted in the cloud handle a lot of the data that enters and leaves your company. SECaaS providers with an emphasis on email security can shield you from dangers and hazards that are inherent to email, like *phishing, harmful advertising, targeted assaults*, and *data breaches*.

- **Antivirus solution**: Your company's endpoints include laptops, smartphones, servers, and other computing equipment. They are frequently the subject of cyber-attacks since they have numerous vulnerabilities that a criminal might leverage. Due to this fact, endpoint security software is essential, and the most popular type of endpoint protection is the usage of antivirus software. Beyond antivirus, robust SECaaS security includes **endpoint detection and response services (EDR)**.

- **Cloud Access Security Brokers (CASBs)**: In the field of cloud-based security services (SECaaS), **cloud access security brokers (CASBs)** are integrated packages. Vendors of CASBs often provide a variety of services aimed at assisting your business in ensuring that its cloud infrastructure and data are always protected. Software such as CASBs hosted on-premises or in the cloud between cloud service customers and providers, imposes security, enforcement, and governance requirements for cloud applications. These technologies serve as security for and monitor all cloud applications used by a business.

- **Security auditing**: Finding potential security holes that can be fixed later is possible with cloud services. Tools that monitor and carry out security assessments can be used by security as a service delivery model. This gives your business access to priceless data and the advantages of long-term security.

- **Network security**: Network security provides a wide range of services to meet the various network requirements of each client. These special requirements are properly handled thanks to security as a service. Physical and virtual devices can both provide network security when using cloud technology. Technologies for *cloud-based network security* give your company the ability to monitor traffic entering and leaving its servers, spot dangers early on, and stop them in their tracks. The *hardware-based firewall* might already be in use by you. However, having many levels of security is a smart idea due to the vast array of threats that are currently proliferating throughout the internet. This layer will include but is not limited to **Intrusion Detection System (IDS)** and **Intrusion Prevention System (IPS)**.

- **SIEM**: SIEM performs information security analysis and correlation as part of **Security-as-a-Service (SECaaS)**, supports incident response procedures, and gathers *logs*, *events*, and *flow data* from devices. The ability to use the SIEM service to recognize threats acting against their environment, clouds, or others is made possible by providing *flexible*, *real-time access* to SIEM information. With this definition, it is then possible to take the necessary precautions and steps to lessen the hazard.

- **Web security**: To add a layer of protection for web security, software, and hardware can be put up in the cloud and traffic can be sent to a cloud provider.

- **Vulnerability scanning**: When employing cloud-based apps, you need to safeguard not only your data and infrastructure but also the applications and digital assets you own and administer, such as your website. You'll be susceptible to assaults and breaches in this area as well if you use standard endpoint and firewall security. The purpose of these tools and services is often to identify and correct bugs in your websites, online applications, or corporate portals and intranets.

- **Encryption**: Clients do not want any intrusion of their personal information; hence encryption is utilized to secure it. All necessary data and messages will be fully protected thanks to cloud encryption as a service.

Potential benefits and concerns you should be aware of

It's crucial to comprehend how SECaaS differs from on-premises security as well as self-managed security before going into the specifics of several key SECaaS categories. Think about the advantages and drawbacks beforehand.

Potential benefits

Here are a few of the benefits you should be aware of when adopting SECaaS for your enterprise:

- **Benefits of cloud computing**: SECaaS can benefit from all of the typical cloud computing advantages, including *lower capital costs*, *agility*, *redundancy*, *high availability*, and *resiliency*. The extent of these advantages depends, like with any other cloud provider, on the security provider's cost, execution, and capabilities.

- **Personnel and knowledge**: Many businesses have trouble finding, developing, and keeping security specialists with the necessary domain knowledge. Limitations of regional markets, high costs of hiring specialists, and juggling daily requirements with the rapid pace of attacker innovation can all make this worse. As a result, SECaaS providers offer the advantage of in-depth subject expertise and research that may be unreachable for many firms that are not completely focused on security or the particular security domain.

- **Intelligence-sharing**: SECaaS providers can exchange data intelligence and data among their clients while simultaneously protecting several clients. As an illustration, if the provider discovers a malware sample in one client, they can add it right away to their defense platform, safeguarding all other clients. Practically speaking, this isn't a magic wand because the effectiveness will vary depending on the category, but the upside is possible because intelligence-sharing is a feature of the business.

- **Flexibility in deployment**: Given that SECaaS is a *cloud-native paradigm* that uses wide network access and elasticity to deliver services, it may be more suited to handle changing workplaces and cloud migrations. The majority of the time, services can handle more flexible deployment methods, like supporting distributed locations without the complexity of *multi-site hardware* deployments.

- **Clients' insulation**: SECaaS may be able to stop assaults before they directly impact an organization in specific circumstances. Attackers and the enterprise are separated by measures like *spam filtering* and *cloud-based web application firewalls*. Before an assault even reaches the client's assets, they can stop it.

- **Cost and scale**: With the *Pay as you Grow approach* that the cloud model offers to the user, businesses can concentrate on their core competencies and leave security issues to the professionals.

Potential concerns

Since SECaaS has a ton of benefits, it also comes with a few concerns that you and your enterprise should understand before adopting the same:

- **Inadequate visibility**: Services frequently offer less visibility or data compared to running one's own company because they operate apart from the customer. The SECaaS provider may withhold information about the specifics of how it controls its environment and implements its security. This might lead to variations in data sources and the level of detail accessible for things like monitoring and incidents, depending on the service and the supplier. The customer's usual sources of information can seem different, have gaps, or do not exist at all. The customer's objectives might not be met by the actual proof of compliance and artifacts, as well as other investigative data. Before concluding any deal, all of this may be ascertained and ought to be done.

- **Data leaking**: There is always a risk of data from one cloud user leaking to another, as with any cloud computing service or product. Although SECaaS providers should be held to the highest standards of multitenant isolation and segregation, this danger is not specific to SECaaS due to the extremely sensitive nature of security data (and other regulated data possibly exposed in security scans or incidents). Legal proceedings, police inquiries and other discovery circumstances are also likely to involve security-related material. Customers want to be certain that their data won't be disclosed when these circumstances involve another user of the service.

- **Differential regulation**: Given the extensive regulatory requirements around the world, SECaaS providers might not be able to guarantee compliance in every country or region where an enterprise conducts business.

- **Regulation of data handling**: Customers will also need reassurance that any regulated data that may be removed as part of routine *security scanning* or a *security incident* is handled following any compliance requirements. This handling must also take into account the aforementioned differences in international jurisdiction. For instance, employee monitoring is more restricted in *Europe* than it is in the US, and even routine security monitoring practices may be unlawful there. Additionally, if an SECaaS provider moves its operations due to a change in data centers or load balancing, it can violate rules that place limits on where data can be located.

- **Alternating providers**: Changing SECaaS providers may appear to be simpler than replacing on-premises hardware and software, but enterprises may be concerned about *lock-in* since they risk losing access to data, especially historical data required for compliance or investigative support.

- **A changeover to SECaaS**: The transition to SECaaS as well as the boundary and interface between any internal IT department and SECaaS providers must be carefully planned, put to the test, and maintained for enterprises that already have security operations and on-premises traditional security control solutions.

Major categories and feature sets under SECaaS

The phrase *Security as a Service* refers to a broad range of goods and services. This has also been depicted in the following diagram (*Figure 8.1*):

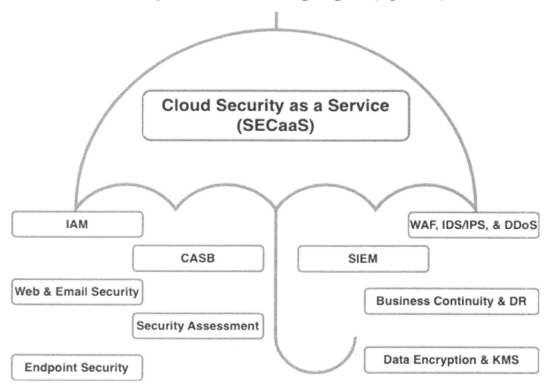

Figure 8.1: SECaaS major categories

While not a definitive list, the following lists several of the more typical categories and feature sets that are prevalent today:

- **Services for managing identity, entitlement, and access**: **Identity-as-a-Service** is a general term that refers to one or more of the services that may make up an identity ecosystem, such as **Policy Enforcement Points (PEP)**-as-a-service, **Policy Decision Points (PDP)**-as-a-service, **Policy Access Points (PAP)**-as-a-service, services that give entities with identity, attributes (such as **Multi-Factor Authentication (MFA)**), and reputation-building services.

  Federated Identity Brokers are one of the most popular subcategories that are frequently utilized in cloud security. These services aid in bridging IAM between the numerous cloud services that a company uses and its *internal* or *cloud-hosted directories*, which serve as identity providers today.

  They offer web-based **Single Sign-On (SSO)**, which can help reduce some of the complexity involved in connecting to a variety of external services that make use of various federation configurations.

  Two additional types are frequently used in cloud deployments. Strong authentication services leverage infrastructure and apps to streamline the integration of multiple strong authentication alternatives, including mobile device apps and tokens for MFA. The other type makes use of cloud-based directory servers as an organization's identity supplier.

- **Cloud Access Security Broker (CASB)**: To monitor *activities, enforce policy*, and *identify and/or prevent security risks*, these products either directly connect to cloud services through API or intercept communications that are aimed at them. Most of the time, they are employed to oversee both authorized and unauthorized SaaS offerings by a business. Although there are on-premises CASB solutions, the service is frequently provided as a *cloud-hosted service*.

  To assist companies in identifying, evaluating, and possibly blocking cloud usage as well as unauthorized services, CASBs can also connect to on-premises technologies. To assist customers in understanding and classifying hundreds or thousands of cloud services, several of these solutions provide risk-rating capabilities. The assessments made by the provider, which may be weighted and paired with the organization's priorities, are used to determine the ratings.

  Inherently or through partnerships and service interaction with other services, the majority of suppliers also provide fundamental data loss prevention for the covered cloud services.

The word CASB may also be used to refer to *Federated Identity Brokers* depending on the organization using it. Confusion arises from the fact that, even though the *security gateway* and *identity broker* capabilities can and do combine, separate services with those two capabilities continue to dominate the market.

- **Secure endpoints**: **Endpoints** refer to all the computing tools that your company uses, including laptops, smartphones, servers, and other technology. Due to the numerous vulnerabilities, they have that can be exploited by criminals, they are frequently the subject of cyber-attacks.

  Endpoint security software is necessary because of this reality. Endpoint protection most frequently takes the form of *antivirus, EDR, data encryption*, DLP, and *other technologies*.

- **Web security**: *Real-time protection* is provided through web security, either on-premises through the installation of appliances and/or software or in the cloud by proxying or rerouting online traffic to the cloud provider (or a hybrid of both). This offers an additional layer of security on top of other security measures, such as *anti-malware software* to stop malware from infiltrating the business through actions like online browsing. It can also enforce policies governing the kinds of web access that are permitted and the permitted times for that access. For online applications, application authorization management can add another degree of contextual and granular security enforcement.

- **Email security**: Email security should give users control over both *inbound* and *outbound* email, safeguarding the company from threats like phishing and harmful attachments, as well as enforcing corporate policies like acceptable use and spam prevention, and offering choices for business continuity.

  The solution might also integrate with different email server systems and allow policy-based email encryption. **Digital signatures**, which allow for identification and non-repudiation, are another feature that many email security solutions offer. This category covers the entire spectrum of services, from basic anti-spam capabilities to fully integrated email security gateways with cutting-edge virus and phishing protection.

- **Security assessment**: The term *security assessment* refers to independent or client-driven reviews of cloud services or evaluations of on-premises systems using cloud-based services. Traditional security evaluations of *infrastructure, applications*, and *compliance audits* are widely defined and backed by numerous standards, including NIST, ISO, and CIS. There is a toolkit that is quite developed, and several utilities have been created utilizing the SECaaS delivery model.

Customers who subscribe to that model receive the normal advantages of cloud computing, including *variable elasticity*, *little setup time*, *low administration overhead*, and *pay-per-use* with low upfront costs.

Security assessments fall into *three* primary categories:

- Conventional assessments of security/vulnerability for assets deployed on-premises or in the cloud (such as virtual machines/ instances for patches and vulnerabilities).

- **SAST**, **DAST**, and **RASP** management for application security evaluations.

- Tools for evaluating cloud platforms that connect directly to the cloud service through API and evaluate not only the assets deployed in the cloud but also the configuration of the cloud.

- **WAF**: Customers use DNS to direct traffic to a service that filters and analyses it before sending it to the target web application in a cloud-based **Web Application Firewall (WAF)**. Anti-DDoS capabilities are a common feature of cloud WAFs.

- **IDS/IPS**: Systems for detecting and preventing intrusions keep track of behavior patterns using *rule-based*, *heuristic*, or *behavioral models* to look for activity anomalies that could endanger the organization. Instead of the client having to analyze events themselves, IDS/IPS as a service delivers the data into a service-controlled provider's platform. In-cloud IDS/IPS can leverage virtual appliances, host-based agents, or already installed hardware for on-premises protection.

- **Prevention of Distributed Denial of Service (DDoS)**: DDoS defenses are typically cloud-based by nature. They work by redirecting traffic via the DDoS service to neutralize attacks before they impact the client's infrastructure.

- **SIEM**: SIEM systems collect log and event data from virtual and physical networks, applications, and systems (through push or pull processes). Following the correlation and analysis of this data, information about events or information that may call for intervention or other sorts of responses are reported in *real-time*, as well as these occurrences are alerted to. Instead of using a customer-managed, on-premises system, cloud SIEMs collect this data in a cloud service.

- **Data encryption and Key Management Services (KMS)**: These services deal with encryption keys and/or data encryption. To facilitate *customer-managed encryption* and data security, cloud services might provide them. They might just be capable of securing assets hosted by that particular cloud provider, or they might be usable for broader encryption management across several providers (and even on-premises, through API). There are also encryption proxies for SaaS in this category, which intercept SaaS traffic and encrypt specific data.

Encrypting data outside of a SaaS platform, however, may limit how well the platform can use the data.

- **Disaster recovery and business continuity**: This topic focuses on assisting a firm in quickly recovering from a cyber-attack or other incident that interrupts its IT services. Every second that your website is unavailable due to an attack costs your customers. The goal of business continuity and catastrophe recovery effort is to promptly resume normal operations. The objective is to arrive at this result so quickly that you fail to detect a problem.

Cloud BC/DR service providers back up data to a cloud platform rather than local storage or shipping tapes from individual systems, data centers, or cloud services. With the cloud service acting as the ultimate repository for worst-case scenarios or archive purposes, they may use a local gateway to expedite data transfers and local recoveries.

Key considerations for enterprise while selecting SECaaS

Similar to how cloud services for general IT gained popularity a few years ago, the SECaaS model, which delivers essential information security operations as a hosted service, is becoming more and more common.

The new model presents a chance for security companies to outsource duties that have grown too *expensive, complex,* or *understaffed* to handle on their own. However, SECaaS has its limitations and warnings, especially for businesses in regulated industries, just like other cloud-hosted services. If you are planning to consider SECaaS for your environment, here are a few of the key considerations.

Knowing how to check out your vendors

When choosing a vendor to provide managed security services, be sure you are prepared with the right questions to ask. This entails learning more about the vendor's security certifications and how they handle compliance with regulations like **GDPR**, **HIPAA**, and **PCI**.

Asking about a vendor's procedures for protecting data, especially PII, across its full lifecycle, from creation to deletion, is important while conducting vendor due diligence. Make sure that its encryption and key management systems are up to date, and find out how it handles identity management, identity federation, and multi-factor authentication.

Verify that they can offer thorough log file information for your service and see if other services can change that information. The **Cloud Security Alliance (CSA)** questionnaire is a good resource for this.

A vendor with expertise in your business should be sought out. The shift to a managed security model may be facilitated by having a provider that is knowledgeable about how your company runs and generates revenue.

Clarifying the roles you must play

SECaaS enables businesses to delegate management of security tasks but not accountability for them. A *shared responsibility* approach is crucial to the success of your SECaaS engagement since you are still largely responsible for your organization's security posture and any failures.

You must be aware of who oversees what security while thinking about SECaaS. Know who has access to your data, what data they can access, and where audit logs, user credentials, and other crucial data are kept. You should also be aware of how to access the data.

Your contract should be very clear about who owns the data, what the obligations are to secure the data, and how they will be enforced. Before committing, ascertain whether the security vendor's coverage will have any holes and how those gaps will be filled.

Understanding what to outsource

Although managed security service providers can offer a vast and growing range of capabilities, be aware that some are probably best kept in-house.

You shouldn't outsource any security functions that are based on an unusual or internal company circumstance, for example. The service provider may not be in the greatest position to identify whether what is happening in your network is an attack or just regular traffic in an emergency.

Similarly, to this, security operations like **SIEM** and **UEBA** can be challenging for a third party to manage without a thorough understanding of your network and endpoint's typical behavior. If, as many large firms do, they have hundreds of rules surrounding the technologies, they must exercise caution even when moving activities like network and web application firewall administration to the cloud.

Developing a risk management strategy

Regardless of the measures you take to reduce the danger, outsourcing security has some level of risk. As a result, in addition to assessing the value offered by the SECaaS model, you also need to have a complete grasp of all the business risks connected to employing that model and choosing how you want to manage them. Common approaches include accepting the risk, reducing it by administrative, technical, or physical control, avoiding actions that increase risk, or transferring risk to a third party, such as *insurance*.

Risk tolerance levels should be assessed against enterprise-acceptable risk and tolerance levels before being permitted for use in choosing and deploying a SECaaS solution.

Anticipating a learning curve

SECaaS-adopting organizations risk being caught off guard by the changes if they are not ready for them. A significant architectural change that can have an impact on your other current IT controls and procedures is having security supplied as a service.

The largest issue in the market is the learning curve businesses experience when utilizing new security services. While some SECaaS, like application firewalls, offer a well-known service in a new format, other SECaaS require you to reconsider security in more basic ways, like how DevOps alters the *patch management paradigm*.

SECaaS working principle

SECaaS operates similarly to other cloud models by letting users provide resources to a third-party data center where services are integrated with local network infrastructure. **Infrastructure-as-a-Service (IaaS)** and SECaaS complement one another since hardware and the necessary security technologies may be deployed in the cloud. Organizations that use *cloud-based cybersecurity* might save hundreds of thousands of dollars while still making sure the IT environment is protected from real-world cyber threats. Cybersecurity resources are expensive, and frequently the team that oversees them is even more expensive.

The selection of a provider is the initial action for an organization. *Google Cloud Platform*, *Amazon Web Services*, and *Microsoft Azure* are just a few of the major cloud service providers that offer cutting-edge cybersecurity. Before signing up, the company should audit and evaluate the provider of cybersecurity solutions that they have selected. Unwinding an integrated system and implementing a different one is complicated and time-consuming.

Enterprise customers can provision and deploy cybersecurity infrastructure using a common dashboard provided by cloud providers. Any number of identity access controls, antivirus and anti-malware software, storage encryption, monitoring, and email security can all be established and managed by users. In only a few minutes, businesses may deploy cybersecurity technologies and configure each one to meet the specific needs of the network environment. Costs are substantially lower than implementing internal cybersecurity technologies in-house because suppliers only charge for resources used.

By utilizing the resources of the cloud provider to build a testing and staging environment, organizations should evaluate *cybersecurity as a service*. These testing environments can be used by users to implement cybersecurity protections to make sure the infrastructure interfaces with the production environment without any issues. Cloud-based tools function in the same way as internal ones, except they do so online.

Any cloud-provisioned resource may be withdrawn at any time from the main dashboard. The provider will make sure that the most recent upgrades are accessible, but it is the organization's responsibility to ensure that cybersecurity resources are configured effectively and adhere to legal requirements. Expert auditing and disaster recovery drills that simulate an actual assault are typically required for this level. Auditing ensures that resources set up to safeguard and monitor data are configured and working correctly if the company is the victim of an attack.

SECaaS framework

This section introduces a paradigm for evaluating and effectively providing cloud-based security services to businesses. First, we provide a detailed explanation of the framework's components, followed by a lifecycle. We suggest the SECaaS framework as a fresh approach to cloud computing. Our definition of SECaaS is the ability to use security products from suppliers that are hosted on cloud architecture and accessed via an interface.

The objective is to create a framework that makes it easier to provision *cloud-based security* apps and specifies how to combine security applications from various providers to create useful solutions.

Customers must have the option to create their security policies and risk management frameworks for SECaaS to qualify as a practical cloud solution. Customers must be able to categorize, evaluate, quantify, and order their system risks. In addition to providing security services that are independent of any platform and adaptive to continuously changing cloud settings, cloud providers must also make sure that their security protocols are not overly complicated to allow for efficient resource deployment. Customers must research the security precautions that a cloud service offers and what additional security services are required to address any potential vulnerabilities before using them. These assessments can help customers determine which service providers they can trust with their common security needs.

Depending on the cloud delivery model, it is possible to compare a cloud service to a set of security controls to ascertain which rules are already in place and can be obtained from either the customer or the cloud service provider, and which controls require contacting additional cloud providers.

The *risk assessment module*, the *discovery module*, the *integration module*, and the *monitoring module* are the *four* essential parts of the proposed framework, as indicated in the following image (*Figure* 8.2). The *security risk assessment module* is in charge of locating, analyzing, and recommending security measures to address threats and their potential repercussions. The possibility that a given threat source would exploit a specific possible vulnerability and the subsequent impact of that unfavorable occurrence on the organization are the *two* components that make up risk:

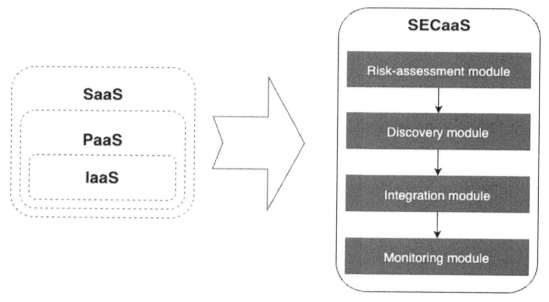

Figure 8.2*: SECaaS framework*

To gauge the scope of potential threats and the risk associated with an organization, customers utilize *risk assessment*. A thorough risk analysis is used by the customer to determine which security software and controls are required to protect the organization. The customer then chooses which security apps will run locally and which security applications should be used with cloud service providers.

The system is characterized, threats are identified, vulnerabilities are identified, controls are analyzed, likelihood is determined, impacts are determined, risks are determined, and control recommendations are made. Security managers can secure their specific solution using the basic building blocks provided by the suggested security controls.

Finding service providers who offer the necessary security services specified by the security *risk assessment module* is the goal of the *discovery module*. Customers can obtain a list of services and their features that are stored in a public repository for this purpose. *Three* considerations should be made when seeking the right services: *lowest cost*, *best fit*, and least *detrimental effect*.

Customers search the public repository for services that best meet their requirements; service providers are then graded according to these criteria, and the best options are selected. Customers can use this module to compare the services that various cloud providers offer and to get assurance from particular cloud providers. A collection of security services possibly from many cloud service providers that this module produces will be supplied as input into the integration module.

Following that, the *integration module* customizes the security services that have been selected from the *discovery module* to complete the security building blocks that security administrators are creating for the company. The system's security architecture is the module's output, and it contains an orchestrated security solution made up of several security building pieces to fulfil different security requirements. At this point, the security architecture is integrated into the evolving larger solution architecture. Data and service privacy and confidentiality should be upheld throughout the integration process.

Continuous security service monitoring is the responsibility of the monitoring module. This is a *real-time security monitoring solution* that continuously tracks adjustments to system specifications that can have an impact on security controls and re-evaluates control efficacy. It controls the *migration*, *configuration*, and *contextualization* of service components as a consequence of changes in context and/or SLA, among many other things that may have an impact on the company. It also monitors SLA commitments and context changes.

It is also in charge of managing processes for handling incidents and business continuity. Considerations should be made for issues like recovery priorities and dependencies pertinent to the restoration process to maintain continuity.

A component of business continuity management is *incident management and response*. With the help of this procedure, unexpected and potentially disruptive occurrences should have less of an impact than is unacceptably high for the business. The ability of an organization to lower the likelihood of an information security incident occurring or lessen its negative effects is assessed.

SECaaS framework lifecycle

To make the market for security services more accessible and open, the framework provides a *standardized, open interface*. The SECaaS framework's lifecycle is represented in the following image (*Figure 8.3*):

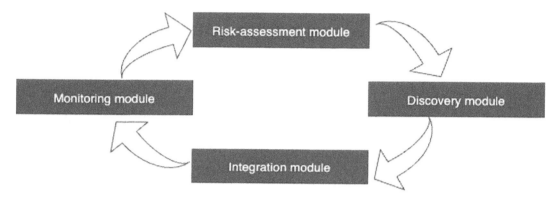

Figure 8.3: *SECaaS framework lifecycle*

- **Determine the requirements for security and evaluate security risks**: Before recommending security controls, identify risks, assess them, and consider their effects.

- **Learn about security services**: Locate companies that provide the services you need, and pick the best companies.

- **Integrate security services**: Adjust the previously identified security services and complete the security architecture.

- **Monitor security services**: Keep an eye out for modifications to the specifications that might have an impact on security controls.

An organization can use this framework to undertake a risk analysis on the services it requires, balance their advantages and disadvantages, and make an informed decision regarding which assets can be secured using cloud-based SECaaS and which are too *risky* and *expensive* to be based on SECaaS. The SECaaS evaluation approach, for instance, might be used by an organization to decide to just use SECaaS to secure its network and information assets, leaving the rest of its assets to be protected by existing or future non-cloud services.

The *next* step is to use our *risk-analysis approach* once more for each of the categories to assess different SECaaS suppliers that are currently on the market after choosing which types of assets a company would like to purchase for which SECaaS vendors are accessible. The organization should weigh the advantages and disadvantages of each IPS and firewall as a service offered by different providers before making a final decision. It is necessary to develop unique, enterprise metrics depending on the needs of the enterprise to use our risk assessment framework when deciding which assets to safeguard using SECaaS. The *next* step is to develop unique, tailored enterprise KPIs for each selected type of asset to assess the SECaaS services that are currently offered in the market.

Security and governance for SECaaS

Understanding the roles that a company and its cloud service provider share is necessary for successful cloud migration. One of the most important factors for businesses moving to the cloud is security and governance due to the alarming increase in cybersecurity threats and data breaches.

While the majority of cloud service providers give their customers a wide range of storage, access, and security options, as well as authorized access, data protection, and training support, we will restrict our discussion to the crucial SECaaS building pieces aligned to the overall security and governance layer:

- **Managing identities and access**: Network stability, availability, and other crucial metrics are monitored by DevOps engineers as they oversee the *development*, *testing*, and *operationalization* of data platforms. Managing numerous libraries and versions of code, accounting for proper deployment parameters to prevent application failure, and customizing scripts in a short amount of time to ensure maximum performance are a few of the main issues faced by DevOps teams.

  Controlling which resources can be accessed, who can access them, and how is a crucial security requirement for any organization going to the cloud. For efficient management of users and access rights, cloud service providers offer a wide choice of options. This helps to manage:

  - Identity and access to the resources and services
  - Handling *multi-account setup* (for a group of companies or having a segmented business approach)
  - Handling **Single Sign-On (SSO)** experience
  - User accounts handling for Mobile and web experience

- **Continuous logging and observation**: Data collection for measurement and governance is a component of logging and monitoring. As they gauge the functionality of physical components and software programs, they are crucial in contemporary businesses. It takes a lot of management and works to create a monitoring solution that works. To make this process simpler, cloud providers offer an *end-to-end monitoring solution* that aids in the monitoring of all cloud-deployed resources, from infrastructure to applications.

- **Encryption and data security**: Making data illegible with the use of an *encryption algorithm* and *encryption key* is the process of *encryption*. Enterprises must create a *key management system* that can maintain the keys in a secure, long-lasting, and highly accessible manner to guarantee the security of the encrypted data. But doing this can be a time-consuming and challenging procedure. Cloud providers offer a **Key Management Service (KMS)** that is tightly linked with its other services for seamless key management and encryption. The typical use case includes:

  - Encrypted key management
  - HSM-related task
  - Certificate management
  - Secret and password management

- **Network and perimeter security**: Controlling the request's path via various components and the parties authorized to send requests to resources is a key component of the *network* and *perimeter security*. To maintain a robust infrastructure, this is essential since it can guard against unauthorized access and network threats including *denial-of-service*, *malware*, and *spam*. Cloud providers offer several services that consumers can employ to create a safe networking infrastructure. A few of them include but are not limited to:

  - Provision and manage private network (**VPC** or **V-Net**)
  - Direct connect services to have connectivity to the existing private data centers or HQ
  - Web application firewall
  - Cloud-based DDoS protection

- **Conducting governance and compliance audits**: An organization's adherence to legal requirements is thoroughly examined via a *compliance audit*. In the course of a compliance audit, audit reports assess the robustness and thoroughness of compliance preparations, security guidelines, user access restrictions, and risk management practices. This is a vital requirement because consumers moving to the cloud are often concerned about following legal requirements. Services for auditing, resource compliance, and report building are offered in a variety of ways by cloud service providers.

Organizations can successfully use the cloud's advantages by having a solid understanding of the fundamental principles of *security* and *governance*. Additionally, adopting an automated strategy for security and governance-related functions can assist prevent risks including *security lapses, excessive maintenance costs*, and *wasted resources*. It is equally important to comprehend architectural best practices while making plans to build a cloud infrastructure because they contribute to the development of an ecosystem that is *highly available, sturdy, secure*, and *cost-effective*.

Best practices around SECaaS

For SECaaS security and implementation to be successful, your IT infrastructure must be under your control. The integrity and resilience of your IT systems can be ensured using the best practices listed as follows:

- **Periodic assessments**: When you initially adopt an SECaaS solution, it is only logical to evaluate how to improve your company's security. Evaluations should be conducted continuously and regularly, nevertheless. There is a security flaw in an out-of-date application. Before a patch is released by a program, cybercriminals may find a vulnerability. These evaluations can be carried out automatically by a SECaaS system, and suggestions can be made. To swiftly learn about new threats and determine whether your IT systems are in danger, they can also provide threat intelligence solutions.

- **Data guidelines**: SECaaS solutions must include data protection as a key component. Establishing your data policy is part of this. *Do you need to back up your data every day or more frequently? Where are the copies kept? Who can access this information? The data is encrypted? What is your policy regarding data storage?* Together with your SECaaS partner, develop a data strategy to guarantee that your sensitive data is safeguarded and recovered rapidly in the event of an attack.

- **Security guidelines**: Developing security guidelines for utilizing and accessing the IT resources and assets of your company is a part of setting up an SECaaS solution. Security guidelines are not something you set once and then forget about. Security guidelines ought to be revised over time. If you decide to integrate the SECaaS solution into your systems, you might need to enhance current policies; alternatively, you might discover that some policies impede company efficiency and demand revision. You should be able to adapt your security policies with SECaaS software.

- **Access control and identity management**: *Who has access to your IT systems? How much access do they have to private systems and information?* In your SECaaS platform, address the **identity and access management (IAM)** challenge. IAM's IDaaS subset addresses the particular problems faced by users who must manage several passwords for access to diverse software applications. The best identity management software assists in meeting IAM needs as a component of a comprehensive SECaaS solution.

- **Disaster recovery**: It's imperative to have a plan in place for recovering from attacks and other IT disasters. You will undoubtedly encounter a difficulty that severely disrupts your IT infrastructure at some point. The *disaster recovery component* of SECaaS solutions is required. Disaster recovery offers *storage*, *data backups*, and the *capability* to restore software to its pre-disaster state.

- **Alerting and reporting**: For any software platform, reporting is crucial, and SECaaS is no exception. One-page views of your present security posture and analyses of system vulnerabilities are two examples of the reports offered by SECaaS solutions. Your security depends on alerting as well. Alerts provide the *real-time knowledge* you require to be aware of a potential assault.

SECaaS may assist companies of all sizes in obtaining an all-encompassing IT security solution at a set cost. It streamlines the intricate and dynamic realm of IT security, reduces the workload of the IT department of the company, and helps it to be ready for security compliance assessments. Boosting computer uptime will assist in better illuminating security activities within a company and boost worker productivity.

Conclusion

SECaaS is a dynamic industry. You must choose the correct vendor based on your company's needs because no one vendor excels in every aspect of IT security.

You must determine the IT security requirements for your firm to receive a comprehensive SECaaS solution. Add the necessary security software to your SECaaS collection after that. When doing this, make sure the SECaaS options you choose enable software interoperability.

In this chapter, we covered the important security standards that businesses must meet. A framework is required to help security managers choose from a variety of security and privacy services offered by various cloud service providers and to help cloud providers deliver their security services more effectively. While security and privacy services in the cloud can be customized and managed by experienced experts, they may not be as effective as they could be in terms of security management and threat assessment. To help people accept the security services provided in the cloud, we have suggested an SECaaS structure. The framework was introduced, its elements were discussed, and it demonstrated how security managers might effectively use it to request security apps from various cloud providers that are necessary for businesses.

In the next chapter, we will learn about various recommendations and best practices one should consider and adopt for the cloud security journey.

Questions

1. Define Security-as-a Service terminology.

2. Explain the need to have SECaaS for your enterprise.

3. Explain cloud SECaaS with a few examples considering the cloud landscape.

4. Differentiate between potential benefits and concerns on SECaaS.

5. What are the different features one can adopt through the SECaaS model?

6. Explain in detail the key considerations an enterprise should factor in while adopting SECaaS

7. Define the working principal model for SECaaS.

8. Explain the SECaaS framework along with the lifecycle for adoption.

9. Why are security controls and governance important for the SECaaS framework?

10. Explain a few best practices for SECaaS that one should adopt for your enterprise.

CHAPTER 9

Cloud Security Recommendations and Best Practices

Introduction

We are coming to an end, and this is going to be the last chapter in this book but certainly not the least. By this time, I am sure you must have gathered comprehensive knowledge of Cloud security along with adoption techniques for the associated frameworks. To move ahead and ensure that you have a mature landscape, we must also understand the best practices and recommendations defined by these cloud service providers. You must consider them in the journey of cloud adoption and cloud security enablement.

This chapter will talk about the various best practices and recommendations across the entire landscape of cloud security. We will also touch base few of the recommendations based on real-life challenges, business scenarios, and alignment with business verticals. To start with, we will help your slate with the next steps and the way forward in this journey of defining the security boundary and upliftment engagement.

Structure

In this chapter, we will discuss the following topics associated with Cloud security:

- Overview and need of the hour
- Key considerations for Cloud security adoption - best practices on strategy
- Cloud Security Assessment

Overview and need of the hour

Enterprise ecosystems have seen a significant transformation as a result of the increasing adoption of public clouds, which have increased agility and creativity. Nowadays, businesses employ a wide range of cloud services, operate across numerous public and private clouds, and can have hundreds or even thousands of developers who have an impact on their cloud infrastructure— sometimes inadvertently. In addition to cloud providers launching new services and capabilities at a record rate, cloud users also have to traverse complicated regulatory compliance requirements. Keeping track of all the settings and configurations required to secure every single service soon becomes burdensome due to the rapid accumulation of complexity.

Cloud data breaches and exposures are a very typical occurrence, which is not surprising given the lack of access and control over constantly changing configurations. Due to incorrect settings of cloud infrastructure, more than 30 billion customer records have been exposed in roughly 200 breaches over the past two years. Almost all effective attacks on cloud services make use of various organizational errors and misconfigurations.

Although cloud service providers go to considerable lengths to ensure the security of their products, most organizations lack the procedures or tools required to use them efficiently. Some of the biggest cloud breaches at businesses like Imperva, Capital One, and CenturyLink came as a result of straightforward configuration errors, such as an open AWS S3 bucket or a configuration with too many rights. According to Gartner, up until 2025, at least 99% of cloud security breaches will be the responsibility of the client, and 90% of businesses that don't manage their public cloud usage would improperly expose sensitive data.

This chapter discusses the security issues businesses are now experiencing with their cloud IaaS setups, potential solutions to these problems, best practices to adopt, and the significance of Cloud Security Posture Management (CSPM) throughout the process.

Key considerations for cloud security adoption

While these apply to the overall security landscape, with Cloud in the mix, these security practices become very evident, and enterprises must adopt them in their overall BAU and operations.

The procedures address customer concerns about cloud security, as shown by several recent cloud security events. All organizations, regardless of size, can utilize the offered practices to increase the security of their cloud usage. The presented practices are targeted toward small and medium-sized businesses. This article focuses on hybrid deployments, in which some IT applications are moved or deployed to a CSP while others stay in the organization's data center. Assuming that small and medium-sized businesses have constrained resources, these best practices explain implementation strategies that might work well under such conditions.

When organizations deploy or move applications and systems to a cloud service provider, there are risks, threats, and vulnerabilities that need to be addressed (CSP).

The four recommendations made here do not include all the steps required for using cloud computing securely. These four procedures take care of the particular hazards that the particular threats that were examined in the mission threads brought about. These four principles should be supplemented by practices offered by CSPs, general cybersecurity practices, legal compliance standards, and practices established by cloud trade organizations like the Cloud Security Alliance.

The four crucial techniques are:

- **Exercise due diligence**: Consumers of the cloud must exercise due diligence by fully comprehending the security ramifications of adopting or transferring applications and systems to a CSP. Customers must comprehend how to employ CSP services to support corporate operations while safeguarding information.

- **Control Access**: To control access to resources in a way that allows users to carry out their responsibilities while safeguarding resources from inappropriate or unauthorized use, it is necessary to identify the various user categories that exist in an IT environment based on the cloud, determine the responsibilities of each user category, and identify the user categories themselves.

- **Protect Data**: The prevention of unintentional or unauthorized disclosure of data and the maintenance of access to vital data in the event of mistakes, failures, or compromise are two issues that data protection solves for consumers.

- **Watch and defend**: CSP and cloud users must collaborate to monitor cloud-based systems and apps to detect unwanted access to data or unauthorized usage of resources.

Risk examples from the real world

These procedures deal with common consumer concerns about cloud security. Examples of well-known cloud security incidents are shown in this section. References to the methods used to reduce the danger of each sort of incident are included in each illustration.

- **AWS Storage Services that are not secure**:

  It has been proven that poorly configured AWS Simple Storage Service (S3) and leaving data available are two causes of unauthorized data exposure to the Internet.

  According to a September 5, 2017, report in *The Register*, a contractor neglected to effectively secure an Amazon cloud database, "leaving information on roughly four million Time Warner Cable consumers access to the public Internet." Due to improper access policy setup, data in the AWS S3 bucket was open to public access. According to press coverage of this occurrence, consumers frequently misconfigure AWS resources. Perform Due Diligence, Manage Access, Protect Data, and Monitor and Defend practices are some of those that might lessen this risk.

  Sensitive files were discovered to be freely accessible online on June 1, 2017, by a security researcher. In an Amazon S3 bucket without any password protection, the files were kept in plain text. Co-founder and CEO of the cloud infrastructure security firm Dome9, Zohar Alon, stated that "Yet the security of S3 buckets to prevent accidental data exposure is often poorly understood and badly implemented by their users, even someone as technically astute as an engineer with one of the world's leading defense contractors." Perform Due Diligence, Manage Access, and Monitor and Defend are practices that would lessen this risk.

- **Compromised Deloitte email**:

  The worldwide consulting company Deloitte3 was "the victim of a cybersecurity attack that went unreported for months," according to a report in *The Guardian on September 25, 2017*. The company's Microsoft Azure-hosted email system was accessed by the attack via a compromised system administrator credential. Only a password was used to authenticate the administrator account. (Practices that would lessen this risk include Monitor and Defend and Manage Access.)

- **Data Loss Through Accident**:

  The US-EAST region availability zone's EBS volume had 0.07 percent of the data that was permanently lost on April 21, 2011. A large decrease in network bandwidth occurred within an EBS cluster as a result of a maintenance operation error [AWS 2011]. In the end, a race condition caused by this bandwidth decrease led to the failure of the EBS cluster nodes. Most client data may be recovered by Amazon after the EBS cluster is repaired. There was, nevertheless, a minor amount of missing consumer data. The "Protect Data" practice might help to reduce this risk.

- **System and Data Destroying Code Spaces**:

Developers of software could access Git and Apache Subversion through Code Spaces, a CSP that offers source code management tools as a service. AWS was used in the development of Code Spaces' SaaS solution. 2014 saw the theft of an AWS credential belonging to a Code Spaces privileged user. Most of Code Spaces' data was permanently wiped within 12 hours of the intrusion, as were all of its virtual machines. Data belonging to Code Spaces' clients were lost, and as a result, the company was forced to close. Perform Due Diligence, Control Access, and Protect Data are examples of practices that would reduce this risk.

- **Data Breach at OneLogin**:

Businesses can get SaaS **Identity and Access Management (IAM)** services from OneLogin, a CSP. AWS is used by OneLogin's products. The business reported that in May 2017, a hacker used a third-party vendor to gain access to a set of AWS keys. These keys allowed the hacker to get access to and breach every file stored by OneLogin at its U.S. data center. Manage Access, Protect Data, and Monitor and Defend are practices that would reduce this risk.

- **Ransomware Makes Use of the Cloud**:

Despite reports of only a few confirmed occurrences to date, it appears that ransomware developers are actively leveraging cloud backups to exfiltrate data that can be ransomed rather than only encrypting victims' files locally. The Doppelware and Maze ransomware operators apparently targeted and/or employed cloud-based backup software as a standard attack strategy to steal or destroy backups. Perform Due Diligence, Manage Access, Protect Data, and Monitor and Defending are practices that would lessen this risk.

- **Attack on the supply chain by SolarWinds**:

A provider of network, system, and information technology management products for businesses is SolarWinds. The SolarWinds software supply chain was hacked by sophisticated threat actors during an infiltration campaign, according to a threat analysis published by FireEye on December 13, 2020, allowing access to international private and governmental networks. Attackers then gained unauthorized access to victim Microsoft

365 cloud environments using on-premises access. Least privilege access would have been enforced and unlawful access may not have happened if zero trust explicit verification controls had been imposed. Perform Due Diligence, Manage Access, Protect Data, and Monitor and Defend are practices that would lessen this risk.

Double-click on important security practices - how to adapt

Since we have seen real-life examples, let's talk about the four major and important techniques we were referring to in detail.

To ensure the security of cloud-based systems and applications, the practices provided in this section outline important consumer obligations.

Due diligence

Due diligence must be carried out throughout the lifecycle of apps and systems being deployed to the cloud. This covers tasks that fall within the following four categories: planning, development and deployment, operations, and decommissioning.

Planning

A successful cloud deployment starts with choosing an acceptable system or application to migrate to, integrate into, or purchase from a CSP. For a first-time cloud implementation, getting this step correctly is difficult. You may learn from others' experiences and should employ a cloud adoption framework to make the most of cloud services. The framework for cloud adoption offers a method for finding applications, choosing cloud service providers, and managing the continuing operational duties related to public cloud services. Frameworks for adopting cloud services could be CSP-specific or CSP-neutral.

To identify the key risk factors connected to the adoption of the cloud and attempt to limit or manage those risks, a risk taxonomy is also helpful. The best method to minimize the risks is to adequately inventory them during the planning stage and then take appropriate action as soon as the adoption process begins.

AWS offers a methodology for cloud adoption that takes six viewpoints into account: business, people, governance, platform, security, and operations. Although this approach is relevant to CSPs, most of the knowledge and suggestions apply to any cloud adoption, not just AWS. The noteworthy CSPs are all equipped with unique adoption frameworks.

A framework can be used to help a business comprehend the effects of cloud computing. All staff involved in the deployment must receive training on the fundamentals of the chosen CSP, the CSP's architecture, the services offered, and the tools available to aid in deployment after using a cloud adoption framework to identify a target system or application for cloud deployment and a CSP. Employees need to be aware of the shared responsibility model used by the CSP and how it will affect how they participate in the cloud deployment. Clear communication is facilitated when all team members are knowledgeable of the foundations of the selected CSP, with a focus on the other three practice areas.

Growth and implementation

It is crucial to train the development and deployment teams on how to properly utilize CSP services. Best practices for using CSP services are outlined in documentation and provided by CSPs. Follow the CSP's recommendations when constructing a new system or application if you're creating one. Review the architecture and implementation of any current applications or systems that you plan to migrate in light of the CSP's recommendations to identify any adjustments that must be made to deploy the application effectively. For the CSP's technical support team to comprehend the adjustments you need, it could be necessary to discuss the deployment.

In the event of failure, CSPs offer solutions to ensure resilience. Ensure that the team understands how to utilize these tools properly, but there are abundant examples that demonstrate no amount of customer skill can completely prevent disruptions that are the CSP's responsibility. One instance is a five-hour AWS Kinesis outage in US-EAST-1 that adversely affected clients and the CSP by briefly halting updates to its Service Health Dashboard. Another illustration is an Azure Active Directory authentication outage brought on by an authentication key that was tagged to "retain" as part of a difficult migration, but that ordinarily is removed on a schedule and exposed a flaw where the "retain" state was not honored.

To ensure security, CSP services frequently need particular setups. Make sure the team comprehends and fully applies these setups. Customers who neglected to properly establish the storage service's access policy and fail to encrypt the stored data were to blame for cases of unsafe AWS storage services outlined in the previous section. This incident highlights the need for personnel to have thorough training in how to use CSP resources. AWS has modified S3 to encrypt data by default to help decrease these issues.

Examine the organization's security policy and the methods being used to apply security controls right now. Before adopting the on-premises security method in the cloud, consult the CSP's recommendations. First, be sure the on-premises strategy would be successful if it were applied on the cloud. Afterwards, determine whether CSP services offer a superior implementation strategy that still satisfies security policy objectives.

Moving to a cloud environment could come with dangers that weren't present when apps and systems were deployed on-premises. Identify any new security controls that will be required to address these risks by keeping an eye out for them. Once more, evaluate the benefits of the control implementations offered by CSP.

The risk exposure of such on-premises resources varies when you integrate your on-premises IT with cloud-deployed systems and apps. Examine the security measures in place in your on-premises IT environment to make sure they sufficiently handle dangers that arise when using a CSP.

When utilizing contracted resources to migrate an existing application or create a new application using cloud services, the personnel of the organization must effectively manage the contractor. Staff members must have a good knowledge of the CSP services utilized in the application as well as a solid comprehension of Planning, and the CSP's fundamental architecture, to provide supervision.

Operations

Applications and systems need to be securely run after they have been built and deployed.

The software determines the cloud virtual infrastructure instead of actual servers, discs, and networking hardware. Since it is a source code, the infrastructure can be considered as such. Use a source code management system to control the software that defines the virtual architecture of the cloud. Software development management has been successfully carried out using source code control systems.

The CSP's tools must be mastered by system administrators to run systems and applications. The integration of operational methods for on-premises and cloud-based apps and systems calls for the development of new procedures.

A service that defines infrastructure using software is AWS CloudFormation. Virtual computers and virtual discs that make up a virtual data center are examples of the cloud infrastructure described in Cloud Formation templates. Since these templates are merely text files, they can and should be managed and configured the same way as other applications. To effectively use template language and secure resource configuration, system administrators must acquire these skills. Furthermore, they require precise guidelines for when and how to verify templates in and out of source code management systems.

Decommissioning

A system or application that has been deployed in the cloud may need to be retired for a variety of reasons. It's possible that the CSP won't survive. Key services that the application depends on could be stopped by the CSP. Price hikes in the CSP could make the current deployment unaffordable. For whatever reason, before launch, preparation for decommissioning a cloud application or system should be done. Each CSP now offers a unique set of cloud services. A significant effort will therefore be required to move a system or application from one CSP to another.

Although there are specific concerns against this approach that are mentioned later in this section, developing a multiple-CSP strategy is one way to address this issue. Several chief information officers offer their opinions in a CIO.com article on the necessity of a multi-CSP strategy (CIOs). When choosing the initial CSP, they advise considering the possibility of deploying the chosen application to many CSPs. Consider how a system or application might be deployed to Microsoft Azure or AWS, for instance. Despite differences in the specifics of each product, there is a large amount of overlap between AWS and Azure's service offerings.

An application that was designed for one CSP may be ported to another using mappings between CSPs, which are easily accessible on the Internet. Even though the application or system may only be deployed to one of these CSPs, it makes sense to keep track of deployment components that are specific to the chosen CSP and would need to be redesigned if transferred.

Even if you are not deploying to numerous CSPs, think about the implications of quitting one. Any application or system's data storage and processing components are its most crucial components. It is crucial to comprehend how data can be taken out of one CSP and transferred to another.

Many cloud service model types make this extraction challenging. The cost might be a significant problem even for those, like IaaS, where the user has a lot of control over how and where the data is stored and the capacity to create software that can extract the data from storage. Data transfers into and out of CSP services are often subject to fees. Charges may be asymmetrical, with lower fees for transfers into the CSP and higher fees for transfers out of the CSP, to incentivize the usage of CSP services. CSPs offer some tools for transferring to their platforms, but extracting anything more complex than the most basic data is likely to remain a major barrier to leaving a CSP.

Since the CSP stores consumer data whether and wherever it sees fit, SaaS creates a particularly significant difficulty. The consumer entirely relies on the source CSP to provide a data extraction tool that exports data in a format that can be ingested by the destination CSP to migrate data from one SaaS service to another. Before storing years' worth of data in a CSP's SaaS application, it is best to be aware of how to do this.

Key considerations

The following are the main things to think about when completing due diligence:

- To find apps that are appropriate for the cloud and choose a CSP, use a cloud adoption framework.

- Provide staff with in-depth training on the design, application, and management of CSP services.

- Manage cloud resource configuration, compliance support, and a continuous authority-to-operate (C-ATO) attitude using a source code control system and change control procedures.

- Implement a zero-trust security paradigm as soon as the planning stage is complete. Prior to implementation, plan for transferring apps and data from the selected CSP to another CSP or back on-site.

Restrict access

As mentioned, and covered in the preceding chapters, both CSP and cloud user share responsibilities for security in cloud computing. Managed access to physical resources, including computers, network storage systems, and the virtualization system used to offer service to customers, is entirely the CSP's responsibility.

It is a shared duty to have access to build, maintain, and destroy virtual resources like virtual storage and machines. Who has access to these acts must be specified in the consumer's policy. The CSP is required to offer tools for enforcing the consumer's policies.

The consumer completely should create access controls and put enforcement measures in place for those restrictions, which apply to both apps and operating systems. The implementation of all three components correctly and fully is necessary to fully control access to resources.

Who has access to resources and what they can do with them is controlled by access management. The capacity to identify and authenticate individuals, the ability to grant users access rights, and the ability to develop and enforce access control policies for resources are the three capabilities that are often necessary for access management.

User identification and authentication

User identification and authentication serve as the foundation for access management. Credentials are provided to authorized users, tying their identities to an authenticator. A username and password, which the user alone knows, are the most typical form of identification. Using valid user credentials, particularly privileged user credentials, to obtain access is one of the most efficient ways to attack an organization's information systems. Given that administration interfaces can be accessed through the Internet, such credentials can be particularly helpful for logging into cloud services. The administrative interfaces used by clients are likewise accessible via the Internet, even if an organization may employ a private connection to the CSP. An attacker is capable of managing and configuring cloud consumer resources with stolen privileged user credentials.

Attacks using stolen credentials can be seen in the Deloitte email compromise and the OneLogin data breach covered in the previous section. These breaches frequently go unnoticed for months, as was the case with Deloitte, because all access seems to be being carried out by authorized, genuine people. Passwords and other credentials that are purely dependent on the user's knowledge are particularly vulnerable to theft because the legitimate user has no visible means to detect a breach.

Utilize credentials that leverage various authentication methods to limit the risk of credential compromise (multi-factor authentication or MFA). Due to the requirement that an adversary has numerous, independent elements before they may compromise a credential, MFA lowers the risk of a credential being compromised.

MFA in cloud computing usually combines a password with something the user has, like a text message delivered to a previously registered mobile phone. Credential compromise becomes more challenging and is more likely to be immediately discovered as a result of the second point. The MFA feature is available from many cloud providers.

A further change to the entire cybersecurity picture that MFA presents is the chance to introduce the concept of zero trust. One of the core principles of zero trust is the stringent implementation of access controls using per-session explicit authentication and authorization. MFA account alignment, IP restriction, and device complaint should all have helped to safeguard the security issue in the instance of Solorigate, which compromised user and vendor accounts as well as vendor software.

The compromise of privileged user credentials is especially worrying since they provide user control over the IT environment. An attacker's chances of gaining persistent access through software installation or user account creation are increased if they have the proper privileged user credentials. Start with privileged users if using multi-factor credentials for all users is not practical. Microsoft, as an illustration, enables Azure multifactor authentication for users of Microsoft 365. The Microsoft 365 admin center makes it simple to enable this authentication. By banning legacy MFA techniques, Microsoft's security defaults feature forces all users to adopt MFA with the Microsoft Authenticator app.

AWS also provides a variety of MFA choices. The simplest method is to use a tablet or smartphone app as a virtual MFA device that adheres to the open **time-based one-time password (TOTP)** standard. AWS does, however, provide extra-cost options that make use of unique hardware tokens.

The initial privileged credential that a consumer receives from CSPs often allow them to carry out all privileged operations. This credential is comparable to a "root" or "admin" credential in Linux or Windows, respectively. Although this credential grants authority over one or more devices, the range of privileges that go along with it is significantly wider.

Access rights for users

Create a group of roles that will fulfill both shared and client-specific obligations. CSPs and other organizations, like Gartner, offer guidance on creating roles. As much as it is practical, these responsibilities ought to guarantee that no single person may negatively impact the entire virtual data center. This division might be implemented in a conventional data center by designating separate operating systems, storage, and network managers. A technique that separates resource definition from resource deployment to production, however, might be more effective given that all of these resources are virtual in an IaaS cloud and can be managed by writing code.

Resources shouldn't be accessible at will by individual developers or system administrators. A compromised credential or a malevolent insider's impact can be reduced by limiting access. Developers should be limited to the projects they have been given. The resources they are given should be limited to system managers. For managing services, CSPs may offer advice on the proper privileges and roles to use. The least privilege concept should be used while defining roles. Only assign roles the privileges that are specifically required for them to carry out their duties. Give services and programs only the permissions necessary for them to function, in a similar manner. The privileges assigned to service and application roles shouldn't be raised.

Credential and user access management can be implemented in a variety of ways with CSPs. The CSP's system's users, credentials, and roles are all defined via one method. In total contrast to on-premises users, credentials, and roles.

Another strategy involves moving all or a portion of the on-premises **Active Directory (AD)** to the cloud. A third method federates the cloud environment with the on-premises capabilities by using the current on-premises users and credentials, augmenting them with roles and groups relevant to the cloud environment, and using the on-premises users and credentials as before. Consideration should be given to each of these strategies in the context of the organization because they each have advantages and disadvantages.

There won't be any inadvertent user migration from the on-premises system to the cloud because users, credentials, and roles are managed solely in the cloud for access to cloud services. But it can lead to running two separate identity and access management systems. Users' experiences may also be hampered by the fact that they require different login credentials for access to on-premises and the cloud. It might raise the possibility of making mistakes, which might compromise security. For privileged users who build, administer, and remove cloud-based virtual resources, this separation is suitable.

Establishing and implementing resource access policies

Access policies that are customized to a given cloud service may be needed. The danger associated with unsafe AWS storage services illustrated in the preceding example was due to incorrectly configured AWS S3 access policies. It's crucial to comprehend the conditions for configuring access policies for cloud services. Furthermore, users need to be aware of any upgrades to cloud services that modify the access policy configuration. Cloud service updates or maintenance may add, remove, or modify access policy parameters. CSPs provide a variety of storage service types, including content delivery services, virtual drives, and blob storage. To safeguard the data they store, each of these has certain access policies that must be set up.

AWS recommends using AWS identity and access management as an example of all the steps a customer should take to manage access. The fundamental actions apply to many CSPs, even though the suggestions are particular to AWS. Microsoft and Google both offer more advice on managing identities and access.

Key considerations

The following are the main factors to think about while managing access:

- Utilize multifactor authentication.
- Implement a zero-trust real-time policy, explicit verification, and a set of roles that enable clear separation of responsibilities.

- Verify that all storage services have their access policies properly set up.

Watch and defend

When systems and applications are delivered to an IaaS or PaaS, it is obvious that the CSP and consumers share equal responsibility for the monitoring. Monitoring is made more difficult by cloud deployment. To properly monitor and protect cloud-deployed systems, users must learn to use the monitoring data supplied by the CSP, supplement it as needed, analyze both cloud and on-premises monitoring data, and work with CSP security operations employees to resolve incidents.

The CSP is in charge of keeping an eye on consumer-facing infrastructure and services. Monitoring the systems and applications developed utilizing the offered services is the consumer's responsibility. A CSP incorporates extensive instrumentation into its cloud services. This instrumentation is required by a CSP to defend the infrastructure and services it manages as well as to provide metered service, one of the five fundamental aspects of cloud computing. According to this reasoning, the CSP gives the customer monitoring data that is pertinent to the customer's use of cloud services. This CSP-provided data serves as the first line of monitoring to

- Identify users who have access to or use systems and applications that are inappropriate or unauthorized,
- Identify users who unexpectedly use systems and applications, and
- Detect any inappropriate or unauthorized behavior.

The consumer's system, services, and data usage must be profiled for this monitoring to be effective. Once a profile of typical operations has been created using CSP monitoring data, the consumer can use the monitoring data supplied by the CSP to spot any unexpected or improper behavior.

For instance, AWS offers the CloudTrail service, which logs every AWS API call made within a user's AWS resources. The action requested, the requester, and the outcome of the request are all recorded by CloudTrail. There are various resources for searching and looking at CloudTrail data. AWS can transmit CloudTrail data to an S3 storage bucket where a user can use other tools, either one they have on hand or one that is bought and sold, to further examine the data. Operating systems and apps that are installed on AWS must include routine monitoring and analysis of CloudTrail logs.

Information about user and administrator activity in Exchange Online, SharePoint Online, OneDrive, and Azure Active Directory is available in audit log reports from Microsoft Office 365 through Security Center. To check for anomalous or suspicious behavior connected to a user's Office 365 services, these reports can be queried using tools in the Office 365 Security and Compliance center.

Data collected for on-premises monitoring differs from that provided by CSP. Customers must therefore learn how to protect their cloud-based assets using the new data. This entails comprehending the meaning of the data, figuring out what is typical for the cloud deployment, and being proficient with the CSP's given tools for spotting anomalies.

In addition to creating and marketing virtual versions of their products that are already integrated with CSP services, traditional security product suppliers. These items are typically already aware of automation, which can save time.

Some components of monitoring and detection are also starting to be automated by CSPs. AWS provides the Macie service, which tracks user access to data stored in S3 buckets, creates patterns of expected access, and sends alarms when user access deviates from historical norms. Macie automates the identification of typical access patterns, freeing the user from having to keep track of and examine S3 accesses.

The Stackdriver service, created by Google, can analyze both AWS and Google Cloud Platform monitoring data. Data collection, detection, investigation, and response are all automated and orchestrated by Azure Sentinel.

Analyze monitoring from both the cloud and on-premises

To get a complete picture of the organization's cybersecurity posture with a hybrid cloud deployment, which retains many resources on-premises while moving some to a CSP, monitoring data from the CSP, consumer cloud-based systems and applications, and consumer on-premises monitoring data must be combined. While this enclave might be deployed on-site or in the cloud, there might be benefits to doing so.

CSPs frequently charge more for transfers into the cloud than they do for transfers out, to promote a continued and maybe expanding usage of their services. It may therefore be less expensive to move data from on-premises monitoring into the cloud than it is to move it out to an on-premises enclave, depending on the volume of data involved. Second, cloud storage for huge amounts of data may be less expensive, particularly for storage of archived material that is being maintained but not being used right now. Last but not least, customers can profit from the inherent elasticity of the cloud, which enables them to quickly increase analytical capacity when required and decrease capacity to save money when it is not.

Key considerations

The following are the main factors to consider when observing and protecting cloud deployments:

- As the main method of cloud monitoring, use the data and services offered by CSPs. only where necessary, enhance CSP's capabilities.

- To give total security situational awareness, combine data from on-premises and cloud monitoring.

- Work together with the CSP to coordinate investigations and responses to events.

- To reduce unwanted access, use zero trust automation and real-time detection techniques.

Double-click on important security practices - what to adopt

To ensure a secure adoption of cloud computing, it is crucial for businesses moving to the cloud to adhere to security discipline at multiple levels. The goal is to draw attention to some industry best practices in cloud security that may be incorporated into the architecture of the enterprise cloud and need to facilitate a sense of security and boost trust in cloud adoption.

In this section, we'll look at the standards to embrace or understand when selecting the cloud for service delivery and the best practices to be followed at various stages of a cloud deployment architecture.

Businesses should adopt a layered approach to have cloud security for their enterprise IT. From physical facilities through the deployment and configuration of IT infrastructure components within the Enterprise, IT security covers the lowest security layers. Networking, computation, and storage security are the fundamental elements on which cloud computing is based.

It's critical to understand the CSP's infrastructure security requirements. In the shared security paradigm, it is the provider's job to keep the physical, abstract, and orchestration layers of the cloud secure (that is, the person who manages the private cloud platform). While highlighting the top cloud security practices for each level mentioned earlier in this part, we'll also talk about privacy as a crucial factor to consider when it comes to cloud-based security.

The following diagram (*Figure 9.1*) represents the various layers that should be considered while defining the best practices on cloud security and the overall cloud adoption journey:

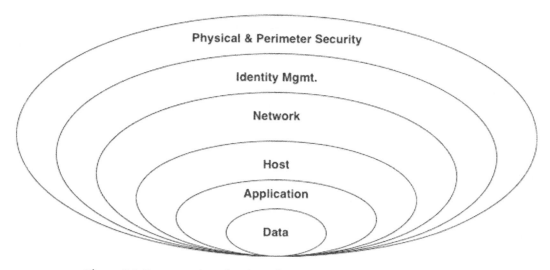

Figure 9.1: Best practice adoption – layered approach for cloud security

In the subsequent section, we will learn more about these layers.

Data protection

There is no need for any fresh methodology for cloud data protection methods. The protection of data in the cloud is quite comparable to that of data in a conventional data center. In the context of cloud computing, data protection techniques include identity and authentication, encryption, access control, secure deletion, data masking, and integrity checking.

The key to a successful cloud is maintaining data control. Nowadays, thanks to virtualization and the cloud, data may be logically under the authority of the Government or federal, but physically live on infrastructure owned and managed by another business. The key driver behind the need for new methods and strategies to ensure enterprises can maintain data security is this change in control.

To get past any hesitation about cloud data security, enterprises may establish certain data protection measures such as:

- Businesses should be aware of the types of data they handle, and they should consider how to safeguard that data from unauthorized access, deletion, and backup by categorizing and deploying pertinent data on the cloud as needed. vulnerabilities, data leaks, hacked administration interfaces, malware assaults, and so on.

- Organizations should develop a data usage policy that explains the different types of data access, who has access to the data, and what circumstances may constitute proper data usage. For violations of policy and the ensuing impact-based penalties, there ought to be safeguarded.

- One of the most fundamental aspects of data protection in the cloud is access control, for which the enterprise or individual business is accountable for implementing Administrative and Technical Controls to regulate data access on the cloud.

Secure data

Create a data security strategy that considers both on-premises and cloud data to protect data. Make periodic assessments to confirm that the strategy's implementation mechanisms are in place. Data protection comprises two distinct challenges:

1. Avoiding unwanted access, and

2. Keeping essential data accessible even in the face of mistakes and failures.

Stop unauthorized access

As already noted, the example of the risk associated with unsafe AWS storage services in the preceding section was caused by a lack of or insufficient AWS S3 access policies. Due to this error, the S3 buckets' data was accessible by unauthorized parties. The information kept in the S3 buckets would not have been revealed if the data had been encrypted, though. Data storage choices with many CSPs typically have encryption enabled by default, which is a good practice to prevent disclosure due to unauthorized access. For data stored in S3 and other data storage services, AWS offers several encryption options. The storage services offered by other CSPs include encryption features.

Multiple cloud services may need to have their data encrypted to encrypt cloud data at rest. The IaaS environment is filled with sensitive data that needs to be protected. The blue folders represent the original locations of the data, which are the file server, application server, object/blob storage, and database. Data spread as it is accessed to the web server and the content delivery network, which are represented by the yellow folders. Data from the database, application server, and file server is copied to the backup service to preserve availability. The archive service ultimately receives backups. Red folders indicate archives and backups.

To safeguard sensitive data, closely examine the cloud deployment to identify any potential copies or caches of the data. To make sure that the data is secure no matter where it is kept, you must be aware of and utilize the encryption features of all the services to which it may have been copied.

Of course, properly managing the accompanying encryption keys is necessary for encryption to function. CSPs give customers the option of using consumer- or CSP-managed keys. While CSP-managed keys are practical, they provide the user with no control over where or how the keys are kept. Consumer-managed keys put more responsibility on the user but provide them with better control. Consumer-managed encryption keys shouldn't be kept in the cloud together with the information they are meant to secure. By doing this, the chance of key compromise and illegal access to data is increased. To create and store encryption keys in the cloud, CSPs provide **hardware security modules (HSMs)**. HSMs are designed to target customers who have strict security requirements or who may need to adhere to regulations like the **Payment Card Industry (PCI)** Data Security Standard or the **Federal Information Processing Standard (FIPS)**.

Third parties provide KMSs for usage with different CSPs in addition to providing KMSs for key lifecycle management. A cloud native key management system, external key origination, a cloud service leveraging an external KMS, and multi-cloud KMS (MCKMS) are the four common KMS patterns identified by the **Cloud Security Alliance (CSA)**. It is advised that enterprises think about their ability to pivot, migrate, or embrace new patterns of cloud KMS because each design can have various strengths and challenges, and the cloud KMS space is moving quickly. The best KMS to use will depend on the context, however, the CSA advises using cloud-native KMS by default because it is the easiest. Other patterns should only be used if the customer has compelling reasons to do so.

Make sure critical data is available

Significant guarantees are offered by CSPs about the preservation of persistent data. The fact that some big cloud companies have unintentionally lost customer data shows that no system is faultless. In addition to CSP problems, cloud users may also commit errors that cause data loss. To ensure they satisfy the needs of the firm, it is crucial to comprehend CSP data backup and recovery methods. The firm might need to add more backup and recovery steps to CSP procedures. CSPs offer services that customers can customize to carry out backup and recovery tasks.

Amazon advised customers to restore data from their own backups in the example of a data loss risk that was previously mentioned. As a method of backing up EBS volumes, AWS offers the capability to snapshot EBS volumes to S3. To back up S3 data and lower storage costs, S3 data can also be moved to near-line storage in Amazon Glacier.

Similar to on-premises backups, cloud consumers are responsible for determining the criticality of data and making sure that the proper backups are carried out by the CSP, the CSP, and the consumer together, or by the consumer alone.

Another example from the earlier discussion emphasizes how crucial it is to assess the criticality of data and make sure that adequate backups are available to enable business continuity.

In this instance, it appears that Code Spaces' infrastructure for both production and backups was fully reliant on AWS. The crucial data to its operation was deleted by a single breach. Without that information, Code Spaces had to stop doing business. Given the importance of the data, it would have been wise to implement a backup strategy using a second CSP or on-premises storage.

Currently, major CSPs offer backup services that can manage a variety of data types and workloads (for example, VMs, block storage, and databases). The best practices for Azure Backup from Microsoft call for considering the architecture, vault design, backup policy, security, network, governance, and monitoring and alerting.

Refrain from sharing deleted data

The cliché *the Internet never forgets* applies to cloud-based storage, despite being overused. To maintain permanence, cloud storage services replicate data. The replication and distribution of data through services during regular system operation must be considered when sensitive data must be destroyed or resources containing sensitive data are retired.

Determine what needs to be done to ensure that any copies of sensitive data that may have been copied or cached are removed by carefully analyzing the cloud deployment. To avoid unintentional data loss, some systems may keep data after deletion for specified retention periods. Verify that the data is indeed removed for these services after the retention term.

In the end, data is kept on storage devices like solid-state or magnetic discs. These media players can and do frequently break down, necessitating replacement. Consumer data is still present on the device even after it has malfunctioned. It's critical to comprehend how the CSP manages storage media that has been taken out of production. For instance, AWS permanently removes all media from the service. Degaussing or other techniques may be used by other suppliers to sterilize magnetic media. As mentioned earlier in this section, encrypting data at rest makes sure that any residual data is unusable even if data is not completely removed or the storage media fails and is not destroyed or cleansed.

Conclusion of data protection

Here are a few key takeaways that you should be using as summary points:

- To safeguard and secure both data at rest and data in transit, encryption is essential.
    - CSP can implement various encryption methods, including **Full Disk Encryption (FDE)**, **Format Preserving Encryption (FPE)**, Application layer Encryption, File Encryption, Database Encryption, and so on.
    - Use encrypted connections (HTTPS, SSL, TLS, FTPS, and so on) or opt to encrypt sensitive data before sending it to the cloud to secure the contents of data in transit.
    - Enterprises can easily encrypt private information before storing it to protect data at rest.
- Consider utilizing service provider-managed encryption options. Use customer-managed keys where you can because they provide you with more control.
- Consider adding a layer of data protection using data classification (Restricted, Confidential, Sensitive, and Unclassified).
- Ensure data integrity while replicating between sites.
- Establish a policy for data usage (data access control management, repercussions of policy violations, correct usage of data, and so on).
- Perform periodic recovery operations to verify accuracy and frequently back up (Full, Incremental, Differential) data to ensure data availability.
- Ensure that data-level monitoring is in place and that logs adhere to all applicable compliance standards set forth by the Business.

Application security

Independent virtual computers are used to host applications. Applications and sensitive data are more susceptible to cloud systems since they share resources with other users. To protect the client's environment, special security measures and controls are needed. When using a shared cloud model, cloud service providers make sure that users and the business only have access to the data that they are authorized to view.

The use of micro-service architectures improves security even more. Developers can instead create more, smaller virtual machines, each focused on a particular function or service while minimizing the use of real servers by customers is not a requirement. This offers granular security measures and reduces the attack surface of individual VMs.

The goal of the cutting-edge application development methodology known as DevOps is to fully automate the process from conception to deployment. Version control management, change management, and increased security operations are all made possible by DevOps, which also creates several opportunities for security. This goes beyond merely the development and operations teams in DevOps. If IT security is involved throughout the whole development life cycle of the application, the agility and responsiveness of a DevOps methodology may be fully used.

The topic of why businesses need DevOps in their ecosystem may now arise. In the past, the responsibility for security was delegated to a particular team at the end of the development process. That wasn't a huge issue when waterfall development cycles were used. Even the most effective DevOps projects might suffer from obsolete and traditional security procedures. DevOps ensures frequent and quick development cycles (often lasting weeks or days), followed by Continuous Integrations and Continuous Deployments.

Online application security is the process of securing web applications and services that are accessed using a browser and are accessible over the internet. It defends against a variety of security risks that prey on holes in both core and non-core applications. The main targets of assaults are content management systems, sensitive data, and other management and administrative applications. Applications used by the business are protected from intrusion by using important tools. A web application firewall monitors and filters HTTP traffic between a web application and the Internet to assist in securing online applications. Usually, it defends against attacks like cross-site scripting, SQL injection, file inclusion, cross-site forgery, etc. It is put into practice with a predetermined set of laws or policies for security.

DevSecOps

Let's now discuss DevSecOps. By assuring an efficient software development life cycle, DevSecOps is significantly changing the IT sector (SDLC). DevSecOps asks for security integration across all phases of the software development process chain, breaking the conventional pattern of having security as a segregated process and addressing security problems from the very beginning of every stage. The DevSecOps approach to cloud security calls for meticulous planning and a culture shift in an IT environment, particularly for security automation and setup of cloud assets.

The following variables control the effectiveness of DevSecOps deployment in a cloud environment:

- **Code analysis**: Continual program updates necessitate thorough code reviews.

- **Automated testing**: Automated testing ensures little effort and time savings. Automated testing, a key component of the DevSecOps methodology, accelerates and streamlines the testing procedure through the effective execution of repeatable test cases.

- **Change management**: Encouraging teamwork so that every team is aware of how the other team functions. It can help in timely addressing potential vulnerabilities if developers are informed about security-related activities from the beginning.

- **Monitoring of compliance**: Compliance continues to be crucial to the development of an organization. Regulations support source code alteration and code generation. This facilitates real-time auditing.

- **Threat analysis**: To assess an organization's level of security readiness, a threat analysis is essential. To handle common security concerns, enterprises must keep a careful eye on spotting potential threats, performing regular security scans, and reviewing their code.

- **Personnel Training**: By providing teams with the necessary subject-matter expertise, organizing practical training sessions and certification programs strengthens the business.

Conclusion of Application security

Here are a few key takeaways that you should be using as summary points aligned with Application security.

- Develop security as the application is being designed. Making Cloud Native applications offers a chance to start using cloud-based security right now.

- Security testing will be integrated with the deployment process.

- Management of all private and public encryption keys through encryption key administration. Businesses need to be aware of the new architectural possibilities and cloud-based services. The business shouldn't just try to enforce current standards strictly on a model, but should instead change its standards and security policies to support them.

- When establishing an application on the cloud, a web-facing application should be hosted in a DMZ (De-militarized) zone, and a database server should be deployed in a protected zone.

- Use of Web Application Firewall for online portals and Web applications.

- Integration between applications and data transfer over secured API channels.

- Interface security and API security.

- Keep track of API calls via logging.

- Automation of security measures can be achieved by using software-defined security.

- Whenever possible, automate the discovery and correction of security flaws by using event-driven security, such as antivirus software.

Host and Compute layer

Workloads are processing units that can be virtual machines, containers, or other abstractions. Processor and memory resources are used by workloads. Workloads are a collection of different processing jobs, ranging from ordinary apps running in a virtual machine under a common OS to workloads that are highly GPU intensive. It is advised that for the majority of operations, a virtual machine may be treated as though it were a physical machine. The fact that virtual machines are equally susceptible to threats like data loss or corruption, hardware malfunctions, viruses, and hackers should be noted.

The following are descriptions of various cloud computing offerings of different types:

- Dissociating the operating system from the underlying hardware is the responsibility of the virtual machine manager (hypervisor). To impose isolation while enabling high-performance activities, hypervisors can connect to the capabilities of the underlying hardware. Certain memory attacks are susceptible to virtual machines; however, this is getting harder because isolation is being strengthened by continual hardware and software improvements. The security controls provided by virtual machines on today's hypervisors are typically effective, and developments in secure execution environments and hardware isolation for VMs are enhancing these capabilities.

- Code execution environments, known as containers, share the resources of an operating system while running within that OS (at least for the time being). A container, as opposed to a virtual machine (VM), which is a precise abstraction of an operating system, is a contained area where different processes can execute while leveraging the kernel and other features of the parent OS. One virtual machine can host multiple containers, or containers can run on hardware without an operating system.

- The term *serverless* describes a scenario in which cloud users merely access exposed functionality without controlling any of the underlying physical or virtual computers. They still make use of features like virtual machines, containers, or specific hardware platforms, but, in retrospect.

There will always be many workloads operating in memory and on a given processor, frequently from distinct tenants. The same physical compute node is shared by multiple tenants, and various levels of hardware stack segregation are available.

Conclusion on Host and Compute layer

Here are a few key takeaways that you should be using as summary points aligned with this section:

- For crucial workloads, guarantee high availability across all deployment tiers, including computing, firewall, and load balancers.

- The deployment of a new application server should be followed by the activation of security scans and the addition of the servers to continuous monitoring, according to Enterprises.

- As you create VM images, incorporate security testing and policies.

- Put an end to remote access after application configuration.

- For all Virtual Machines (VM), Containers, and VM images implement the proper role-based access controls and strong authentication.

- Use pre-certified VM images from the cloud platform where pre-certification would be a continuous effort.

- Choose patching VM images above patching active instances. Check to see if your operating system, database licenses, and other patches are current.

- Ensure VM-level encryption using Bitlocker, LUKS, etc. to protect VM security in the event of a compromise.

- Check the Operating System On the virtual machine, hardening is done.

- Take VM snapshots regularly and store them in a secure location.

- Prefer using file integrity monitoring to assure authenticated changes and identify unauthorized file changes.

- Keep logs, especially audit logs, separate from workloads.

- Install antivirus software on the virtual machine and make sure to do routine patches.

- Conduct recurring vulnerability assessments and penetration tests (VAPT) on the enterprise's cloud infrastructure.

- Plan for disaster recovery if business-critical applications are used (DR).

Network layer

Virtual networks come in many forms, from straightforward VLANs to fully developed **Software-Defined Networks (SDNs)**. Additionally, the network layer must provide security for the data that is in transit. For data transmission and reception, a cloud service provider needs to be aware of the enterprise network traffic plan. Businesses must confirm that CSP has put strong security controls in place for internal and external network segregation and communication. CSP is responsible for ensuring effective network segmentation that divides networks with varying degrees of sensitivity. SDN is now widely used to virtualize networks on cloud computing platforms. As a result of SDN's abstraction of the network management strategy from the underlying physical infrastructure, many conventional networking limitations are eliminated. As an illustration, an enterprise might overlay different virtual networks over the same physical hardware while correctly isolating and segregating each type of traffic.

Additionally, SDNs are defined via software settings and API calls, supporting orchestration and agility. Virtual networks and physical networks differ in that they both run on physical networks, but abstraction enables more profound changes to networking behavior that have an impact on security procedures and technologies.

Data transfers to the cloud must be secured. Enterprises must ensure data security as they transfer their data to the cloud. Understanding the CSP's data migration processes is necessary since doing so can often be more affordable and secure than using "manual" data transfer methods like **Secure File Transfer Protocol (SFTP)**.

Several alternatives for in-transit encryption exist, depending on the capabilities of the cloud platform:

- Client-side encryption, or encrypting data before transferring it to the cloud, is one alternative.

- Network encryption (TLS, SFTP, and so on) is an additional choice. Transport Layer Security (TLS), a crucial security feature, is used by default in the majority of CSP APIs.

- A third alternative is proxy-based encryption, which controls encryption before data is transferred to the CSP and places an encryption proxy between the cloud consumer and CSP in a secure location.

Isolating and scanning the data before integrating it is a smart technique. Due to the faster pace of change in the cloud, logs must be offloaded and externally gathered more promptly. The enterprise would be protected from losses by implementing a procedure like gathering logs in an auto-scale group before the cloud controller terminates such unnecessary instances.

The CSP cloud computing resource must be protected from the denial-of-service threat, which is typically an external threat to public cloud services. A **distributed denial-of-service (DDoS)** assault is a malicious attempt to obstruct the regular flow of traffic on a targeted server, service, or network by saturating the target or its surrounding infrastructure with an influx of Internet traffic. Consequently, the company must implement CSP's Anti-DDoS services.

Conclusion on Network layer

Here are a few key takeaways that you should be using as summary points aligned to Network layer security.

- Use a virtual private network (SSL or site-to-site) to access cloud infrastructure and services.

- Avoid turning off any personal firewalls on any machines used by the business that are networked.

- Use IP Whitelisting to accept connections from specific IPs and reject those from all others as necessary.

- Pre-certifying extra load balancers, firewall ports, and VLANs.

- In comparison to conventional data centers, separate virtual networks and the cloud account for lower security threats.

- Whenever possible, it is necessary to restrict traffic between workloads that are part of the same virtual subnet using a firewall policy.

- Reliance on virtual appliances that limit elasticity or result in performance bottlenecks must be reduced.

- Put in place regulations and internal security measures to prevent unauthorized traffic monitoring, changes to consumer networks, and agreements with third parties.

- Businesses are responsible for ensuring that all new network segments are included in continuous monitoring after registering for security checks at the time of deployment.

- It's important to set up an automatic defense against attacks and gather more details on intrusions. One example of a procedure under such an automatic response is IP blocking, connection termination, and signature analysis.

- Implement a SIEM or routinely check network traffic logs to receive security alerts in real-time sent by network and application devices.

- Using SDN capabilities for numerous virtual networks and multiple cloud accounts/segments will boost network separation.

Identity management

Defining and controlling a user's access privileges on a network, as well as the conditions under which they are allowed (or denied) such privileges, is known as **identity and access management (IAM)**. These users could either be inside the business or external (like citizens) (for example, employees). One digital identification for everyone is the main goal of IAM systems. The maintenance, modification, and monitoring of that digital identity throughout each user's "access lifespan" is of the utmost importance once it has been created.

The following would be among the security measures for identity management and access control:

- Utilizing Multi-Factor Authentication (MFA)
    - MFA may be used, allowing for the definition of a conditional access policy and authentication that is subject to LDAP or AD authentication. Identify any potential weaknesses that could compromise the identity of the Business. Automated reactions can be set up to recognize suspicious behavior connected to Business IDs. Investigating suspicious situations is crucial and solving them requires taking the right steps.
    - As using a single factor (password) for cloud services carries significant dangers, MFA provides a way to reduce account takeovers.

- Making use of Access Control Techniques
    - Any Enterprise that uses cloud services must carefully manage access to its cloud resources. Role-Based Access Control (RBAC), for instance, is a recognized access management methodology that aids in controlling end users' access to cloud resources, what they may do with the resources that have been assigned to them, and the regions to which they have access.
    - Assigning tasks to specific Cloud roles helps eliminate confusion, which frequently results in human and automated errors, potentially posing a security risk.

- Active observation of suspicious activity
    - Identity monitoring systems are entrusted with quickly detecting questionable behavior and subsequently setting out notifications for additional actions.

○ As a best practice, Enterprises should have a mechanism for spotting brute force assaults, sign-in attempts from various locations, suspicious IP addresses, and sign-ins from infected systems to their cloud deployments.

The organization must institutionalize a detailed plan that lays out in detail how user identities and Cloud service authorizations will be managed.

Physical and Perimeter Security

The main goal of perimeter defense is to manage network traffic entering and leaving a data center network. A tiered system of defenses that cooperate is one of the best practices. Beyond a router, which links internal and external networks, the perimeter protection provided by a firewall serves as primary layer of defense. A firewall filters out potentially harmful or unknown traffic that might pose a threat based on a set of rules regarding the permitted source and destination addresses on the network. The use of intrusion detection or intrusion prevention systems (IDS/IPS), which scan for suspicious traffic after it has passed past the firewall, is another service offered by data center providers.

Unauthorized physical access to hardware may result in a cloud service interruption. CSP needs to use availability techniques to protect its data center infrastructure and take resilience into account. Where a cloud service provider hasn't put in place sufficient secure or remote working environments from internal and external sources, the threat grows.

The enterprise must ask the chosen CSPs for confirmation that the required security controls are in place. CSPs are required to offer assurance by using pertinent audits and assessment reports.

The CSP is responsible for maintaining the physical security of the Data Center and its perimeter following numerous standards including ISO 27001 and PCI-DSS, among others.

Unauthorized personnel entering the data center will compromise it, so the CSPs must make sure that there are enough security precautions in place there to prevent unauthorized or coerced entry into the data center's premises, such as security guards, secured fencing, security scanners, biometric access, CCTV surveillance, Access Logs, and so on.

Conclusion on Physical and Perimeter security

Here are a few key takeaways that you should be using as summary points aligned to Physical and Perimeter security:

- Physical infrastructure needs to be kept in secure locations; CSP must make sure perimeter and building security are in place to prevent unwanted entry. Having physical entry controls that guarantee only authorized people have access to areas with sensitive infrastructure falls under this category.

- Protection from environmental threats – CSPs must offer protection from hazards like floods, earthquakes, lightning, fire, natural catastrophes, civil unrest, and other dangers that could impair a data center's ability to function.

- Controls for the security of the IT infrastructure in data centers must be in place, and the CSP must make sure that they are, to prevent asset loss, theft, compromise, and other forms of loss.

- Safety from equipment failure – CSP must ensure that the required safeguards are in place to carry out preventative maintenance on every piece of data center equipment to prevent service interruptions brought on by observable equipment breakdowns.

- Procedure for data center asset removal/theft – CSP must ensure that the necessary safeguards are in place to prevent the removal or theft of sensitive assets.

- Safe disposal or reuse of data center equipment – CSP must ensure that the required safeguards are in place for the proper disposal of any data center equipment, in particular any devices that may contain crucial data, including storage media.

- Security measures for DC employees – Appropriate measures must be put in place for every employee working at a CSP's facilities, including any temporary workers.

Cloud security assessment

As noted in the preceding section, enterprises may prioritize conducting a security assessment for their Cloud projects while institutionalizing procedures surrounding cloud security. During each stage of the security assessment, they must ask themselves as well as their cloud service providers several important questions. This section outlines the enterprise's effective process for assessing the CSPs' security capabilities and their particular threats. The following collection of guiding questions (*Table 9.1*) is intended to help businesses evaluate each of the specified security domains.

Phases	Assessment Questions
Verifying the existence of processes for governance, risk, and compliance	1. What guidelines or requirements for information security apply to the territory of the business? 2. Is the business using cloud services in accordance with any governance and compliance procedures? 3. Is the CSP complying with the enterprise's obligations about the governance and incident notification protocols for its services? 4. Does the Master Services Agreement and Service Level Agreement specify the obligations of the supplier and the client in detail?
Verification and Reporting	1. Do the cloud services provided by the CSP have a report from an impartial auditing firm? Does the audit data meet one of the recognized ISO 27001 requirements for security audits? 2. Does the CSP have procedures in place to inform clients of regular and unusual conduct about the services it provides? Having security implications, are all necessary events and actions logged? 3. Are customer-facing management interfaces covered by security controls in addition to the cloud services themselves? 4. Is there an incident reporting and incident handling procedure in place that satisfies the needs of the client?
Managing Roles and Responsibilities	1. Do the services offered by the provider provide fine-grained access control? 2. Does the provider offer multi-factor authentication? 3. Is the provider able to produce reports to track user access? 4. Can client identity management systems be federated or integrated with the provider's identity management capabilities?

Phases	Assessment Questions
Data and Information Protection	1. Does the cloud environment include a list of all the data that will be utilized or kept there? 2. Have the responsibilities and tasks of the various data management stakeholders been established? 3. Has the management of all data types, particularly unstructured data like photos, been considered? 4. Is data belonging to several customers properly segregated for structured data stored in databases in a multi-tenant cloud environment? 5. Were the proper safeguards for data use or storage in the cloud, including those for confidentiality, integrity, and availability, implemented?
Policy around Data Privacy	1. Will PII be handled or stored by cloud services? 2. Is the Business aware of all applicable data protection rules and regulations? 3. Are there adequate procedures in place for managing PII for the CSP's services? 4. Is the cloud service agreement clear about who is responsible for handling PII? 5. Does the Cloud Service Agreement contain the necessary restrictions on data residency? 6. In the event of a data breach, are our roles and responsibilities for notification and resolution, along with deadlines and priorities, clearly defined?

Phases	Assessment Questions
Cloud application security evaluation	1. Is it obvious who, the business or the CSP, is in charge of the security of the apps based on the cloud services model that is being used?
	2. If the business is responsible, are there policies and procedures in place to guarantee that each application has the proper security controls?
	3. If the CSP, does the cloud service agreement specify the obligations and demand that particular security measures be used on the application?
	4. Does the application, in either scenario, employ suitable encryption methods to safeguard the data and the user's transactions?
Cloud Network Security	1. Can network traffic be screened?
	2. Do the CSP's defenses against distributed denial-of-service attacks exist?
	3. Is intrusion detection and prevention present on the CSP's network?
	4. Is there a facility in place for the CSP to track network activity and provide notifications? Is it possible to separate network traffic in a shared multi-tenant provider environment?
Physical Infra. security controls	1. Is the CSP able to show that the right security measures have been taken to protect their facilities and physical infrastructure?
	2. Does the service provider have the necessary infrastructure to maintain service in the event of equipment malfunctions or environmental threats?
	3. Does the CSP have the required personnel security controls?

Phases	Assessment Questions
Managing Security in the overall Service agreements	1. Does the cloud service agreement outline the enterprise's and CSP's security obligations? 2. Does the service agreement include performance and efficacy metrics for security management? 3. Does the service agreement specifically outline the notification and handling processes for security incidents?
Exit clause understanding	1. Is a written exit procedure included in the cloud service agreement? 2. Is it obvious that at the conclusion of the leave procedure, all customer data from cloud services is erased from the provider's environment? 3. Is client data in cloud services safeguarded from theft or breach during the exit process?

Table 9.1: *Cloud Security Assessment Questionnaire*

Conclusion and way forward

While Security is a never-ending topic and you love discussing and writing about it. Having said that, we need to put an end to this chapter and hence, I would like to conclude the next steps after all we spoke about so far.

The next steps once you have adopted the native cloud security practices to your ecosystem, you should consider thinking about Zero-trust framework adoption and maturity. While a lot of homework has already been done by you by adopting the cloud security practice, you still have a lot of room to uplift your overall security posture.

As businesses quickly migrate to the cloud, managing risks requires a grasp of specific cloud security challenges. Finding the appropriate tools to effectively handle them, nevertheless, is a challenge for many businesses. Manual configuration is inefficient and, at a large scale, impractical due to the dynamic cloud environments' ever-increasing complexity and the present rate of change. In such a situation, cloud security becomes essential for addressing security problems throughout the IaaS cloud architecture.

With the use of proper tools and automation, businesses may identify hundreds of threats in their cloud accounts while also managing and monitoring their security posture across the multi-cloud architecture. Weaving it into a bigger cloud-native security plan that includes your complete technological stack, from infrastructure to workloads, is crucial to maximizing the benefits and protecting your data.

A comprehensive strategy is needed to secure contemporary agile environments. This entails integrating security throughout the full lifespan of the program, starting with the initial build phase and continuing through to the run-time environment. Full-stack security can be achieved across all of your cloud-native deployments by combining cloud workload protection for VMs, containers, and serverless with cloud infrastructure best practices.

When compared to how most businesses secure their on-premises apps and data repositories, cloud services can offer security that is on par with or better. Organizations must be aware of and fulfill their security obligations when employing the services of their CSP to achieve these outcomes. Although prospective cloud customers frequently worry about the security risk of entrusting a CSP to carry out some security responsibilities, experience has shown that security mishaps are more frequently caused by users neglecting to use the security measures supplied.

Using some of the components that make up on-premises computing, cloud computing is a novel way of computing. Assuming that cloud computing functions exactly like on-premises computing, that it can be secured using the same tools used on-premises, or that it is entirely secure by the CSP is naive and dangerous. It takes expertise and practice to use cloud computing effectively and securely, just like any other new technology or method. Utilizing well-established, mature CSPs also aids in lowering the risks connected with moving apps and data to the cloud for small and medium-sized businesses.

Index

Made in the USA
Middletown, DE
05 September 2024

60432223R00203